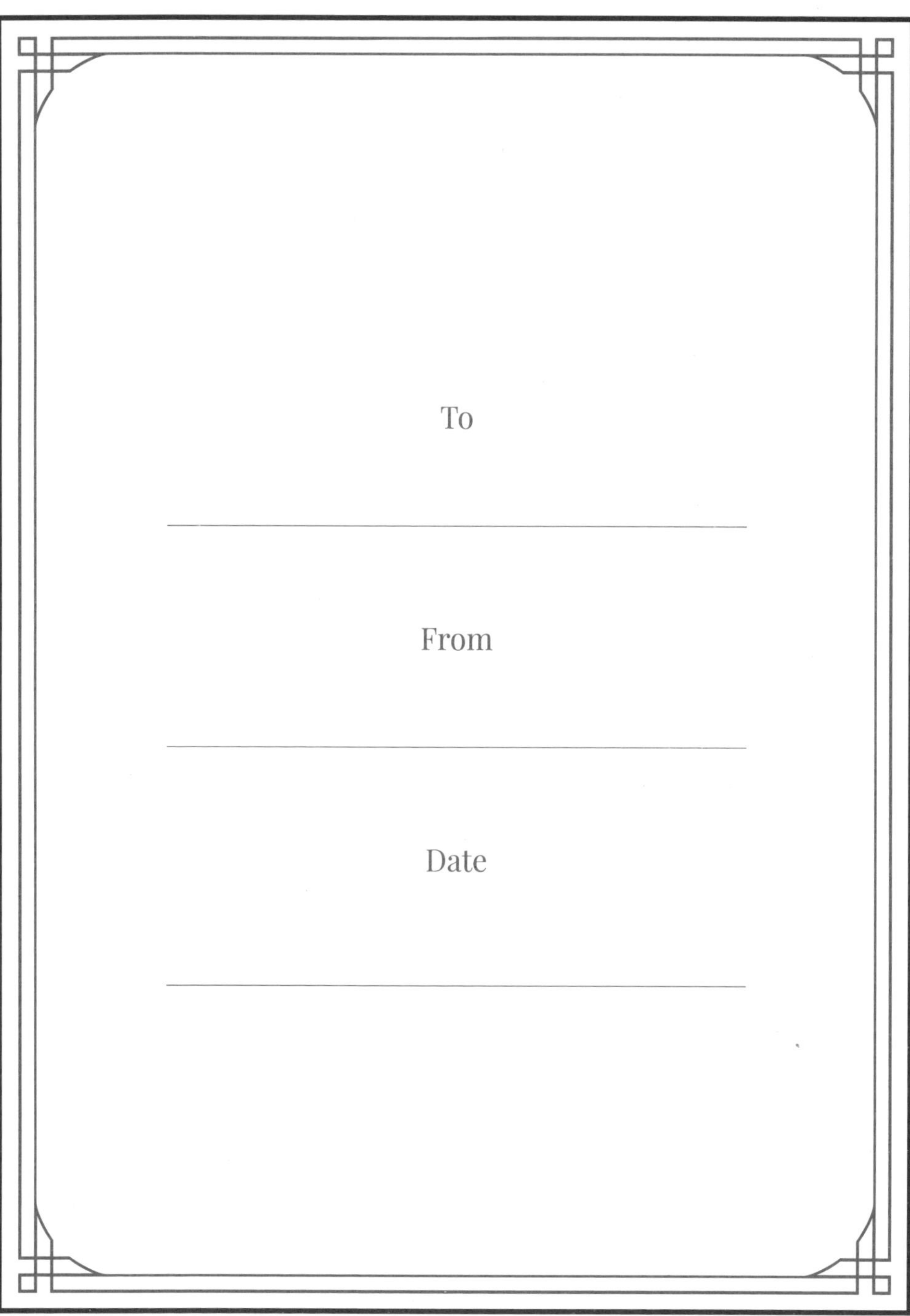

To

From

Date

Visit Christian Art Gifts, Inc., at www.christianartgifts.com.

*Ten Minutes with God for Men: 365 Devotions*

Published by Christian Art Gifts, Inc., Bloomingdale, IL, USA.



Published in association with the Books & Such Literary Management, www.booksandsuch.com.

First edition 2025.

Designed by Christian Art Gifts, Inc.

Cover and interior images used under license from Shutterstock.com.



Most Christian Art titles may be purchased at bulk discounts by churches, nonprofits, and corporations. For more information, please email SpecialMarkets@cagifts.com.

ISBN 979-8-89678-195-0

Printed in China

30 29 28 27 26 25
10 9 8 7 6 5 4 3 2 1

365 DEVOTIONS

# Ten Minutes WITH GOD

— FOR MEN —

CHAD MOORE

Dedicated to my sons, Josh and Jackson.
I love you and I'm proud of you.
You're both my favorite.

*Friend,*

I'm grateful that you picked up this devotional. It's written man to man to help you spend ten minutes with God each day. To get the most out of it, you don't have to be a big-time reader, or a theologian. You just have to be consistent. You can do ten minutes a day! That compounds over time to 3,650 minutes over the course of a year, which adds up to over sixty hours of Bible reading and prayer. It's bite-sized chunks. You got this.

Each month has a focus and is designed to help you get direction from God within the various categories that make up a man's life. Sometimes there are very specific instructions from the Lord, and sometimes the application will be a different way of thinking. Read, think about the bottom-line points, and then use the short prayer as a prompt to talk to God about it through the rest of your day.

As you build the habit of ten minutes a day, you'll start to see things differently. You'll get God's vision for your life and the more you see what He sees, the more you'll do what He says. Commit to the ten-minute journey. You'll be a better man for it.

Walking with you,
*Chad*

# January

## TRAINING

Physical training is good, but training for
godliness is much better, promising benefits
in this life and in the life to come.

*1 Timothy 4:8 (NLT)*

# TRAINING

*No, I strike a blow to my body and make*
*it my slave so that after I have preached to others,*
*I myself will not be disqualified for the prize.*
1 CORINTHIANS 9:27

My youngest son and I just started taking boxing lessons. I signed us up for what's called the "buddy plan." That means we have a trainer and do the workout together. I love it and hate it all at the same time. I'm fifty-two years old and my son Jackson is sixteen. Someone asked me the other day if I'm going to be fighting anyone, and I responded that so far, just the workout itself is kicking my butt. I wanted to do this to share an experience with my son and to get in shape. I want Jack to be formidable. It's important for a man to know he can defend himself and defend those he cares about. This is going to require a lot of discipline and training.

The Christian life requires a lot of training too. For some reason, we think it's supposed to come easy, but frankly, living for Jesus is much more difficult than boxing. The apostle Paul says in our verse for today that he disciplines his body like an athlete to follow Jesus. I don't know about you, but my body wants to do things that Jesus doesn't want me to do. This is true in the realm of food, sex, and all-around laziness. If we're really going to follow Jesus, our bodies are involved, and this requires discipline. When you read the Bible, read books like this, go to church, or pray, you're training. When you say no to sin, you are disciplining your mind and body and getting spiritually stronger.

*Today I will remember:*

- Following Jesus requires training.
- When I read the Bible, read books like this, go to church, or pray, I'm training in trusting Jesus.

*Jesus, I choose to do a workout each day in godliness.*
*Help me to discipline my mind and body to follow You.*
*Help me to be intentional and consistent.*

# PROTECTIVE PRAYER

*When tempted, no one should say, "God is tempting me." For God cannot be tempted by evil, nor does he tempt anyone; but each person is tempted when they are dragged away by their own evil desire and enticed. Then, after desire has conceived, it gives birth to sin; and sin, when it is full-grown, gives birth to death.*

JAMES 1:13-15

God doesn't tempt us. We are tempted by the enemy, by our own evil desires, and by the world. Let me give you some very sobering news: You will never outgrow temptation. How do I know? Well, Jesus was tempted, and we'll never outgrow Jesus. Temptation is going to be part of our lives this side of heaven. We must learn to combat it because the stakes are so high. Giving in to temptation is destructive as sin can steal your future and your family.

Ephesians 6:11 warns that the Devil is scheming against us. Let's give the Devil his due—he is an excellent schemer. Satan and his minions are working behind the scenes to trip us up and destroy our lives. We also have a sin nature, and we rationalize things, which means we'll tell ourselves rational lies. Lastly, the world and culture are trying to shape us, and we must combat this too. The ways of the world are not the same as the ways of God, so we must ask God to help us see where we're more worldly than with Him.

*Today I will remember:*

- God doesn't tempt me.
- I am tempted by the schemes of the enemy, my own sin nature, and by the world.

*Jesus, protect me today from the schemes of the Devil, from myself, and from the ways of the world. Help me to seek You and Your truth. Help me to flee from evil and cling to righteousness. Give me the grace and strength to fight the good fight of faith.*

# A SIMPLE MYSTERY

*Those who live according to the flesh have their minds set on what the flesh desires; but those who live in accordance with the Spirit have their minds set on what the Spirit desires.*

ROMANS 8:5

God guides our lives through the teachings of His Word and the guidance of His Spirit. The Holy Spirit indwells every follower of Jesus, and He is a counselor, comforter, and friend to those who trust in Him. But sometimes being guided by the Spirit can seem mysterious. I think that's because we way overcomplicate it.

Following the Holy Spirit is as simple as thinking about the things He desires for us. There is a war going on inside all believers. It's the tug of war between our flesh, or old sin nature, and what it desires versus what the Holy Spirit desires. It's not an angel on one shoulder and the Devil on the other like in the old cartoons. This conflict is like having our souls stretched in two different directions. The key to the Spirit winning this war is your thought life.

Perhaps you've heard the story of the missionary talking with a tribal chief who was a new believer in Jesus. The chief said there were now two dogs fighting within him. The missionary asked which one wins. The chief responded, "The one I feed the most." Your soul is constantly being fed by an outside source. Feed the things of the Spirit, and the Spirit wins. Feed the things of the flesh, and the flesh will win.

*Today I will remember:*

- When I think about the things of God, the things of God will be evident in my life.
- My life goes where my mind goes.
- I will guard my thoughts.

*Holy Spirit, fill me with Your desires. Help me to think on the things that are pleasing to You. I choose to focus on You today, and I pray that Your fruit would be evident in my life.*

# DO WHAT IT SAYS

*Do not merely listen to the word, and so deceive yourselves. Do what it says.*

JAMES 1:22

I love the book of James. James is a cut-to-the chase, no-frilly-language, in-your-face, straight-up dropping-truth-bombs-like-they're-hot kind of dude. He just tells it like it is. It's a great book for guys to start with. Frankly, there's not a lot of room for interpretation. It's very clear.

James was the half-brother of Jesus and did not become a believer until after the resurrection. That makes sense to me. After all, what would your brother have to do to prove to you that he was God? That's a hard sell. He'd have to rise from the dead or something. You get the picture. James would go on to be a powerful leader in the church, and it all began with his testimony that he had seen the risen Christ.

James says in our verse today that we deceive ourselves, and here's the catch: We deceive ourselves *while we're listening to the Bible.* What does he mean? If I were to ask you to describe a spiritual man, what would you say? My guess is most of us would describe someone who goes to church, reads his Bible, and prays. Someone who spends a lot of time listening to the Word. James says these things can be deceiving. A spiritual, godly man listens and does what the Word says. The power is not in the listening, but in the doing. We think ourselves spiritual because we know some Bible. James warns us to remember that it's not just what you know, but what you show. Don't deceive yourself; what God is after is obedience.

*Today I will remember:*

- I must do what the Bible says.
- Maturity is less about knowing and more about doing.
- My actions speak louder than my words.

*Lord, help me not just be a hearer of the Word, but a doer. Let me not deceive myself. Loving You is about obedience.*

# BORN FREE!

*It is for freedom that Christ has set us free.*
*Stand firm, then, and do not let yourselves*
*be burdened again by a yoke of slavery.*
GALATIANS 5:1

This past summer I celebrated the honor of having pastored the same church for the past twenty years. Some of those days have gone by slowly, but the years have gone by fast. My wife encouraged me to celebrate by doing something special for myself. I thought about it and got her permission to buy a motorcycle. I had an Indian Chieftain years ago and missed the freedom of going for rides in the desert mountains of Arizona where I live. So I shopped around and bought a Harley Road Glide Special. I call my Harley time "wind therapy." There's a sense of freedom you feel when you're out on the open road on a bike, and yes, I always wear a helmet!

What makes you feel free? Our verse for today says that Christ has set us free. Free from what? A yoke of slavery. The apostle Paul is talking about freedom from shame and sin. Free of the burdens of past mistakes. Freedom from the weight of guilt. In Jesus, we have moved from a transactional arrangement with God as His subjects to a relationship through Jesus as His sons. We are no longer slaves, but children of God. We are now empowered to break away from sin because we are loved. To be born again is to be born free.

*Today I will remember:*

- I am not a slave, but a son!
- Jesus has set me free from guilt and shame.
- To be born again is to be born free.

*Jesus, thank You for Your great love.*
*Thank You that You covered all my sin through*
*Your sacrifice on the cross. I am free to live for You!*

# ACCOUNTING

*So then, each of us will give an account of ourselves to God.*
ROMANS 14:12

For some, it's scary to realize that God is watching us and that we will give an account for everything we do. Perhaps you hear the band Police right now singing, "Every move you make. Every step you take, I'll be watching you." But the aim of our verse today is not to make us afraid, but to keep us humble. It's a warning to avoid arrogance and self-righteousness.

We often judge people for things the Bible doesn't specifically condemn. We might do this to feel better about ourselves, but the truth is it's sinful. The apostle Paul is reminding us here to not get cocky. At the end of the day, we'll all stand before a holy God and give an account of our lives.

Therefore, we might want to show a little humility and embrace the fact that we don't have it all together. Is there any area where you judge people apart from the Bible? Perhaps it's politics. You think people who vote differently are not as smart or righteous as you. Maybe it's church culture. When I was kid, the rule was you "don't smoke, drink, or chew, or go with girls that do." None of which the Bible addresses. The point is this: Be careful how you judge others, because God is going to judge you.

*Today I will remember:*
- I can be right but still be wrong in how I go about being right.
- I will give an account to God for how I treat others.

*Jesus, help me to love others the way that You love me.*
*May I treat the Bible as a mirror to examine my own life*
*instead of as a microscope to inspect everyone else's.*

# FOLLOW YOUR HEART?

*The heart is deceitful above all things*
*and beyond cure. Who can understand it?*
JEREMIAH 17:9

I was talking to a young woman the other day on our church patio. She was a single mom with three kids in tow and as we shook hands, I noticed a tattoo on her arm. It read, "follow your heart." I mentioned it, and she began to tell me that following your heart will never lead you astray. I then asked about her three children and their ages, and she told me her story about being in love when she was young, marrying an abusive man everyone had warned her about, and how hard her life had been since. I felt great compassion for her and got her connected with a ministry in our church that helps people in recovery. As I left that conversation, I wondered if she made the connection. Following her heart had led her astray. Instead of listening to the wise counsel of others, she listened to her heart and made poor decisions that caused great pain.

Our hearts will lie to us. In fact, no one will lie to you more than you. We even have a word for it: rationalizing. I pray regularly for self-awareness and wish I could give this gift to others. Your heart will lead you astray. While emotions are important, we can't live our lives by them. We need God's Word and the wisdom of people who love us to help us see what we can't see. I encourage you not to follow your heart, but to follow the Scriptures.

*Today I will remember:*

- My heart will lie to me.
- I need the Bible and others to help me see what I can't see.
- Christians don't follow their hearts; they follow Jesus.

*Jesus, give me the wisdom of Your Word.*
*Help me to know the truth and to walk in it even*
*when my feelings say otherwise. You always know best.*

# DYING TO SELF

*Then Jesus said to his disciples, "Whoever wants to be my disciple must deny themselves and take up their cross and follow me."*

MATTHEW 16:24

All growth, maturity, and learning require death to self. There is no advancement of any kind without some type of personal surrender. To win in battle you must surrender your fear, die to it, and bravely advance. To learn a skill, you must die to your pride because you're probably going to look a little foolish at first. Any time you follow a personal trainer or are being led by a coach, you choose to die to your way and submit yourself to theirs.

Our verse today is about dying to self and following Jesus. It's a daily decision to submit to His way of life and His leadership. I used to think this verse was about suffering. It might include that at times, but it's mainly about submission. An apprentice, student, or disciple submits to the way of his master. We learn to be with the master, think like the master, and do what the master would do if he were in our place. Discipleship is continually being in a state of submission, growth, and change.

The truth is, we are all dying to ourselves already. Every one of us is already taking up a cross of some sort. We do this for more money or to get the corner office; we die to reality and present a false image of ourselves so others will think well of us. Followers of Jesus, however, choose to die to themselves and trust in Him.

*Today I will remember:*

- All growth, maturity, and learning require death to self.
- Taking up my cross is dying to my way of life and learning from Jesus His way of life.

*Jesus, everyone follows something or someone. I pray that I would trust and follow You. You are my coach and trainer in how to live. You are Lord.*

# FAITH

*Now faith is confidence in what we hope for*
*and assurance about what we do not see.*

HEBREWS 11:1

There's an idea out there that Christianity is about blind faith. The myth is that you must accept all of it without critical thinking. That's not true. Christians are to have a blind love. We're to love people regardless of race, culture, or socioeconomic background. Our faith, however, is not blind; it is based on what we know. Faith is about being confident in the person of God and convinced of His faithfulness, despite not knowing all of the details. Faith isn't wishful thinking, but a logical, rational trust.

If you have ever flown in an airplane, you practiced faith. You made a faith decision based on the evidence. You presumed the plane had been flown before, so you trusted in it. You assumed that the pilot was well trained and had lots of experience. You trusted that trained mechanics were keeping the aircraft in top condition. You had no conclusive proof of any of these things until you landed safely at your destination. Until that moment, you were living by faith.

Faith is about trust in the evidence: taking people at their word or taking God at His word. Many say they must see it to believe it. That's not true, and it's hypocritical. Faith is confidence and assurance of what we do not see, but it is not totally blind. Where does the evidence point? To head in that direction is to walk by faith.

*Today I will remember:*

- Faith is about being confident in the person of God and convinced of His faithfulness.
- Faith isn't wishful thinking, but a logical, rational trust.

*Father, I choose to trust You because of what*
*I see and know of You. Help me to know*
*You more, so that I might trust You more.*

# GOOD EYES

*"The eye is the lamp of the body. If your eyes are healthy, your whole body will be full of light."*
MATTHEW 6:22

I've worn glasses since I was nineteen. Most people don't recognize me without them. My boys used to call me "backwards Superman." If we were in a restaurant and I wanted to remain incognito, I would take my glasses off, unlike Superman, who put them on when presenting himself as Clark Kent.

Our verse today is not about 20/20 vision, but about focus. Healthy eyes here mean healthy focus. Our focus either fills our lives with darkness or with light. The world wants to keep us laser-focused on all kinds of unhealthy things. Everything from whether we're keeping up with the Joneses or lusting over women on a computer screen. The darkness is all around us. Healthy eyes are about healthy choices. Here are a few suggestions:

1. Go the first hour of every day without looking at your phone. Instead, pray, and perhaps read a devotional like this one. Go for a walk. Listen to good music or even just sit in silence. Start your day with good focus.
2. Limit your screen time. Television and social media can fill us up with dark things. The tricky thing is, it's a slow fade. Many times, it starts innocently but can quickly go awry. Limit your screen time.
3. Get a couple of good friends who will help you check your eyesight on a regular basis. Your eye can't see your I. It's easy to be self-deceived, so schedule regular checkups.

*Today I will remember:*
- Healthy focus makes for a healthy soul.
- What I focus on is what I move towards.
- Good focus leads to good things.

*Father, I pray I would practice good sight habits. Help me to protect my vision, so that my soul may be full of light. May my focus always be fixed on the things of You.*

# JUDGMENT BLOCKING

*Therefore, let us stop passing judgment on one another. Instead, make up your mind not to put any stumbling block or obstacle in the way of a brother or sister.*

ROMANS 14:13

There are no jerks for Jesus; there are just jerks. Have you ever met someone who was passionate about his faith, zealous even, but his approach was terrible? I have. A friend of mine calls people like this a "jerk for Jesus." They might be right in what they are saying, but they're wrong in how they are saying it. This happens on social media all the time. I'm embarrassed at times for my Christian brothers who argue online. This rarely accomplishes anything other than pushing non-Christians further away. I mean, has anyone who has been argued against online ever actually changed their mind? Maybe, but it's a safe bet that those moments are few and far between.

Being hyper-judgmental can be a stumbling block to many coming to faith. Sometimes we can be so passionate about our position that we forget to love. In those moments, we must remember that our goal is not to win arguments, but to win people. Have you ever been right about something, but completely wrong in how you presented it? Yeah, me too.

We must make judgment calls all the time, but we can do that and still represent the truth winsomely. It's been said that one great cause of atheism in the world is Christians who do not represent the love of Christ. I think there's truth to that statement. We want to lovingly invite people into the kingdom of God, not be a stumbling block on the path to them getting there.

*Today I will remember:*

- There are no jerks for Jesus.
- It is not our goal to win arguments, but to win people.

*Jesus, help me to represent Your kingdom well. May my life help people and not hinder them in coming to faith. Help me to love people I disagree with.*

# GOOD TALK

*Do not let any unwholesome talk come out of your mouths, but only what is helpful for building others up according to their needs, that it may benefit those who listen.*

EPHESIANS 4:29

I saw a T-shirt recently that said, "I love Jesus, but I cuss a little." The funny thing was it was an older woman who goes to our church who was wearing the shirt. That made me laugh. I can relate. I don't always say wholesome things. How about you? I guess we're all still a work in progress.

Most people think this verse is simply about cussing. It includes that, but it's much more than that. For example, church people might see this verse and immediately think they don't use foul language, so all is good. At the same time, they might gossip, say self-righteous and judgmental things to people who sin differently than they do, and maybe speak ill of people because they're of a different race. These things are more harmful than a culturally-frowned-upon adjective or noun.

Here's the bottom-line question: Do we build people up with our words, or do we tear them down? "Unwholesome talk" is tear-down talk. It doesn't benefit those who hear it. It harms them. The litmus test of our words is whether they help or hurt others. Jesus cares much more about how our mouths affect others' lives than what's culturally acceptable or mannerly in church. You could never say a cussword in your life and still have an unwholesome mouth. Choose today to bless people with your words. Be an encourager. Say things that benefit those around you.

*Today I will remember:*

- My words can build others up.
- Wholesome talk is about encouraging others and blessing them with what I say.

*God, make my words a blessing today to all I encounter. Help me build others up and not tear them down. May my words be pleasing to You.*

# KILLING COMPARISON

*"You shall not covet your neighbor's house. You shall not covet your neighbor's wife, or his male or female servant, his ox or donkey, or anything that belongs to your neighbor."*

EXODUS 20:17

Our verse is part of the big ten. It's one of the Ten Commandments. Any time you see one of God's commands, I would encourage you to think like my sons when they were around five years of age. I would tell them to do something, and they would ask why. It wasn't defiance; it was curiosity. Do what God says and be curious as to why He says it. The more you understand the why, the more mature you will become. Why does God want us not to covet? Because comparison kills joy. It has been said that where comparison begins, contentment ends. Nothing squashes gratitude and contentment like comparing and coveting.

We live in the age of coveting. Social media is fueled by it. It's easy to get jealous of other people's lives when you're scrolling through pictures on Instagram and Facebook. People seem to have better marriages, better kids, better vacations, better toys, and better lives. Beware of this. Any time we look at social media, we're comparing the worst of our lives with someone else's highlight reel. Most people are giving you the just right light, the right angle, and they're most likely painting a picture that is not the full reality of what's going on. You're facing reality, and they're giving you a facade.

Think about your life for a moment. What are you grateful for? It can be simple, shallow, deep, or profound. Gratitude is the antidote to coveting and comparison. Make gratitude your go-to response, and contentment will increase. Celebrate others' blessings and be grateful for your own.

*Today I will remember:*

- Where comparison begins, contentment ends.
- Gratitude should be my go-to response.

*Father, thank You for Your blessings. Help me to make gratitude my go-to response and learn to celebrate others' blessings. Forgive me for coveting.*

# MOTHER NATURE?

*In the beginning God created the heavens and the earth.*
GENESIS 1:1

As I write this, I'm sitting in my home office at six in the morning drinking a cup of coffee and waiting for a friend to pick me up. We're headed to the Arizona mountains today to prep our deer stands for an archery hunt we'll do in a few weeks. I was inspired last year by a podcast of Cameron Hanes, probably the best archery elk hunter in the world. I listened to his stories of bow hunting and decided I wanted to learn as well. So I called Jeff, a guy from my church, and asked him to teach me. He kindly entered the fray of being my bow hunting coach. I went with him last year for the first time, and I got a deer on the first morning of the first day, at thirty-two yards, on my knees, and from a ground blind. Epic!

There's something special about being in nature. It connects me with God like nothing else. When I want to spend time with God, I don't journal. I go for a hike. How about you? Sometimes men think they must be a reader or a seminary professor to know God. That's not true. After all, some of the most devout followers of Jesus throughout history were illiterate. They were taught the Word of God and did what it said. Discipleship is about obedience.

I'll be in my deer stand soon praying, listening, and just being still in the presence of the Father. After all, it's not Mother Nature who made the beauty of the world; it's Father God.

*Today I will remember:*

- Growing in God is about doing what He says.
- I can connect with Him anywhere, at any time.

*Lord, thank You for the beauty of creation. I see Your artistry in the mountains, trees, and oceans. Thank You for sharing these things with me. I want to enjoy them more and more with You.*

# LIVE FOR GOD

*Do not conform to the pattern of this world, but be transformed by the renewing of your mind. Then you will be able to test and approve what God's will is—his good, pleasing and perfect will.*

ROMANS 12:2

How do we know God's will? How do we find it? Many think that God's will is elusive. That it's a mystery to be solved, a riddle we must figure out. Our verse today teaches us something different. God's will is not something we have to find; it's something that finds us. If we live for God, God's will lives in us.

If we're going to live for God, then we must live a different pattern. What are the patterns of your life? What does your daily rhythm look like? Our patterns or habits conform and shape us. For example, if you make New Year's resolutions, do they look any different than those of someone who doesn't believe in God? Is there any difference in the pattern?

The world shapes us to its ways. We must not let it conform us. Instead, by giving God our minds, we must allow Him to transform us. The more we follow the pattern of getting into His Word, the more our minds are renewed. We begin to see things differently, and we begin to live differently. God's will is not something we have to find; it's something we choose to live. It's not a vision of the future that we find in a crystal ball; it's a decision to live each day for Christ. If we choose to live for God, His will lives in us.

*Today I will remember:*

- God's will is not something we have to find; it's something we choose to live.
- When I live for God and obey Him, His will lives in me.

*Father, help me to live Your patterns. I'm always being shaped by something, and I choose to be shaped by You. Following Your will is simply doing what You say.*

# IT'S NOT HOCUS POCUS

*Those who live according to the flesh have their minds set on what the flesh desires; but those who live in accordance with the Spirit have their minds set on what the Spirit desires. The mind governed by the flesh is death, but the mind governed by the Spirit is life and peace.*

ROMANS 8:5-6

The Christian life is about learning to live by the Spirit. When you see the word *Spirit* in your Bible, if it begins with a capital "S," it's talking about the Holy Spirit. If it's lower case, it could be talking about your spirit or angels (because angels are spiritual beings). The Spirit leads us away from sin and empowers us to live for God. In the church I grew up in, we didn't talk much about the Holy Spirit. I always thought that things about Him were in the realm of hocus pocus. Perhaps you can relate. But the Holy Spirit is a person in the Trinity. God is triune and is Father, Son, and Holy Spirit. Just as Jesus was with His disciples to teach and to comfort them 2,000 years ago, the Spirit is with us today.

Look at our verses for today. Simply put, the guidance of the Spirit is not about hocus pocus, but focus. He is the Spirit of Jesus. We think about Jesus continually and ask the Holy Spirit to lead us. What is your mind focused on? Whether we work, play, or rest, we are called to fix our minds on Jesus. This allows His Spirit to guide us. Yet if we focus our minds on sin, our sin nature will guide us. Think on the things of the Spirit, and the things of the Spirit will be evident in your life.

*Today I will remember:*

- Those who live by the Holy Spirit think on the things of the Holy Spirit.
- It's not hocus pocus, but focus.

*Holy Spirit, guide me. Help me to focus on Jesus today and empower me to live for Him. The more I think on You, the more Your ways will be evident in my life.*

# NUMBERED DAYS

*Teach us to number our days, that we may gain a heart of wisdom.*
PSALM 90:12

Zach, who is ninety-four, was my counselor during a rough season in my life. We built a friendship, and he became a member of the church where I pastor. We get together once a quarter or so for lunch, coffee, or just to talk. Zach is wise. Years ago, he was an Army tank commander who suffered from alcoholism. As a result, he lost his marriage; but in all that pain, he met Jesus, got sober, and became a licensed counselor so that he could help others. I love Zach! He has told me that time seems to speed up as you get older. He assumes it's because you're measuring current time against all the time that has passed. He told me that in your senior years, the days get slower, and the years get faster.

Our verse for today is a short line from a prayer of Moses. Life is short. Our time here on this earth is limited. The mortality rate for every man still hovers right around one hundred percent. It is good for us to number our days because it helps motivate us to make the most of them. Here's a big question: What are you doing with your one and only life? Don't waste it! Invest it. If you knew you were going to die soon, what conversations would you have? Who would you spend time with? How would you live your remaining days? Go ahead and do those things now. After all, your days are numbered.

*Today I will remember:*
- I should make the most of the time I've been given.
- My days are numbered.

*Father, teach me to number my days so that I might live wisely. I don't want to waste my life. I want to invest it for You.*

# MIRROR CHECK

*Anyone who listens to the word but does not do what it says is like someone who looks at his face in a mirror and, after looking at himself, goes away and immediately forgets what he looks like. But whoever looks intently into the perfect law that gives freedom, and continues in it—not forgetting what they have heard, but doing it—they will be blessed in what they do.*

JAMES 1:23-25

My wife and I just got back from a trip to Las Vegas. We live in Phoenix, and it's a very short flight. We like to go to the Cirque du Soleil shows, enjoy nice dinners, shop, and walk around. Through the years it's become a three-day date event that is good for our marriage. As I read our verses today, I thought about the mirrors in the bathroom of the hotel we usually stay in. One side is normal, but flip it over and you have a super mirror! The super mirror blows your face up to massive proportions so you can see every pore, every wrinkle. I swear if I tilt my nose up, you can probably see my brain!

Our verses for today show the importance of obedience. First, we're to treat the Bible like a mirror. It's not a pair of binoculars that we use to look at everyone else but a mirror to examine our own lives. Second, the goal of looking in the Bible is to adjust ourselves accordingly. To read the Scriptures and not change anything is like having a terrible case of bedhead, seeing it, and then going on with our day without combing our hair. Have you ever seen anyone in public and thought *I guess they don't have any mirrors at their house*? Do what the Bible says. Make the proper adjustments.

*Today I will remember:*

- I must trust and adjust.
- Reading the Bible is necessary for the adjustments God wants me to make.

*Father, give me wisdom from Your Word*
*so that I might adjust my life accordingly.*
*Your ways are best and bring freedom and life.*

# PRAYER WRESTLING

*Epaphras, who is one of you and a servant of Christ Jesus, sends greetings. He is always wrestling in prayer for you, that you may stand firm in all the will of God, mature and fully assured.*

COLOSSIANS 4:12

I prayed for you today. Most likely, we've never met, and I don't know you, but God does. He knew that you would be reading this sentence at this moment even while I'm writing it. Pretty cool. The verse here says that Epaphras wrestled in prayer for the people in this church in Colossae. He's wrestling because that's where we fight the spiritual war, in prayer. I want friends who will wrestle for me, and I want to be a friend who wrestles in prayer for others.

This wrestling doesn't mean that the prayer is so intense that we're out of breath. It doesn't mean drops of sweat are pouring off our heads as we body-slam the Devil and his army to the proverbial spiritual mat of the cosmos! It simply means that we earnestly pray that people will be strong in the Lord and that they would do His will.

Who are you wrestling for? Start by wrestling for your family today. Maybe as you drive to work, choose to turn off the radio, podcast, or audiobook and pray instead. This is part of what it means to fight for our families, we wrestle for them in prayer. Wrestle for a few friends. Pray for the men in your life who are more like brothers and ask them to pray for you. Wrestle for your country. Pray for the nation and its leaders. Part of fighting the good fight of faith is to wrestle in prayer for others.

*Today I will remember:*

- When I pray for others, I fight for them.
- Prayer is a powerful weapon to support the people of God.
- This is how I fight against the enemy.

*Holy Spirit, guide me as I pray for others. Help me to wrestle according to Your will. I pray for my family and friends. Give them strength to do Your will.*

# THE SECRET DISCIPLE

*Joseph of Arimathea, a prominent member of the Council, who was himself waiting for the kingdom of God, went boldly to Pilate and asked for Jesus' body.*

MARK 15:43

I first learned of Joseph of Arimathea in a movie. He's talked about in *Indiana Jones and the Last Crusade* as the one who first took hold of the Holy Grail. The Holy Grail is *not* the stuff of the Bible; it's the stuff of folklore and legend. Legend has it this was the cup that Jesus drank from at the Lord's Supper and later was filled with the actual blood of Christ. Anyone who drinks from it is blessed with immortality. It's not true, it's legend. But it does make for a cool movie.

The Bible says Joseph of Arimathea was a disciple, but a secret one. Now being a secret disciple of Jesus is better than not being a disciple at all, but disciples were not made for secrecy. Jesus desires His followers to go public with their faith. This requires courage. The verse above is a courage moment for Joseph. He goes public with his faith and loans Jesus his family tomb for three days (all that Jesus needed).

Are you similarly courageous with your faith? Faith is personal, but faith in Jesus is not meant to be private. We're to go public with it! We're not salesmen; we're just witnesses of what Jesus has done for us. Go public with your faith.

*Today I will remember:*

- Faith is personal, but it's not meant to be private.
- I am not a salesman for Jesus, but a witness to His grace in my life.

*Jesus, give me the courage to be a good witness. I want to give good testimony about Your grace in my life and how You've blessed me.*

# REST

*"Remember the Sabbath day by keeping it holy."*
EXODUS 20:8

In the Bible, rest is not a suggestion but a command. That's because God loves you and wants you to enjoy your life. God first commanded the Sabbath to former slaves. God's people had been in bondage for four hundred years and they had a mentality of slavery. They continued to think and act like slaves because all they knew was slavery. God, however, rescued them and began establishing a new way of life for them. Part of the rhythm of that new life was a day of rest, the Sabbath.

The command to take a day off every week is about trusting God as our ultimate provider and enjoying the gifts He has given us. It is a day to have fun, laugh, love, and bless our family and friends. God's will is that you work hard, do your best, and practice the rhythm of one day a week chilling out and enjoying His blessings. If you think you can't do that, then you're thinking and acting like a slave. Choose to repent and trust God.

Of course, religious people tend to ruin God's good plans. Over time, the religious leaders of God's people added a myriad of rules and regulations about what you could and could not do on the Sabbath. What God designed as a blessing, the religious leaders turned into a burden. Jesus challenged their thinking by loving and healing people on the Sabbath. It is God's commanded day of rest because He loves you. It doesn't matter which day, but it does matter that you take a day. Remember the Sabbath!

*Today I will remember:*

- God loves me and wants me to enjoy life.
- He has commanded me to take one day a week for rest.
- This is a time to enjoy my family, friends, and all that He has blessed me with.

*God, give me understanding of Your love for me. I choose to practice a day of rest and enjoyment at least once a week. Thank You for Your good gifts. May I choose to really enjoy them.*

# PUSH THROUGH

*Not only so, but we also glory in our sufferings, because we know that suffering produces perseverance; perseverance, character; and character, hope.*

ROMANS 5:3-4

Pain is hard. I never wish for it for anyone. It's also part of life. We live in a broken world because of sin. The weather is broken, the political system is broken, and I'm personally broken. I can't live up to my own standard, much less God's. However, pain can also be profitable. Nothing grows us up more than trusting God in seasons of pain. Notice the flow of our verses today. Pain produces perseverance, which builds character, which brings hope. Pain will change you, but not necessarily for the good; we must choose that.

The most fertile soil for real life change is a season of suffering. When we trust God in those times and stick to His path, He does something in our souls that otherwise would not have been possible. In times of pain, you must choose to keep doing the things you know He wants you to do. You don't vote with your feelings; you vote with your feet. You share how you feel, your frustrations and fears, and you stick to God's path. You choose to grow through whatever you're going through. Most men don't do that. Instead of facing the pain, they medicate it. We try and drink it away, or sex it away, or anger it away. None of that helps us grow. When we do these things, we're wasting the pain. Don't waste it, invest in it. It's OK to get help, talk to trusted, mature men, go to counseling, whatever you need. Face the pain and let it produce maturity in you.

*Today I will remember:*

- God gives me the strength to persevere despite what I'm going through.
- God wants me to grow through seasons of difficulty.

*Father, give me the grace to not avoid pain, but to grow and push through it. Help me to persevere and grow in character and in hope.*

# SHOWING UP IN PRAYER

*"This, then, is how you should pray: 'Our Father in heaven, hallowed be your name.'"*

MATTHEW 6:9

If you're like most men, you're intimidated by prayer. I remember talking with a man in my church who told me he was going through something difficult. I asked if he had prayed about it. He said, "Oh, man, do you think it's come to that?" I responded that everything has always come to that. We usually pray when things are bad, when we're desperate, but that's about it. Why? Because we're intimidated by prayer and are not sure how to do it.

Start simple. What if you began to pray simple, short prayers on a regular basis? Simply tell God some things that you are grateful for and ask Him to guide you each day. That's it. Nothing too profound. You don't have to be long winded. Just thank Him for a few things and ask for guidance in some area of your life. But here's the deal—do it every day at the same time and place. It's your daily meeting with God. Start to practice this, be consistent and see where it goes.

As you do, remember that God loves you and wants to spend time with you. When my boys were small, I wasn't constantly evaluating how they spoke to me. They weren't thinking about how they could use the right words when addressing Dad. They just wanted to spend time with me, and I wanted to spend time with them. Prayer is like that. Your Heavenly Father loves you. Spend time with Him. He likes it when you show up.

*Today I will remember:*

- God wants to spend time with me.
- Prayer is me simply showing up to talk with my Heavenly Father who loves me.

*Father, teach me to pray. Help me to see prayer as simple.*
*It's me spending some time with You and You with me.*
*Thank You that it's not about fancy words, but,*
*like a son with his dad, it's about time together.*

# PEACE BROTHER

*"Blessed are the peacemakers,*
*for they will be called children of God."*
MATTHEW 5:9

I've never met a blessed troublemaker. Have you? Troublemakers are on edge. They're looking for something to get upset about and they usually find it. I try to avoid people like that. I've got enough troubles, and I don't want them adding more. I think social media is a breeding ground for troublemakers. They thrive on it.

Sometimes a clip from a podcast or sermon of mine will go viral on Instagram. I don't pick the posts; we have a Comms Team that does that. Occasionally, I do something foolish: I read the comments. Big mistake. I'm amazed that people have so much time on their hands to go around angrily criticizing something they didn't really listen to or are taking out of context. Of course, then the pile-on happens. Have you ever seen the pile on? Hundreds of people arguing about it. It's so crazy! Makes me wonder if troublemakers travel in packs, at least online.

Jesus says that being a peacemaker blesses you. It reveals that you're a child of God. Followers of Jesus aren't called to make trouble. We're called to make peace. In fact, we're to be ambassadors of peace to a world full of trouble and chaos. Sometimes when I preach on this, someone will say, yeah, but we must fight to defend the truth! No. Truth is very strong and can take care of itself. We don't have to defend truth; we have to unleash it. We lovingly share the truth of Jesus and live it out. Beware the temptation to become a self-righteous online troublemaker. That doesn't bless anyone, especially you. Jesus is the Prince of Peace, and His followers are secure enough in Him to be people of peace.

*Today I will remember:*

- I'm called to be a peacemaker.
- This calling is a blessing for my life.
- Peace comes from the security I find in Jesus.

*Jesus, help me to represent Your peace in a broken*
*world full of chaos. May I be strong, kind,*
*and peacemaking in all my interactions.*

# THE CHIEF VIRTUE

*All of you, clothe yourselves with humility toward one another, because, "God opposes the proud but shows favor to the humble."*

1 PETER 5:5

Humility is the chief virtue of the Christian life; all other godly virtues flow out of it. If you want God's "favor," or grace, you must practice humility. What is humility? If you win the award for humility and then choose to accept it, does that mean you lose it? After all, wouldn't it be weird to show off your trophy of humility? I can see it now: "Out of all my trophies and accolades, I'm most proud of this humility award. It was the little people who made it possible."

Is humility timidity then? Must we constantly shrug off compliments with an "awe shucks" demeanor? Or worse yet, does humility simply allow us to be walked on by everyone else? Does it mean never standing up for yourself? No.

Humility is not timidity. Nor is it the absence of a healthy pride in accomplishment. Humility is simply reality. Pride is about pretending, and humility is about what's real. Think with me here. God is real and only operates in what's real. He will not show grace or favor to who you are pretending to be, because that person does not exist. God loves the real you. He knows the reality of your life past, present, and future. Humility is simply living in the truth of that reality before God and others. What are you pretending is not a problem? Step out of that pride and get help from God and others in your time of need.

*Today I will remember:*

- Pride is about pretending, and humility is about reality.
- The only way to experience the real God is to be courageous enough to be the real me.

*Father, I never want to oppose You. Help me to walk in the truth and continually be in the flow of Your grace. Forgive me for pretending and faking it. Thank You that You love the real me.*

# THE PROFOUND PATH

*There is a way that appears to be right,*
*but in the end it leads to death.*

PROVERBS 14:12

At the beginning of each year, people all over the world make resolutions. In principle, this is a very good thing. In the Old Testament, God established certain times of the year for His people to remember certain things and practice a reset in their lives for the days ahead. While we tend to do this at the start of each new year, it follows the same principle. Know this, every day is an opportunity for a reset. Every day is an opportunity to evaluate the direction of our lives and choose to be on God's path.

What needs to reset in your life? Our verse today tells us that appearances can be deceiving. What do people usually want to change? Often, it's in the realm of losing weight and gaining money. Those things are fine and good, but they don't bring life to one's soul. What we really need is contentment and peace. We want the profound, but this cannot be experienced on the puny path of the same old resolutions. It can only be experienced on the profound path of following Jesus. If you're looking for a reset, repent and choose to live for God. Each day is an opportunity to walk His path, a path that leads to peace.

*Today I will remember:*

- Only God's path leads to the profound.
- Pursue repentance over resolutions.

*Lord, I choose to walk Your path and live for You today.*
*My soul longs for You more than things of this world.*
*Your path leads to life and peace. Help me to walk it with You.*

# TRAINING DAYS

*Everyone who competes in the games goes into strict training. They do it to get a crown that will not last, but we do it to get a crown that will last forever.*

1 CORINTHIANS 9:25

The Christian life requires training. Most guys do not realize this. They think it's about trying. Every year they commit to trying harder. The problem is that the goal is to reflect Christlike character. Trying to be like Jesus would be like me going out right now to run an ultramarathon. It wouldn't matter how hard I tried; the task would be impossible, given my current conditioning. However, if I train each day, then over time, with a good coach, I might have a legitimate shot. The same is true of being more like Jesus. Trying doesn't work, but training does.

Training is doing what I can today, so that in the future I'll be able to do what I can't do today. Training brings growth. So stop trying and start training. The word *disciple* is the root word for discipline. What are you doing to train in godliness?

You're training right now as you read this book. You train when you go to "team meetings," which is church. A Bible-based church gives you inspiration, teaching, and coaching in following Jesus. All of this is in partnership with the Holy Spirit. He empowers you to do character-wise what you could never do on your own. Put together a training plan and follow it. Prayer, Scripture, time with God each day, church, and good friends to help you along the way. All this trains us in following Jesus.

*Today I will remember:*

- I should choose training over just trying.
- The more I train in Jesus, the more I will trust in Jesus.
- To pray, read, and go to church is to work out in Him.

*Jesus, help me to train in You. Teach me the little things I can do each day that help me live out the big things over the span of my life.*

# THINK ON THE BOOK

*"Keep this Book of the Law always on your lips; meditate on it day and night, so that you may be careful to do everything written in it. Then you will be prosperous and successful."*

JOSHUA 1:8

I used to think meditation was for weirdos. A weirdo by my definition has always been someone who is not like me. I thought meditation was for people who don't eat meat. People who are "artsy fartsy." Skinny dudes in skinny jeans. People unlike me! Weird. God has all types of children with all kinds of personalities, and to keep it real with you, we're all a bit weird in various ways. Meditation, however, is not just for the mystics. It's for all of us. To meditate here is to focus, process, and apply.

In Eastern meditation, the goal is to empty your mind. In Christian meditation, we fill our minds. Specifically, we fill our minds with God's Word. Why? Notice the verse: "so that you may be careful to do everything written in it." We want to think about what the Bible says, focus on it, and process it, so that we might obey it. God tells Joshua here that the result of living out His Word is prosperity and success. There's a flow to it; talk about the Bible, think on it throughout the day, do what it says, and this leads to a better way of life.

How can you keep God's Word at the forefront of your thoughts and conversations today? Look for opportunities to live it out. Have a conversation at the dinner table about something you're learning. Learn to think on the Bible, talk about the Bible, and live out what the Bible says.

*Today I will remember:*

- I grow by talking about the Bible, thinking on it, and doing what it says.
- Doing what the Bible says leads to a better way of life.

*Father, help me to focus on Your truth today, so that I might live it out. Help me to make Your Word a regular topic of conversation. Help me to think on it and apply it.*

# WORK OUT

*Therefore, my dear friends, as you have always obeyed—not only in my presence, but now much more in my absence—continue to work out your salvation with fear and trembling, for it is God who works in you to will and to act in order to fulfill his good purpose.*

PHILIPPIANS 2:12-13

Working out is how you stay in good physical shape. The irony is that your body does not grow stronger and healthier through comfort. Man, I wish it did. Wouldn't it be great if the best thing you could do for your body was lounge around on the couch and eat chips and salsa? If that were the case, I'd most likely be an Olympian by now. The body doesn't grow at rest; it grows through resistance. Rest is necessary, of course, but health comes from a rhythm of resistance and rest. Your soul is the same. We must work out our salvation.

This working it out is at least threefold.

1. We work out our doubts. Christianity not only allows questions, but it also encourages them. People who never doubt concern me. I feel like they are completely self-deceived, or just not thinking very much. As I get older, my faith is stronger than it's ever been, and yet I have more questions than I've ever had. What do we do with that? We work it out. We keep going.
2. We also work out our faith in action. We give and we serve. God works His grace in us, and we work it out among us. We love others as Jesus has loved us.
3. We work out our faith in our pain. Pain will change you, but not necessarily for the good; you must choose that. We must choose to grow through whatever we're going through.

*Today I will remember:*

- Christianity encourages questions.
- We love others as Jesus has loved us.
- We must choose to grow through whatever we're going through.

*Father, help me in my doubts, in loving others, and through times of pain. Help me to continue to grow through whatever I go through.*

# TRAIN YOUR BRAIN

*"I am the vine; you are the branches.*
*If you remain in me and I in you, you will bear*
*much fruit; apart from me you can do nothing."*
JOHN 15:5

At church when I was younger, the pastor would give an inspirational sermon on following Jesus and living for Him. I would leave fired up! I was convicted, motivated, and ready to follow Jesus with all my heart. The only problem was, I didn't know how. I knew there were sins I wanted to stop, but surely following Jesus was more than stopping something. Surely there was more to it than just sin management.

Today's verse is about vines, branches, and fruit. It's a quote from Jesus about how the Christian life works. The fruit is about character and the vines and branches are about power. We stay connected to Jesus. We learn from Him, and His power flows in us and through us, and this changes us.

If you want the Jesus fruit, then you stay connected to the Jesus vine. We train to remain in our brains. The more you fill your mind with the things of Jesus, the more the things of Jesus will be evident in your life. Following is about thinking, and thinking leads to acting. What's going on inside reveals itself on the outside. Apple seeds produce apples. New seeds of thought from Jesus produce the fruit of Jesus. Teach yourself to think about Him continually. Train to remain in your brain.

*Today I will remember:*

- If I want the Jesus fruit, stay connected to the Jesus vine.
- I train to remain in my brain.
- I must train in thinking on Jesus.

*Jesus, I choose to focus my thoughts on You each day. Change the root of my thinking, so that the fruit of my actions matches Yours. Teach me to remain in You.*

# TRUE WORSHIP

*Therefore, I urge you, brothers and sisters, in view of God's mercy, to offer your bodies as a living sacrifice, holy and pleasing to God—this is your true and proper worship.*

ROMANS 12:1

People usually equate worship with music. When was your greatest moment of worship? Maybe you're thinking about a song that gave you the chills. Years ago, I attended a men's conference called Promise Keepers. It was held at the football stadium in San Diego where the Chargers played. Fifty thousand men were in attendance and the music and singing were amazing. I remember standing there as we sang the classic hymn "A Mighty Fortress is Our God." Fifty thousand men there were belting out the chorus! I had chills from head to toe, but that type of worship is not what our verse is about today.

The Bible teaches here that true worship is less about music and more about how we live. Music is important, but real worship is not about the goose bumps. It's about obeying God. We are called to be a living sacrifice. Our greatest moments of worship will probably not be at church, but in the privacy of our own homes. It's when we choose to be honest instead of lie, when we run from lust instead of giving into it, when we choose patience instead of anger. Worship is when obeying God costs us something. It's fueled by remembering God's mercy, and in that remembrance we sacrifice. Songs of worship are good, but a life of worship is better.

*Today I will remember:*

- Real worship is about how I live.
- It's less about singing and more about how I am living.

*God, I want to worship You with my life. When I sing at church, I pray that it's simply a reflection of how I'm living. The more I think of Your mercy toward me, the more I want to live for You.*

# February

## MARRIAGE

Husbands, love your wives, just as Christ loved
the church and gave himself up for her.
*Ephesians 5:25*

# NOT ABOUT ME

*Husbands, love your wives, just as Christ loved the church and gave himself up for her.*
EPHESIANS 5:25

Pop quiz. What would make your marriage considerably better right now? Go!

What thoughts came to mind? If you're like me, you probably had thoughts about what your wife could do better. Possibly even a dream scenario of how she should greet you when you come home or when you wake up in the morning. After all, if she would just do some things differently, then married life would be perfect! Right? This is how we think. We blame our marriage woes on our wives. Blame is lame. That's how it's spelled, b-*lame*.

We can't control anyone else. We can gripe, complain, encourage, and compliment, but, at the end of the day, the only person we can control is us. So what are *we* supposed to be doing? The Bible says we're to lay down our lives for our wives. In fact, we're to love our wives as Jesus loves us. He doesn't sit around and gripe about us. Jesus actively serves us in His grace.

Grace is unmerited favor; it's getting what we don't deserve. Grace is what His love looks like when it meets our imperfections, mistakes, and sin. Graceful love is not focused on what it is not getting. Grace-filled love focuses on what it can give. Perhaps our marriages would be better if we took responsibility for ourselves, how we think, and how we act. Instead of waiting on our wives to love us, we could lead and just choose to always love them first. How does your wife feel loved? It's probably different than how you feel loved. Ask her. Listen well and act accordingly.

*Today I will remember:*

- I ought to love my wife as Jesus loves me.
- My marriage requires me to take the lead and choose to love her first.
- Grace gives and serves.

*Thank You for Your grace, Jesus. May I learn to receive it, and may I give it to my wife. Help me to love her in grace.*

# GOOD LISTENING

*My dear brothers and sisters, take note of this: Everyone should be quick to listen, slow to speak and slow to become angry.*

JAMES 1:19

To listen is to love. For the longest time when my wife would share a problem, I would immediately try to solve it. After all, isn't that why she was sharing it with me? She just needs the solution, right? Over time, I've realized that she mostly just wants to be heard. To be cared for. She wants me to listen.

Listening is a lost art. We're all looking at our phones or jumping onto social media, ready to give our opinion. We're quick to speak. Caring for others means giving them your undivided attention. When I tried this, I could set aside the distractions, but I wasn't very good at the actual listening. If others were talking, I'd be thinking about what I was going to say and not really taking in what they were saying.

Our verse for today gives the solution:

*Be quick to listen* ... Listen first. Make listening your first goal in any conversation. This is going to require intentionality, but after a while you can make it a habit. Look people in the eye and really take in what they're saying.

*Slow to speak* ... Don't get distracted with what you're going to say next. Instead, ask questions to better understand what the other person is saying. Good questions bring clarity and understanding.

*Slow to become angry* ... Most arguments with people we love are really about misunderstandings that come from a lack of listening. Asking good questions and genuinely caring about what a person is saying brings peace.

Choose to practice the art of listening well. It will change all your relationships for the better.

*Today I will remember:*

- Listening should be my goal in any conversation.
- Being slow to speak requires asking questions.
- Genuinely caring about others brings peace in conversation.

*Lord, give me the grace to love people well. Forgive me for the times I'm selfish and passive. Help me to listen well, that I might love well.*

# LOVE IS A VERB

*Love is patient, love is kind. It does not envy, it does not boast, it is not proud.*

1 CORINTHIANS 13:4

What is love? This question reminds me of the SNL sketch guest starring Jim Carrey bouncing his head to the rhythm of the song "What is Love" by Haddaway. How would you answer the question? The Bible teaches that love is a verb while most people think it's a noun. If you think love is just a feeling, you're on the noun route. You feel it, baby! But what happens in your marriage when the feelings begin dissipating? Disappearing? Does that mean that love is gone?

The Bible teaches that love is about what you do or don't do. First Corinthians 13 is known as the love chapter, and the first few verses are read at almost all Christian weddings. This chapter does not define love as much as it describes it. It's a description of what love looks like when it's happening and when it's not. Love is not a noun that describes my feelings; it's an action that I choose to take.

Feelings follow action. Years ago, my wife and I went through a very difficult season in our marriage. I wasn't sure I would ever have great feelings of love for her again. At the time, she was pregnant with our second son. During her first trimester, she got very sick. For weeks, she couldn't do anything, which meant I did everything. I cared for her, our oldest son, and the house, and I worked fifty-plus hours a week. You know what happened? The more I served her, the more I fell in love with her. Feelings follow action. You choose to love, and then the feelings follow.

*Today I will remember:*

- Love is a verb.
- It's not a noun that describes my feelings.
- It's about actions that I choose to take.

*Father, today I choose to love. I won't wait on the feelings; I'll choose to act knowing that the feelings will follow. I decide to love.*

# GROWING UP

*"Therefore what God has joined together let no one separate."*
MARK 10:9

No one plans to separate when they get married. When we get married, we plan on staying together until death do us part. Then do you know what happens over time? Life. People change as their lives go on. My wife has been married to several different men over the past twenty-three years, and they've all been me. I've changed, she's changed, and we must grow and adapt and commit to loving each other.

The most common advice I give when people are struggling in their marriages is don't give up, grow up. Unless there's infidelity or abuse, most marriages still have tremendous potential. Usually, our troubles come from selfishness and unrealistic expectations. Even when there are realistic expectations, no one is sharing what they expect. It's hard to meet an expectation if you don't know what it is.

Other times, we believe the myth that we're supposed to constantly feel in love, that wild sex should be a nightly thing, and that the other person should make me feel complete. If that last sentence applies to you, then it's time for you to grow up. Marriage is a partnership where you learn to grow over time as you give and serve and learn to love the other person for who she is. If most of your thoughts are about you and what you're not getting, then it's time to mature.

We can't control anyone else, but we can only control what we're going to do. God joins marriages together, so they're not meant to be easily separated. How does God want you to grow in your marriage? Commit to that.

*Today I will remember:*

- Instead of thinking about giving up, I will think about how to grow up.
- I am responsible for growing and becoming a better husband.

*Father, help me to love my wife the way that You love.*
*Show me how You want me to grow and change.*
*May I always be committed to growing up.*

# KEEPING IT PURE

*Marriage should be honored by all, and the marriage bed kept pure, for God will judge the adulterer and all the sexually immoral.*

HEBREWS 13:4

Let's talk about lust for a moment (a sentence I know that *no one* likes to hear). Scripture clearly teaches that lust is wrong, yet it resides in all of us. I am writing to men, and I know that lust is part of our day-to-day experience. It is important to remember though, that lust and sexual attraction aren't the same thing. While lust is self-serving, attraction can lead you to serve your wife. It is good for a man to desire his wife and a wife to desire her husband.

At the time of this writing, I've been married for twenty-three years. I love my wife. I desire my wife. Sometimes when I see her, I'm still like a teenage boy, excited and curious. And this is after seeing her almost every day for twenty-three years. However, I also notice that other women are attractive. My guess is you can relate. How do we deal with this? Well, we do what this verse says. We keep it pure.

When we see an attractive woman, we resist and replace. Most of us just try to resist. I'm not going to look! I'm not going to think about that woman! The foundation here is good. We are resisting, but it is insufficient, and our desires run amok. Instead of just saying, *I'm not going to look*, add to it *I'm going to choose to love my wife*. Replace your lustful thoughts by thinking about your wife. Feed the desire, just focus it on the beautiful woman you married. Keep it pure.

*Today I will remember:*

- Purity is not an absence of desire.
- Purity is about properly focused desire.
- I can resist attraction toward others and replace it with the desire I have for my wife.

*God, help me to love my wife purely. I choose to have eyes only for her. Teach me to resist and replace and to live purely.*

# MARRIAGE IS ONE

*That is why a man leaves his father and mother and is united to his wife, and they become one flesh.*
GENESIS 2:24

Marriage is the lifelong journey of two people becoming one. I believe it's meant to reflect the character of God. God is triune. He is Father, Son, and Spirit, and yet He's one God. This being who is three and yet one, one and yet three, creates two in Adam and Eve and then commands them to become one. The Trinity is true and truly mysterious. The Bible says marriage is a mystery too.

When this verse says "one flesh" it has a more profound meaning than just sexually. It's about two souls becoming intertwined and bound together as well as two bodies. God made men and women different. This is a source of strength and it's a challenge. The lifelong journey of becoming one is less about a fifty-fifty arrangement and more about each person surrendering their selfish desires in service to the other. It's about mutual, self-giving love.

Notice also that the verse says we leave something old to start something new. While we're still connected to our families of origin, they are no longer our highest priority. We have started a new family, where the most important relationship is between the husband and wife. We are not called to be one with our parents. We are not called to be one with our children. We are called to be one with our wives. How can you serve your wife today? What are some things that you know make her feel loved? Commit to doing those things. You can't control what she's going to do, but you can control what you will do for her. Choose self-giving love.

*Today I will remember:*

- I am called to become one with my wife.
- This is physical, but also a matter of the soul.
- To serve my wife is to love her.

*Lord, help me to not be selfish, but to make my wife a priority. Help us to live out this mystery of becoming one physically and emotionally.*

# HOT AND HOLY

*May your fountain be blessed, and may you rejoice in the wife of your youth. A loving doe, a graceful deer—may her breasts satisfy you always, may you ever be intoxicated with her love.*

PROVERBS 5:18-19

It is God's will that you enjoy your wife. Her personality, her partnership, and her body. If you didn't catch that in today's verses, then you weren't paying attention. You might want to read them again, commit them to memory, share them with your wife, and tell her that you're committed to living biblically.

Sex was created by God for procreation and for pleasure. If you are uncertain about that, then read Song of Solomon. This Old Testament book is dedicated to the celebration of romance and physical pleasure in marriage. Sex is a gift from God, and to keep it real with you, let me say that I'm grateful for this grace.

But, like all good gifts from God, if we do not trust the Creator of this wonderful gift, then we take what is good and we mess it up. It's like fire. Fire in the right place brings us warmth and deliciously cooked meals. But in the wrong place, it scars, kills, and will burn your house down. Wisdom here teaches us to keep the fire burning with wives. Unfortunately, I sometimes put the responsibility all on my wife. I'll sit around and dwell on how she could do a better job taking care of her man! That's lame. To keep the flame lit, I must take responsibility to light the match. Question: When was the last time you contributed to warming up your wife? When was the last time you romanced her? Keep the flame lit!

*Today I will remember:*

- Loving my wife will be my priority.
- I should romance her and let her know she is loved and desired for who she is.
- I will speak affirmations and accolades over her.

*Thank You, Father, for my wife. She is Your gift to me. Give me the wisdom and grace to help her feel beautiful and loved today.*

# A KIND MARRIAGE

*Be kind and compassionate to one another,*
*forgiving each other, just as in Christ God forgave you.*
EPHESIANS 4:32

I've been watching a documentary on Netflix called *Love on the Spectrum*. It's about the dating lives of people with disabilities. I got to tell you, I love this show. I find myself getting emotional at times. The innocence and sincerity can be very touching. I also find myself learning or being reminded of basic relational principles. In one couple, the man is both autistic and a savant in mathematics; the woman has Down syndrome. They are continuously kind to one another. There's no posturing, keeping score, or negative commentary between them. There is just encouragement and compliments. It's a beautiful thing to behold. He's telling her she's beautiful and funny, and she's telling him that he's handsome and smart. They are consistently loving in the simplest of ways.

If you and I were to simply put into practice our verse today, my guess is our marital satisfaction would go way up. What if we were to stop keeping score, quit bickering over insignificant things, and start choosing to be consistently kind? What if we practiced simple relational common sense each day? Let's be kind and compassionate to our wives. Let's be quick to forgive and quick to encourage. Choose to compliment her in the morning and in the evening. Greet her with a hug and a kiss. Send her an encouraging text during the day. These things are the stuff of relational genius. It's not the big trip, the expensive jewelry, the Hallmark cards, or the love songs. These things are good, but the simple, continuous acts of love are what make for a great marriage.

*Today I will remember:*

- I should be continuously compassionate and kind to my wife.
- There is no scorekeeping in marriage relationships.
- I should be quick to forgive and quick to encourage.

*Jesus, help me to love my wife today. Help me*
*to see that the continuous decision to love in*
*kindness and grace makes for a great marriage.*

# A WOMAN OF CHARACTER

*A wife of noble character who can find?*
*She is worth far more than rubies.*
PROVERBS 31:10

If you're single and looking to be married one day, then I would encourage you to memorize today's verse. Regularly ask God to bring you a woman of noble character. Apply this verse as you date and search for a woman of integrity. Normally when a man is dating, especially when he is younger, he's just looking for someone attractive, or as my sixteen-year-old son says, a "smoke show." Proverbs 31, however, describes a woman of great character. A single man should read, think through, and use this chapter as a litmus test. List the characteristics of the woman you're looking for and then think about the kind of man that she would be looking for. You want to follow the path of character, not just the spark of chemistry.

If you are married, then use this verse as a guide to celebrate the character qualities you admire in your wife. Express your gratitude to her and to God for who she is. We tend to focus on the negative but love blossoms and blooms in the positive. When you think about your wife, what do you focus on? The largest room in the world is the room for improvement, but focusing on those things will not endear you to your wife nor her to you. So make a list today of all the things you love about her, then regularly choose to affirm and celebrate those attributes. Gratitude is the gateway to good emotional vibes.

*Today I will remember:*

- A great marriage is built on great character.
- The character of the woman I marry is much more important than the package she comes in.

*Father, help me to see what You see and to humbly take hold of Your wisdom for me. Thank You for the gift of a woman of character. Who we are is more important than how we look.*

# GREENER GRASS?

*Wisdom will save you also from the adulterous woman,*
*from the wayward woman with her seductive words,*
*who has left the partner of her youth and*
*ignored the covenant she made before God.*

PROVERBS 2:16-17

The grass always looks greener somewhere else. Beware of the temptation to abandon your own yard for the allure of greener grass. Do you know why that grass is so green over there? One word: manure. Lots and lots of manure. You just haven't stepped in it yet.

We need wisdom to be saved from this type of temptation. Let me state the obvious. If wisdom protects us from adultery, then foolishness drives us toward it. Fools cheat. Wise people remain faithful. The only thing that can save us from giving in to the seductive words of an adulterous woman is to think wisely. Wisdom considers the consequences. Wisdom pictures everyone knowing and the painful conversation you'll have with your kids. Wisdom knows that adultery is not just a fling. It's a path that leads to destruction.

Almost every man will be tempted at some point to cheat. There's nothing wrong with noticing attractive women, it's what we do with that attraction that can harm us. To notice and let it go is right. To notice and choose to lust is wrong. To notice it and pursue it can burn your house down, ruin your legacy, and cause years of tremendous pain. The reason that the other yard appears to be so green is because there's a bunch of crap in it. Stay away from it.

*Today I will remember:*

- The wise are faithful.
- Godly men do not dream of greener grass but choose to work on their own yard.

*Lord, protect me from temptations that I know would cost*
*me everything if I gave in. Help me to think and choose wisely.*
*There are no perfect women, just as I am not a perfect man.*
*Help me to joyfully focus on continually improving my marriage.*

# ME TO WE

*In this same way, husbands ought to love their wives as their own bodies. He who loves his wife loves himself.*
EPHESIANS 5:28

I have an internal theme song of my life. I don't sing it aloud or even hum it. The truth is, I'm not proud of it and I try to change the tune regularly, but it always comes back. You ever have a song get stuck in your head that you can't get rid of? It's like that.

The song is not really a song, it's more like what the soloist sings when he's warming up. It's "Me me me me meeeeeeee!" If I'm honest that's who I'm thinking about most of the time. Me! In fact, no other human being on the planet thinks about me as much as I do. If I'm not careful, all my thoughts and all my concerns are about one person: me.

I think most of us are like that. When you got married, you stood in front of God, your family, and your friends and vowed that your life was no longer about you. You vowed that your theme song was now shifting. You vowed that you were moving from "me me me me me" to "we we we," all the way home. Marriage is the mystery of two people choosing to move from *me* to *we*. It's a lifelong journey. It's worth it, but it isn't easy. The most common marriage advice I give is "Don't give up; choose to grow up." Choose a new theme song.

*Today I will remember:*

- We. We. We. My life is no longer about me, but about us.
- *Me* is no longer as important as *we*.
- Don't give up; choose to grow up.

*Father, help me to think of my wife first. It's not my marriage; it's our marriage. Help me to love and lead well, knowing that it's always about us and never just about me.*

# MOUTH MATTERS

*The tongue also is a fire, a world of evil among the parts of the body. It corrupts the whole body, sets the whole course of one's life on fire, and is itself set on fire by hell.*
JAMES 3:6

What would you say is the most sinful part of your body? We're dudes, I know immediately where your mind went. Makes sense, and yes that body part has the potential to get us in lots of trouble. However, the Bible says that the most sinful part of our bodies is our mouth. James is talking about the power of our words.

How many marriages have ended because of the way husbands and wives talk to each other? How many people have lost their jobs and ended their careers because they were reckless with their words? How many children have experienced lifelong hurts because of something stupid their parent said in a heated moment? Words are powerful. How do we manage our mouths, tame our tongues, and watch our words? The Bible teaches that our words simply reflect what is in our hearts.

The greatest evidence of the Holy Spirit working in our lives is not speaking in a tongue we don't know but controlling the tongue we do know. To manage our mouths is to do some heart work. We need to constantly be praying about what's going on in our hearts. Any time we find ourselves running off at the mouth with things that are dishonoring to God and to people, it's time to do some heart work. A mouth matter is a matter of the heart.

*Today I will remember:*

- My words are powerful.
- I will speak love and affirmation over my wife.
- Thinking before speaking is always wise.

*God, purify my heart so that my words are pure. I want to honor You and others with what I say. May thinking precede speaking.*

# MUTUAL SUBMISSION

*Submit to one another out of reverence for Christ. Wives, submit yourselves to your own husbands as you do to the Lord.*

EPHESIANS 5:21-22

Usually when I ask men if they know any verses in the Bible about marriage, they'll mention the second verse listed above. Men tend to know the verse about wives submitting to their husbands. Most men, however, do not know the verse right before it. We are to submit ourselves to one another out of reverence to Jesus. Marriage is about mutual submission.

My wife is better at some things than I am. Let's go with money. She's better at managing it, while I tend to be more gifted at making it. She's great at day-to-day details, and I'm better at the big picture. I would be a fool to think I should manage our money or the day-to-day details of our lives. She is far superior to me at those things. I'm better at looking to the days ahead and shaping our future, so she submits to me in that. It's about a partnership, or, as the Bible says here, in verse 21, mutual submission.

What is your wife better at than you are? Have you ever thanked her for her leadership in that area? There is a biblical principle that men are to lead their families. We'll be held accountable for how we lead, and do you know what good leaders do? They serve. They're humble. They acknowledge their weaknesses and others' strengths. Tell your wife today what she's better at than you and thank her for it.

*Today I will remember:*

- Marriage is about partnership and mutual submission.
- I am not the ruler over my marriage; I am the leader.
- Leaders serve.

*Father, forgive me when I think more of myself than I ought and less of my wife than I should. Thank You for my partner and for the life we are building together.*

# NO SHAME

*Adam and his wife were*
*both naked, and they felt no shame.*
GENESIS 2:25

I always wonder what it was like for Adam and Eve running around the Garden naked. The weather was perfect. There were no thorns or poison ivy. They were just enjoying their marriage and making out in the yard. No one to compare themselves or each other to. Just a long, shameless, naked honeymoon. We don't know, but it could've lasted for decades or even centuries! Sounds pretty good.

Things, of course, are a lot different now. Sin has entered the world and now there are all kinds of opportunities for shame. We don't run around free and naked anymore; we cover that business up! Opportunity for comparison abounds. We are bombarded every day with beautiful people on television, billboards, and in magazines. If we're not careful, we can make our wives feel like they don't measure up.

God, however, desires that there be nakedness and no shame when it comes to you and your wife. Sex is His gift, and it's meant to be life-giving for the both of you. Tell your wife regularly how beautiful she is and how you only have eyes for her. Mean it! If she's curvy, that's what you're all about. If she's slim, then that's what you're totally into. Whether she's tall, short, thin, round, or somewhere in between, then that's what you're crazy about. Help her feel free, desired, and truly loved. Make your marriage a shame-free environment.

*Today I will remember:*

- I only have eyes for my wife.
- I will love her, affirm her, and be devoted to her in both mind and body.
- I will protect her from shame.

*Lord, help me to love my wife in such a way*
*that she feels no shame. Thank You for the*
*gift she is to me. I commit myself to purity.*

# THE LORD'S FAVOR

*He who finds a wife finds what is good and receives favor from the LORD.*

PROVERBS 18:22

God is for marriage. He created it and called it good. Yet many of us make poor decisions and make our marriages not so good. It's like anything God has created. When we do things God's way, His gifts are a blessing. When we do things outside of God's will, those blessings can become bummers. The same is true with marriage.

Our wives are a gift from the Lord, but we must choose to see them in the way the Lord instructs. This keeps a marriage blessed. How do you see your wife? When you think about her, what do you choose to focus on? Now reality is, you married an imperfect woman. You married a sinner, and she probably married an even bigger one. Do you focus on her shortfalls, or how much of a gift she is to you? What we focus on is what we move toward. Here's the other thing: Women generally are extremely intuitive. Whether you say anything out loud or not, she knows what you think of her for better or worse. Choose to focus on the things that are great. Thank God regularly for your wife. Honor her as a gift from the Lord. Your emotions will be positive, and guess what? So will hers. She will begin to sense your shift, and, in most scenarios, she will feel more safe and secure and will respond in kind. How does God want you to see your wife?

*Today I will remember:*

- My wife is a good gift from the Lord.
- I will choose to think on the things that I love about her.
- I will cover her with grace when it comes to the things that irritate me.

*Thank You, Father, for the gift of my wife.*
*Help me to see in her Your grace and favor to me.*
*Thank You for giving me what I need in my wife.*

# DRESSING WELL

*Therefore, as God's chosen people, holy and dearly loved, clothe yourselves with compassion, kindness, humility, gentleness and patience.*

COLOSSIANS 3:12

Does your wife ever make you change your clothes? Mine does. We'll be getting ready to go out, I'll put something on, and she'll ask if that's what I'm going to wear. Now, how I answer at this moment is extremely important. The answer I give is really going to make or break the night. Since I'm literally wearing the clothes that she is asking about, part of me wants to say that her question is dumb and lacks some sense. However, if I choose to answer in this way, it's going to send the night on a difficult trajectory that neither of us wants. So I simply ask her what she would like me to wear. She tells me. I change clothes. Love is in the air and the night is headed toward a preferred destination. I'm giving you gold here.

Our verse for today is about clothing ourselves in the right style. We can choose each day to put on compassion, kindness, humility, gentleness, and patience. This always looks good on anyone. Or we could go with indifference, coldness, harshness, and complaining; no one ever looks good in that. Not even Brad Pitt can pull that off! We choose each day what character qualities we will put on and practice. One style is godly and fashionable; the other is wicked and distasteful. If you practice this verse and put on these qualities each day, your wife will never ask you to change. You will always wear it well.

*Today I will remember:*

- God calls me to put on the right things.
- I choose how I will act each day toward my wife.
- I choose to put on compassion, kindness, humility, gentleness, and patience.

*Jesus, help me to wear Your type of character qualities each day, especially in how I act toward my wife.*

# HOLY SEX

*But among you there must not be even a hint of sexual immorality, or of any kind of impurity, or of greed, because these are improper for God's holy people.*

EPHESIANS 5:3

A teenager in the late eighties and early nineties, I grew up in Texas in a Southern Baptist church. There was a big campaign in churches across America entitled "True Love Waits." The goal was for teenagers to choose abstinence until marriage. Girls wore purity rings on their wedding fingers, and both boys and girls signed commitment cards promising chastity. While the goal was right, an unintended and unhealthy side effect was that teenagers began to form an unhealthy view of sex. In the minds of many, sex became the be all and end all for marriage. Some young people came to believe that there must be something wrong with sex, even in marriage.

The simplest definition for sexual immorality in the Bible is any sexual activity outside of a marriage between one man and one woman. That's immorality. But God is for sexual morality in marriage! God's desire is for husbands and wives to keep it hot and holy with each other. Sex is designed for procreation yes, but also for pleasure and intimacy. A healthy sex life helps us flee from what is unhealthy. So create a healthy sex life with your wife. Pursue her. Talk to her about what she likes and doesn't like in the bedroom. Be humble, not selfish. Make it your desire not to be served but to serve. Care for her soul, love her well, and help her to feel sexy.

*Today I will remember:*

- I will commit my mind and body to my wife.
- God is for sexual morality.
- Sex is a gift to be enjoyed in marriage.

*Father, thank You for the gift of sex. Help me to think about it the way You desire. I pray that I would love my wife selflessly and help her feel cherished, safe, and deeply loved.*

# FIGHT ON THROUGH THE NIGHT?

*"In your anger do not sin": Do not let the sun go down while you are still angry, and do not give the devil a foothold.*

EPHESIANS 4:26-27

Before Katrina and I were married, we worked for a missions agency to the Spanish-speaking world; I was the Director of Development and Katrina helped manage housing for missionaries. Over time, we became close with the staff. Before our wedding, they threw us a shower, and everyone took turns writing pieces of marriage advice on an index card. The one that stands out was written by my boss: "Never go to bed angry. Go ahead and fight on through the night." I don't know that this is the best interpretation of today's verse, but it's pretty good.

The principle here is that we do not let anger fester. Unresolved anger leads to resentment, unforgiveness, and bitterness. It lodges in our hearts, takes root, and causes all kinds of relational issues. Perhaps you need to take a timeout when you're angry, and that might even include a good nap. But you must go back, have a conversation, and resolve the issue. To heal from it, you must deal with it. A man who trusts God and loves his wife does not let things fester. He has the difficult conversation, makes amends, and learns to move on. Should we fight on through the night? Not necessarily. But we do all that we can to lead well and resolve the conflict.

*Today I will remember:*

- To heal from it, I must deal with it.
- I must lead with patience, kindness, and love when resolving conflict.

*Lord, help me to be quick to forgive. May no bad thing take root in my heart. Help me to be levelheaded, patient, and kind when resolving conflict.*

# FAITHFULLY SURRENDERED

*But Ruth replied, "Don't urge me to leave you or to turn back from you. Where you go I will go, and where you stay I will stay. Your people will be my people and your God my God. Where you die I will die, and there I will be buried. May the* L*ORD* *deal with me, be it ever so severely, if even death separates you and me."*

RUTH 1:16-17

These verses speak of Ruth's commitment to her mother-in-law, Naomi, after Ruth's husband died. This commitment would lead Ruth to marry again, and eventually she is listed in the genealogy of Jesus. There is a faithful surrender that God intends to happen in marriage. This statement from Ruth is a great example of this type of godly surrender.

I want to encourage you to have an all-in attitude concerning your marriage. It's you and your wife until death do you part. I'm not talking about marriage as "the old ball and chain," but real love. Love is a choice to be faithfully surrendered. You die to yourself. It's no longer a matter of *your* life as a man but *our* lives as husband and wife. You and your wife are one. Yes, this type of surrender means you give up some things, but in a healthy marriage it also means that you gain more valuable things. To faithfully surrender yourself to give and serve your wife leads to a love and an intimacy far beyond what you could experience on your own.

*Today I will remember:*

- Love is a choice to be faithfully surrendered.
- I choose to be all-in for my marriage.

*Father, my life is about living for You and for my family. I pray that I might understand what it means to become one with my wife. I'm all in.*

# IT TAKES TIME TO LOVE

*If a man has recently married, he must not be sent to war or have any other duty laid on him. For one year he is to be free to stay at home and bring happiness to the wife he has married.*

DEUTERONOMY 24:5

It would be great if we all still practiced this verse. A newly married man would spend the first year of marriage in honeymoon mode. You would take a year off from larger duties to settle in with your new wife. It was a year of ambition, not at work, but at home. You spent time saving and preparing for it in advance because you knew that this first year with your wife would be a time of laying a strong foundation for the years ahead. It takes time to learn marriage and to learn how to love your wife well.

While most would find this practice unreasonable or seemingly impossible today, there is a principle here worth practicing. It takes time and energy to love someone well. Loving well does not happen naturally; it requires effort. I suspect when you first fell in love with your wife, it felt natural. But think of all the effort you were putting in. How often was she on your mind? How hard did you work to win her over? It seemed effortless because it was new and exciting, yet you were putting forth a lot of effort. So how much effort are you putting forth today? Is time with your wife an afterthought, or a priority?

I want to encourage you to continue to pursue your wife. Have a date night each week. Plan getaways for just you and her. It takes time to love, so make the time.

*Today I will remember:*

- Loving my wife well requires planning, time, and effort.
- It is my job to initiate and take the lead.

*Father, thank You for my wife.*
*Help me to put in the time and the*
*wise planning it takes to love her well.*

# BEING A GENTLEMAN

*Husbands, love your wives and do not be harsh with them.*
COLOSSIANS 3:19

The other night while my wife and I were having dinner at a restaurant, we couldn't help but hear a conversation between a couple a table over. The more we heard, the angrier I got. The husband was a total jerk. He was not a gentleman, meaning he was not a *gentle* man. He was harsh with his wife. Unkind, cruel, and unyielding. As I listened, I thought about the times that I've been that way with my wife, Katrina. I thought about God listening and getting angry at me. Humbling.

One of the practices that I learned years ago from a counselor was the notion of taking a timeout. Early on in our marriage, when I would get angry at Katrina and start to lose my cool, I'd have the option of taking a timeout for a few minutes. I would literally say, "I need to take a timeout." I would go for a walk, blow off some steam, and when I had calmed down, I would come back and continue the discussion. Now that I'm older and hopefully have matured a bit, I don't lose my cool very often. But back then, taking a timeout was a good practice. It's OK to get mad. It's OK to have real and raw emotion. But it's not OK to be harsh. Let's choose to always remain a gentle man with our wives.

*Today I will remember:*

- God desires for me to be a gentle man.
- Gentleness is not weakness, but a decision to use my strength to serve my wife.

*Father, forgive me for losing my temper or being harsh with my wife. Help me to always be a gentle man.*

# NOT YOUR OWN

*The husband should fulfill his marital duty to his wife, and likewise the wife to her husband. The wife does not have authority over her own body but yields it to her husband. In the same way, the husband does not have authority over his own body but yields it to his wife.*

1 CORINTHIANS 7:3-4

Most men I know really like these two verses. You're probably wanting to quote them to your wife later in an intimate Bible study, adding, "Let's be biblical!" Well, that's all fine and good, but let me help you think through it a bit more. Anytime we see verses like this we want to think like a servant, because following Jesus always involves serving. This includes the fact that our bodies do not belong to us, but to our wives. If your wife has authority over your body, what do you think she wants to do with it? Not what you wish to do with it. She might desire your body in a different way than you desire hers.

For example, my wife desires my hands to rub her feet. This is important to her. Now to keep it real with you, sometimes a foot rub leads to what I think are better things. But while I desire the next step, she may simply desire a foot rub. Are you catching my drift? She likes a foot rub, or a back rub. The biblical truth that my body belongs to her means she can have it. Sometimes, her authority over my body means snuggling only. Just snuggling. The point: Use your body to serve your wife in whatever way she desires.

*Today I will remember:*

- My body should be used to serve my wife.
- I can love her by serving her without always expecting something in return.

*Lord, help me not to be selfish with my body, but to love and serve my wife with it. Help me to give her selfless affection.*

# PARTNERSHIP

*So God created mankind in his own image, in the image of God he created them; male and female he created them. God blessed them and said to them, "Be fruitful and increase in number; fill the earth and subdue it."*

GENESIS 1:27-28

When I first got married, I thought marriage was about me providing financially and my wife providing domestically. Meaning, it was my job to go out into the world and make money and her job to take care of my home and me. With my parents divorcing when I was eight, I looked to my grandparents as the model to emulate. They basically fit into the roles I mentioned above, and I thought that all marriages should look like theirs. Then I met my wife, Katrina. Katrina is smart. She graduated first in her college class and is a gifted communicator and leader. Wow! However, this attraction became an irritation after we married. I wanted a servant to support my ambitions. She wanted a partner to share her love.

Notice how our verses today are worded. They describe an equal partnership. Here's a quick test: Who should manage the money in your marriage? Answer: The one who is better at managing should take the lead, and you both should be involved in the decisions. Partnership is better than hierarchy. Partners cover each other's weaknesses and lean into each other's strengths. Be humble enough to acknowledge your wife's strengths and love her enough to cover her weaknesses and empower her dreams.

*Today I will remember:*

- My wife is an equal partner in the building of our lives.
- She is better at certain things.
- It's wise for me to follow her leadership in those things.

*Father, give me wisdom to understand our individual strengths and weaknesses. Help us be the best partners we can be. Help me be a wise, humble leader in our marriage.*

# UNHINDERED

*Husbands, in the same way be considerate as you live with your wives, and treat them with respect as the weaker partner and as heirs with you of the gracious gift of life, so that nothing will hinder your prayers.*

1 PETER 3:7

How do you define a godly man? Think about it. What does a godly man do? If you thought a godly man prays, tithes, goes to Bible study, and practices other spiritual disciplines, then you would be right on some level, but not completely. A godly man has some religious practices for sure, but it's not the practices that make a man godly. Godliness is about character, and how a man treats his wife reveals his character. Our verse says that a man can pray and still be ungodly. In fact, a man can pray hindered prayers because of how he treats his wife. A man remains unhindered in his prayers when he does three things:

1. He is considerate toward his wife: kind, caring, and selfless. To be inconsiderate is to be ungodly.
2. He is respectful to his wife. He speaks well of her and honors her when she is around and when she is not around.
3. He treats his wife as an equal. When this verse says *heirs*, it means equality before God. When Peter wrote this to Christian men, women were considered property. Peter is writing something radical here. He's talking about spiritual partnership.

How we treat our wives is so important to God that if we do not do it well, our prayers are hindered. You can skip a Bible study and God will still hear your prayer. Be an unrepentant jerk to your wife and there's static on the line. Love your wife well and remain unhindered.

*Today I will remember:*

- How I treat my wife is very important to God.
- To be inconsiderate is to be ungodly.
- My prayers can be hindered because of how I treat my wife.

*God, help me to be considerate, respectful, and humble toward my wife. Help me be a godly husband.*

# THE ONE YOU'RE WITH

*Love is patient, love is kind.*
1 CORINTHIANS 13:4

I tend to be an idealist. I have in my mind the way things ought to be, should be, and will be if I just make it happen. This can be a good trait in leadership, but not so much in marriage. In fact, when it comes to marriage, it has more to do with my own ego than it does with loving my wife.

When we first got married, I thought my wife Katrina would match my ideal. I had a picture of what I wanted her to be and how our marriage should be. If she did not match this vision, then I would get disappointed, and she would get frustrated. The truth is, I wasn't loving my wife. I was just using her to fulfill some misconstrued, made-up, unrealistic, idealistic, idea of marriage and how it was supposed to make me feel. My parents divorced, so my marriage was going to be perfect. My idea of perfect anyway.

As time went on, I began to grow up a little. God does not call us to live the ideal but to love in the real. In some ways, to say it bluntly, my wife has not been what I wanted. But, in almost every way, she has been what I needed. God in His sovereignty knew better than I did and has called me to love my wife as she is, and she is wonderful. I found out the real her was better than my ideal anyway.

*Today I will remember:*

- God does not call us to live the ideal; He calls us to love in the real.
- A great marriage is about two broken people choosing not to give up on each other.

*Father, thank You for my wife. Teach me to love her well. We are two broken, imperfect people who need You. May I lead us in grace-filled love.*

# LOVE LEADS

*This is love: not that we loved God,*
*but that he loved us and sent his Son*
*as an atoning sacrifice for our sins.*
1 JOHN 4:10

Love does not wait on the other to be worthy. Love gives and serves. As husbands we are to love our wives first. That's what leaders do; they go first, and this is how God loves us. The more we sit around and think about what our wives are not doing for us or how they are not loving us the way we desire, the less we are fulfilling the role that God has called us to.

Often when I train other leaders, I will ask the question, "What do leaders do?" I usually get blank stares. It's not a trick question. In fact, the answer is about as simple as it gets. What do leaders do? They lead. If you want a loving marriage, then love your wife. Don't wait on her to set the tone; you set it. What makes your wife feel loved? Do that. Tell her you love her regularly. Kiss her or hug her before you walk out the door. Love goes first.

God is the prime example in loving first. Our verse today reminds us that He did not wait for us to get our act together. He took the lead. His love is sacrificial. If your marriage seems to be lacking in love, don't blame your wife. Look in the mirror. Take responsibility, choose to change, and lead in love.

*Today I will remember:*
- Love goes first.
- Take responsibility and choose to lead in love.

*God, help me not to wait on my wife to love me,*
*but instead to take the first step in choosing to love her.*
*Leaders choose to lead, and I want to lead in love.*

# MALE AND FEMALE

*God created mankind in his own image,*
*in the image of God he created them;*
*male and female he created them.*

GENESIS 1:27

In recent years there has been a blurring of the lines when it comes to gender. Much of it is based on stereotypes. For example, if you're a boy who likes the arts and prefers music to sports, the blurring says maybe you should question your maleness. *Oh, you're a girl who likes to play sports?* The blurring says maybe you should question your biological gender.

The whole crazy, blurring thing is based on stereotypes and it confuses personality with gender. I like the arts. My wife is an athlete and a huge sports fan. No need to blur gender lines here! I also hunt, fish, and ride motorcycles. She enjoys tea with her girlfriends. Throw the stereotypes out the window; those things are more about personality than they are gender.

I want to encourage you to celebrate your wife's differences. She sees things differently, feels things differently, and acts differently. These differences can be a source of frustration or a source of strength. You choose. It all depends on how you look at it.

I used to get frustrated when Katrina had a different opinion. Now when we disagree, I see it as an opportunity to get a different angle. Our differences make us stronger, not weaker. I'm a better man because of those differences.

*Today I will remember:*

- I should celebrate how my wife is different from me.
- Our differences can be an irritation or a strength.
- How I choose to treat our differences makes the difference.

*God, thank You for my wife and for the*
*fact that we are different. Help me to love,*
*lead, and learn from her in wise humility.*

# NOTHING IN THE FILE

*Love does not delight in evil but rejoices with the truth. It always protects, always trusts, always hopes, always perseveres.*

1 CORINTHIANS 13:6-7

All healthy relationships are built on trust. Whether it's with a parent, with a child, in business, or in marriage, trust is the bedrock of great relationships. Where there is no trust, relationships disintegrate. Truth is what builds trust. No truth, no trust; and when there's no trust, the relationship is over.

A few years ago, my wife Katrina and I were in marriage counseling. I've learned that the weak don't get help, but the strong and wise do. Our counselor described me as having a metaphorical file. The file is called "Things I Can't Tell My Wife." He said most husbands have one, and while we rationalize having the file, it keeps us from true intimacy. His solution? Katrina should regularly ask me if I have anything in that file; if I do, I must commit to telling her the truth. The strongest relationships are honest. Marriage can be as sick as our secrets, and the goal is to have nothing in the file.

At first it was scary, but as time went on, I could truly say I had no secrets. The shocking thing is, the more I trusted Katrina with the truth, the closer we became. The truth is not always easy, but it is always best. It also caused me to think through things with more clarity. I don't ever want to do anything that I feel like I can't tell my wife about. Love blossoms and rejoices in truth.

*Today I will remember:*

- Truth builds trust.
- It is not always easy, but it is always best.
- I will keep nothing in the file.

*Lord, help me be a man of truth. My wife can't love who I pretend to be—that man doesn't exist. Help me to lead the way and build trust.*

# March

## LEADERSHIP AND WORK

Commit to the LORD whatever you do,
and he will establish your plans.
*Proverbs 16:3*

# REAL LEADERSHIP

*Love and faithfulness keep a king safe;*
*through love his throne is made secure.*
PROVERBS 20:28

When people only do what you say because you're the boss, you are exercising the lowest form of leadership. There are lots of employees who work for bosses who have no real sway over them other than the minimal requirements of their jobs. Higher levels of leadership require influence. People take to heart what the leader says. They are inspired beyond the minimum requirements. They want to take the hill with that person leading the charge. Leadership expert John Maxwell famously said, "Leadership is influence. Nothing more and nothing less." I wonder if he got that from the Bible. It's the meaning of our verse for today.

The first step to increasing your influence is caring about the people you lead. Just as data and spreadsheets are necessary in management, loving people is necessary in leadership. If people don't think you care for them, they will not follow you. They might do what you say as a boss, but there will be no loyalty or impact beyond that. In fact, they're probably praying for the day you leave, or possibly even working out a way to help make that happen.

True influence grows with caring for people, developing people, accomplishing goals, and being consistent. Great leaders don't demand respect; they earn it because of who they are. Leaders who love their people are leaders worth following. They serve those in their charge. Leadership is about where we are going. It's also about the vibe everyone feels in getting there. If you're a leader, memorize this proverb. Put it where you'll see it regularly.

*Today I will remember:*

- Real leadership is about influence.
- Great leaders don't demand respect; they earn it because of who they are.
- Leaders who love their people are leaders worth following.

*Lord, help me to truly love the people I lead.*
*You are the Kings of kings, and You loved*
*people enough to give Your life for them.*

# GODLY INTUITION

*When a king sits on his throne to judge,*
*he winnows out all evil with his eyes.*
PROVERBS 20:8

Some of my biggest regrets in leadership stem from when I didn't trust my gut. I felt something, I knew something was off, but I didn't listen to my instincts. People with leadership gifts tend to have a sense of things. They may not be able to explain it, or quantify it, but somehow, they just know. For those who have a relationship with God, this gift increases. In partnership with the Holy Spirit, godly leaders have what I'm going to call sanctified intuition. There's discernment with a leadership bias. You sense a poor decision, an untrustworthy client, or a bad deal. You might also have a gift of spotting good timing, seeing potential in someone no one else sees, or predicting where a trend is headed.

One of the best prayers a leader can pray is to ask God to give him the ability to see what He sees. To see beyond the obvious. My wife has this ability, especially as it pertains to people. If I'm making a big hire, I will invite the candidate out to dinner with my wife and me. I want my wife to meet the person because she sees things I don't see.

Perhaps the most important trait here, especially for senior leaders, is the ability to read a room. To sense where people are currently and how to lead them to where everyone needs to go. Great leaders listen with their ears, but also with their eyes and heart. The Holy Spirit will help you with this if you ask Him.

*Today I will remember:*

- Discernment looks beyond the obvious.
- Great leaders listen with their ears, but also with their eyes and heart.

*Holy Spirit, grant me the ability to*
*not just see things, but sense them as well.*
*Guide me and give me a sanctified intuition.*

# THE POWER OF VISION

*Where there is no revelation, people cast off restraint;*
*but blessed is the one who heeds wisdom's instruction.*
PROVERBS 29:18

Much was written about leadership and the power of vision in the nineties; I read a lot of it. If it was a Christian book, our verse for today was almost always referenced. Some translations used the word *vision* instead of *revelation*, and people would sometimes ask me if I was a visionary. I was a young adult leading teenagers and volunteers in a church; I wanted to become the best leader I could be. Vision felt mysterious and I thought visionaries were supremely gifted at seeing the future. Our verse for today simplifies all this.

A vision is simply a dream with a deadline. Good leaders will share a vision that falls in line with the mission of their organization. It's the "revelation" of what could be. Leaders define reality, dream of that preferred future, design the path from here to there, and then lead people along the path. We make it sound sexy after it's done, but the doing is a lot of hard work, hard choices, and plain, old fashioned grit. People cast off restraint without vision because, without it, there's no need for alignment or grit. Why push hard if we don't know where we're headed? The goals bring focus. The purpose of vision is to focus everyone to move in the same direction to create that better future.

*Today I will remember:*
- A vision is simply a dream with a deadline.
- Goals bring alignment and focus.
- Leaders define reality, dream of a preferred future, design a path from here to there, and then lead people along the path.

*God, grant me the wisdom to see a preferred*
*future and the courage to lead people to it.*

# DECISIVE LEADERSHIP

*A wise king winnows out the wicked;*
*he drives the threshing wheel over them.*
PROVERBS 20:26

Leaders make tough calls. One of my mentors told me that a whole lot of leadership is disappointing people at a rate they can stand. There's a lot of truth to that statement. Leaders are out front. When you're a leader, you see things that people can't see yet. You deal with issues that they are unaware of and carry the burden and weight of being responsible. Everyone is looking to you, and ultimately the decisions rest on your shoulders.

This proverb is about having the strength to make those hard calls. I've learned many times that a breakthrough in our organization is on the other side of a tough call that I've been unwilling to make. But once I suck it up and do it, things begin to move forward again. Is there a tough call that you've been avoiding, or a conversation that you need to have, but you keep wimping out? Your leadership potential is determined by your capacity and willingness to deal with those difficult situations.

Think about it. Leadership is confrontation. We confront current reality to lead to a better future. We must confront people when their attitude or actions are not aligned with our culture. Leadership by its very nature is somewhat controversial. Great leaders understand this. The best can confront, challenge, and lead in a winsome fashion. One of the most important skills for leaders to learn is how to lovingly confront. Any time I teach leadership, I am asked, "What do leaders do?" The answer is simple: they lead. Leading requires courage and strength. Lead on.

*Today I will remember:*

- Leaders must lead, and this includes healthy confrontation.
- One of the best skills I can learn is how to lovingly confront.

*Lord, grant me the wisdom and courage to confront well.*
*Forgive me for tolerating things that I shouldn't.*
*Help me to be both kind and courageous.*

# HAVE A PLAN

*The plans of the diligent lead to profit*
*as surely as haste leads to poverty.*
PROVERBS 21:5

Wise people practice self-leadership. Do you have any hopes or dreams? Would you like your life to be better than it is right now? If so, what's your plan? Hope is not a strategy, and wishing on a star won't get you very far. It's great for Disney movies, but it's not at all close to how life usually works.

The first step to getting what you want out of life is deciding what you want. What are those things? How would you like your marriage to look five years from now? What kind of relationship do you want with your kids? Where do you want your career to go? Decide what you want and write it down. Turn the dreams into specific goals.

The second step is putting a plan together. How will you get from where you are to where you want to be? What is your current reality? What habits do you need to form? What steps can you take? If you keep doing what you've always done, then you will keep getting what you've always gotten. What needs to change?

Decide what you want; that is your future destination. Plan how you will get there from where you are. Then, finally, walk the path to that better life. Very few people are thinking about where things are headed. Wise people plan and then work the plan to a better future.

*Today I will remember:*
- Leadership begins with leading myself well.
- Wise people plan and then work the plan to a better future.

*Father, give me wisdom for the right goals*
*and the right plans for my life. Help me to make big*
*decisions slowly. I pray that I would practice diligence.*

# ANSWERING TO THE OWNER

*By me kings reign and rulers issue decrees that are just;*
*by me princes govern, and nobles—all who rule on earth.*

PROVERBS 8:15-16

As I write today's devotional, we just had a presidential election in the United States. While many people are happy at the result, just as many are disheartened and even afraid. The president wields tremendous power as the commander in chief and the CEO of the wealthiest economy in the world. Yet God says no leadership or authority exists apart from Him, and it is wise for leaders of all kinds to remember this.

Whether God has called you to lead a ministry, a business, a ball team, or your family, your authority and influence come from Him. We are all stewards or managers of what He has given us for a time, and we will give an account for how we managed. Even our breath is borrowed. One day, God, the leader and owner of all things, will take it back and we will answer to Him alone. Remember this as you lead.

Where I lead, we have what we call "Cultural Distinctives." They are priorities and values that shape our behaviors with one another and the people we serve. Here's one of those values: We love first, lead second, but always do both. Godly leadership involves loving the people we lead. This includes compassion, making the tough calls, and (at times) having to let people go. We can do all these things in ways that honor God. Let's remember this every day as we lead.

*Today I will remember:*

- I must love first, lead second, and always do both.
- God is the one who grants authority.
- All leaders will ultimately answer to Him.

*God, thank You for what You have*
*entrusted me. Help me to lead in a way*
*that loves people well and honors You.*

# GOOD PLANS

*Commit to the LORD whatever you do,*
*and he will establish your plans.*
PROVERBS 16:3

This verse is not about magic, but it's about trust. It doesn't mean that we can throw up a prayer of commitment to the Lord and then get whatever we want. It means that if we're committed to God's leadership over our plans, He will guide us.

The first step to getting what you want out of life is to decide what you want. Hope is not a strategy, and it is good to make plans. On the other hand, the best way to predict the future is to create it, and God desires to create the future with you.

This ability to create is part of what it means to be made in His image, and it is part of His will for your life. The key is to honor Him and people when you do it. God is not anti-success; God is anti-sin. He will help you establish righteous success as you involve Him. His principles have worked for thousands of years, and they are found throughout the book of Proverbs. Praying is not about wishing but about working with God's guidance.

Take some time and think about the future. What is your dream and vision for the days ahead? What is your plan? Pray about it, seek wise godly counsel, and commit to the Lord whatever you do.

*Today I will remember:*
- God is not anti-success; God is anti-sin.
- Planning is part of living out God's purposes for my life.

*Lord, give me wisdom for the future. Guide me as*
*I dream, plan, and work. I commit it all to You.*
*Help me to be diligent in living for You.*

# GOOD ADVISERS

*Plans fail for lack of counsel,*
*but with many advisers they succeed.*
PROVERBS 15:22

If you are always the smartest person in the room, you are in the wrong rooms. None of us is as smart as a collective few of us. We need advisers. We need people who cover our weaknesses, help us see what we can't see, and assist us in thinking through how to create a better future. One of the wisest things you can do is learn from those who are ahead of you. I absolutely adore people who invest in others. I want to learn from them and pay it forward by being like them. The mentors and advisers who have saved me from making the same mistakes they made and protected me from paying a costly "dumb tax" are some of my favorite people in the world.

Who are your advisers? Not just at work, but in life. We need advisers in marriage, parenting, finances, business deals, and the like. Talk to smart people. Read good books. Have you ever thought to yourself, "Well, I guess I'll just have to learn the hard way"? We're friends and all, and I appreciate you reading this book, but that's just stupid. I don't want to learn the hard way; I want to learn from people who have already learned the hard way. That's the wise and easier way. Wise people learn from the stupidity of others. They watch, listen, learn, and in humility continue to grow.

It has been said that we become the average of the five people we hang out with the most. Choose wisely. Get some good advisers, and in humility you will become better than you otherwise would have been.

*Today I will remember:*

- Wise people listen to good advice.
- A plan without good counsel is a bad plan.

*Lord, help me to be wise. May I be intentional*
*about seeking good counsel, and may I have*
*the humility to receive good advice.*

# NO SUGARCOATING

*Wounds from a friend can be trusted, but an enemy multiplies kisses.*
PROVERBS 27:6

Unrealistic expectations can cause great harm. This is true in marriage, friendship, on vacation, and at a restaurant. There is nothing worse than when something is overpromised and underdelivered. Continually disappointing one's followers does not a great leader make. (Did I just speak like Yoda in that last sentence?) Bottom line: Good leaders don't sugarcoat things. They live and communicate reality.

When recruiting someone new to your team, don't paint an overly glamorized picture of the job or your organization. Present the opportunity in the best, honest, and realistic light. But don't overcommit or promise what you cannot deliver. In fact, it's better to under promise and then over deliver. That makes for great morale, while the opposite destroys it. You obviously want to communicate the upside when recruiting, but the employees you really want appreciate honest challenges, as well as your transparency.

Everything in life has its challenges and that's okay. People are not perfect. Let's be honest about it. Great marriages, friendships, and teams operate in the context of reality. Let's be kind but not sugarcoat. Truth builds trust. Enemies will lie to you, while people who care for you will love you enough to be honest. This is true in life and true in leadership. Love people well by being kind but not sugarcoating.

*Today I will remember:*
- Truth builds trust while sugarcoating erodes it.
- Great marriages, friendships, and teams operate in the context of reality.
- I can be kind without sugarcoating it.

*Father, give me the grace to be a kind truth teller. I don't want to manipulate people; I want to influence them. May I love people well by telling them the truth.*

# EMPOWERING OTHERS

*Moses listened to his father-in-law and did everything he said. He chose capable men from all Israel and made them leaders of the people, officials over thousands, hundreds, fifties and tens. They served as judges for the people at all times. The difficult cases they brought to Moses, but the simple ones they decided themselves.*

EXODUS 18:24-26

Moses was wearing himself out as the leader of Israel. So he sought advice from his father-in-law, Jethro, who told him to keep the big decisions but delegate the rest. It was a lesson in empowering others. Moses immediately puts this lesson into practice and executes a new and better plan. He still has to do the heavy lifting, but he gives away everything else. This ability to empower separates the big leaders from the little ones. It's not easy, but it's necessary if you want to see growth. In Moses' case, it wasn't about growth, but survival.

To empower literally means to give your power away. Great leaders don't hoard their authority through micromanaging. They give authority to others. If you cannot empower others, you will be the cork in your own bottle of impact, and you will risk mental and emotional exhaustion. Empowering is key to growing a leader's influence and to keeping a healthy amount of personal margin.

There are many excuses for not empowering. Perhaps the most common is the myth that no one can do it as well as you. That may be true on one or two things, but for many things, it's not true at all. What do you need to give away? Whom do you need to empower?

*Today I will remember:*

- Great leaders empower others.
- They don't hoard their authority through micromanaging.
- Instead, they give their authority to the trustworthy.

*God, give me the wisdom and personal security to empower others. Help me continue to grow in leadership. Help me know who is trustworthy and to entrust them with more.*

# DEALING WITH CRITICS

*"The Son of Man came eating and drinking, and they say, 'Here is a glutton and a drunkard, a friend of tax collectors and sinners.' But wisdom is proved right by her deeds."*

MATTHEW 11:19

Leaders always have critics. The only way to avoid criticism is to never say anything, do anything, or stand for anything. When my boys were younger and playing sports, I made a commitment to never criticize their coaches. After all, these were men who volunteered their time to teach and coach my boys in a sport they loved. I appreciated them and encouraged them even when I occasionally disagreed with them. These guys were getting enough unfair criticism from the other parents on the sideline.

Even Jesus was criticized and He always led perfectly because He's, well, perfect. How did He handle it? He usually ignored it. Sometimes He would ask pointed questions to the criticizers, and occasionally He would tell a story in response. Bottom line? Jesus knew His wisdom would eventually be proven right. You will sometimes make decisions that no one will understand in the moment, but that will be celebrated in time. Such is life. Everybody criticizes the watering system, while leaders prepare for the good fruit.

Leaders consider the source. We all need feedback. But if the criticism is coming from someone who has never led anything, done anything, and is the quintessential armchair quarterback, then just let the squeaky wheel squeak. You have more important things to do. Over time, wisdom will be proved right by her actions.

*Today I will remember:*

- Leaders get criticized; it's part of the job.
- Everyone has an opinion, but very few make a real impact.

*Father, give me wisdom. Help me to discern what is good feedback versus people just whining about not getting their way. Help me be a wise leader and a great encourager.*

# BUILDING TRUST

*A tyrannical ruler practices extortion, but one who hates ill-gotten gain will enjoy a long reign.*
PROVERBS 28:16

Leadership is influence, and influence is gained through building trust. If there is no trust, then people will not follow you. This is true at work and especially at home. We build trust through care and competency, yes, but real influence primarily comes through displaying good character. If you want to build trust, then be a truth teller. Be honest.

I have the privilege of leading a large organization. Every week I get to speak to thousands of people across six locations throughout the East Valley of Phoenix, AZ, and thousands more online. It's a great blessing and a great responsibility, but if you were to ask me what success looks like to me, then I would tell you that success to me is when the people who know me best trust me the most. Because the people who know me well, know the truth. They know whether I am a person of integrity or not. Integrity is when our public life and private life match up, they are integrated. If a person has integrity, then their talk matches their walk. They are a person who speaks the truth and lives it.

Some of the greatest influence gains of my life have been when I've screwed up and made mistakes but was honest about them. Especially with my wife and children. They don't expect me to be perfect, but they do expect me to be honest. Impressing others is short lived, but influencing others gives you what our proverb today calls a "long reign." Honesty gives you credibility even in your imperfections. Truth builds trust and trust increases influence.

*Today I will remember:*

- Truth builds trust and trust increases influence.
- I may not be perfect, but I can be honest.

*Father, I pray that my walk would match my talk. Help me to be a person of integrity. I pray that I would admit when I'm wrong. Help me to be a leader worth following.*

# CHOOSE YOUR OWN TEAM

*These are the names of the twelve apostles: first, Simon (who is called Peter) and his brother Andrew; James son of Zebedee, and his brother John; Philip and Bartholomew; Thomas and Matthew the tax collector; James son of Alphaeus, and Thaddaeus; Simon the Zealot and Judas Iscariot, who betrayed him.*

MATTHEW 10:2-4

Jesus chose His own disciples. He picked His own team, and He did so carefully. Yes, one of them would go on to betray Him, but I wish I could choose the right employees eleven out of twelve times. History proves that Jesus did a phenomenal job in choosing His team. And, if you understand God's larger plan of salvation, you know that even Judas, the betrayer, played his part.

If you want a leader to get the job done, then you must give him the right tools. The most important asset on the list is the people who will be on the team. Are you considering a leadership position? Then make sure you will be allowed to build your own team of direct reports. Leading is difficult enough without the handicap of a staff that poorly fits your vision. The last thing you want is a bunch of leftover players from the other guy's team who think they should have gotten your job.

Great senior leaders give their managers the freedom to choose their key people. That could mean replacing the current team, or keeping some while saying goodbye to others. Remember the example of Jesus. Choose your own team and allow those you hire to lead to do the same. It's the best way to increase your effectiveness.

*Today I will remember:*

- Wise leaders choose their own team.
- The most important assets in life are the people I live it with.

*God, give me wisdom to know who*
*needs to be on my team and who doesn't.*
*Help me to love and lead my team well.*

# A FOCUSED LIFE

*Hezekiah turned his face to the wall and prayed to the LORD, "Remember, LORD, how I have walked before you faithfully and with wholehearted devotion and have done what is good in your eyes."*

ISAIAH 38:2-3

If you go back and read the passage before today's verse, you will learn that Hezekiah is sick. The Lord speaks through the prophet Isaiah and tells Hezekiah he's going to die; this prayer above is Hezekiah's response. The Bible says that because of his prayer, God adds fifteen years to his life.

Now there's some theological questions here like: If God knows everything, which He does, then how could He change His mind? I think the simple application is, God knows what's going to happen, but He likes His children to participate. Good fathers will at times act as if they don't know some things with their children because that's what is best for the child. The father wants them to think it out, participate, and grow. What I want you to see here is the overall focus of the prayer. Could you and I pray the same?

A focused life is a life that is wholeheartedly devoted to the Lord. It's a man who is continually striving to do what is right in the eyes of God. It doesn't mean that the man is perfect, but that he is continually striving. What we focus on is what we move toward, this is the key to godly living. To focus on the Lord is to remember Him in all things. It is a rule of life that everything else submits to.

*Today I will remember:*

- What I focus on is what I will move toward.
- I participate in God's plan when I pray.

*Father, I want to walk faithfully before You with wholehearted devotion. I choose to focus on You. You are the priority of my life.*

# BEWARE THE YES MEN

*"You hypocrites! Isaiah was right when he prophesied about you: 'These people honor me with their lips, but their hearts are far from me.'"*

MATTHEW 15:7-8

One of the most dangerous things a leader can do is surround himself with people who only tell him what he wants to hear. We all need honest feedback. If you're only receiving good news, then you're not receiving the whole story. You need people who will tell you the good, the bad, and the ugly. This is news you can really use to make better decisions. We want to be the kind of leaders that celebrate honesty, even when it hurts.

Jesus was the first to use the word *hypocrite* how we use it today. The word comes from a Greek word that refers to actors wearing masks. When Jesus used the word *hypocrite*, that's what people heard, "mask wearers." You want a team made up of true faces, people who tell you what they really think and who will not mask their opinions. If you don't allow that, then you've let your pride get in the way of good leadership.

My friend Larry Osborne says, "You can have the wisdom of Solomon and the wrong information and still make a fool's decision." He's right. More than we need our egos boosted, we need the truth. You cannot lead with wisdom without it.

*Today I will remember:*

- I need honest feedback.
- I want team members who tell me what they really think and who will not mask their opinions.

*Lord, help me to celebrate honest feedback. I will never lead perfectly, and I need the insights of others. Put people around me with honest lips. I need it.*

# MAKING GOOD HIRES

*Like an archer who wounds at random is*
*one who hires a fool or any passer-by.*
PROVERBS 26:10

An old axiom says that when it comes to employees, you want to hire slowly and fire quickly. Old sayings like this last because they're true. Our proverb for today is thousands of years old and has also stood the test of time. Wise leaders are careful about those they choose to bring into their inner circles.

Bad hires will wound you. They will cost you customers and infect the culture of your team. We lose leadership credits when we make bad hires. Some of my biggest mistakes as a leader have been making bad hires and then leaving the wrong people in place for too long. My excuse was our rapid growth. We hired quickly and, because we didn't have enough people in place, I fired too slowly. I learned the hard way that the wrong staff can cause deep wounds. Often a breakthrough was waiting on the other side of a hard decision.

As you look for team members and partners, you need to know the specifics of the job and the type of person you want to fill it. Look for competent people with good character. You also want chemistry with them and a good fit with your organization's culture. Wrong people wound, but the right people help you win. Getting personnel right is one of the hardest challenges of leadership. Take your time, know what you're aiming for, and shoot for the bullseye.

*Today I will remember:*

- Wrong people wound, but the right people will help me win.
- I should take my time, know what I'm aiming for, and shoot for the bullseye.

*Lord, guide me and give me wisdom and courage*
*with my teammates and partners. Protect me*
*from bad hires and bad choices in friends.*

# TYRANTS ARE LIKE TODDLERS

*Like a roaring lion or a charging bear is*
*a wicked ruler over a helpless people.*
PROVERBS 28:15

Show me a tyrant and I'll show you a terrible leader. Tyrants are like toddlers throwing a fit. They haven't yet learned to share and that life is not all about them. There's nothing worse than a leader who throws temper tantrums. They may elicit fear, but they'll never be truly respected. They're like an untamed, rabid animal. Their time is short, and their legacy quickly forgotten.

Great leaders, on the other hand, know that the power they've been given is best used to serve. Wicked leaders are self-focused and selfish while righteous leaders work for the good of others.

One of the best leaders I've ever had the privilege of working with was named Dan. He was the president of the organization I served, and we regularly traveled together. One trip, we were running a bit late. As I was checking in for our flight, I turned and saw Dan, the CEO, carrying my bags to the counter. I'll never forget it. His first question to me in private meetings was usually about my family. Dan wasn't a tyrant; he was a servant, and you know what? I'd take a bullet for that guy. He was driven, he held me accountable to the job I was given, and he loved me. That's a righteous leader; that type of leadership endures.

*Today I will remember:*

- Tyrants are like toddlers.
- Wicked leaders are self-focused and selfish.
- Righteous leaders work for the good of others.

*God, help me to serve the people I lead. To serve*
*is to love and this type of leadership lasts.*

# GOOD ANSWER

*A gentle answer deflects anger,*
*but harsh words make tempers flare.*
PROVERBS 15:1 (NLT)

A mentor once told me that you know you're good with people when you can fire a man and he loves you for it. That takes a lot of wisdom, love, and candor. Through the years, I can name a few people I've had to let go and we've remained friends. I'm grateful for that. I can also name some others who are not fans of me at all. When I see them, they avoid eye contact at all costs. Such is life. Good leaders know how to combine gentleness with boldness. They can confront in a loving way. The ability to do this won't solve all your work problems, but it will greatly reduce them.

When dealing with personnel problems, be cordial, kind, and clear. Gentleness and calmness are contagious. At the same time, anger is even more contagious; it's like pouring gasoline on a raging fire. Choose to carry the water of gentleness instead of the rocket fuel of fury.

Where anger is high, logic is low. One of the best ways to begin a volatile conversation is with the simple statement, "Help me understand." This is a humble beginning. It assumes the best about the other person and acknowledges that there is most likely a simple misunderstanding. Your goal is clarity. You're trying to get to the root of the problem. This approach diffuses anger, helps everyone take a deep breath, and begins to bring some rationale to the situation.

*Today I will remember:*

- Where anger is high, logic is low.
- A cordial, kind, and clear approach is the way.
- It won't solve all my relational problems at work, but it will greatly reduce them.

*Holy Spirit, in moments of anger, would You please*
*help me surrender to Your leadership and guidance?*
*I pray that I would carry the water of gentleness and not*
*the rocket fuel of fury. Help me to be gentle and bold.*

# GLORY TO GOD

*So whether you eat or drink or whatever you do, do it all for the glory of God.*

1 CORINTHIANS 10:31

It's so frustrating when others take credit for your work. After all, they don't deserve the glory; you do. It was your idea, your leadership, and your early mornings and late evenings. It was your work! Now that it has become successful, someone else gets the applause. It is frustrating and demoralizing when someone else gets the glory for what you have done.

Ultimately, everything comes from God. Whether you realize it or not, nothing you have ever done has been apart from Him. He gave you the ability and opportunity. He gave you your very life. In the end, all glory for any good thing goes to Him. This includes our work. Our pride and ingratitude reveal that we have left Him out, taking the full credit and forgetting where it all came from. Working for the glory of God, on the other hand, means including Him. You don't have to be falsely humble or demean yourself in an "awe shucks" kind of way. You just acknowledge God amid the work. You do it with integrity and honesty.

Every day is a take-God-to-work-with-you day. The happiest of men know that He is their business partner. This fills us with gratitude while simultaneously releasing some of the pressure. Glorify God in your work. Involve Him in your decisions. Work in such a way that He is pleased.

*Today I will remember:*

- God gave me ability and opportunity.
- He deserves the glory in everything.
- Honoring this truth brings gratitude and relieves pressure.

*Lord, thank You for the ability to work. Thank You for the gifts and talents You have entrusted to me. All glory belongs to You.*

# GET OVER IT

*A person's wisdom yields patience;*
*it is to one's glory to overlook an offense.*
PROVERBS 19:11

One of the most paralyzing hindrances to success is the inability to overlook offenses. The easily offendable are rarely successful. I've never been criticized by someone who was doing more than me. People ahead of me have encouraged me, while some people who are behind me have tried to pull me down. The easily offended tend to be large on opinions and small on impact. They're so busy managing their insecurities that they can't get anything significant done. Such is the life of the proverbial armchair quarterback. They busy themselves criticizing those in the game to mask the fact that they are too afraid to play.

Our verse for today teaches that it is to your benefit to overlook offenses. To raise your soul so high in your pursuit of God and His purposes that you quickly get over criticisms. God, of course, does not whine, complain, or get paralyzed in negativity. Why? Because those things are not godly. They are separate from who He is and how He works. Life is too short to get stuck in the mire of others' opinions. Stay humble, learn from those you can, and when a small-minded person tries to cut you down to their size, choose to get over it and pursue the large purpose God has for you.

*Today I will remember:*
- The easily offended tend to be very large on opinions and very small on impact.
- Pursuing God and His purposes will allow me to quickly get over others' criticisms.

*Lord, forgive me for when I get stuck in the mire of other people's opinions. Your call and plans are too great for me to live offended. Help me to overlook offenses.*

# FOR THE LORD

*Whatever you do, work at it with all your heart, as working for the Lord, not for human masters, since you know that you will receive an inheritance from the Lord as a reward. It is the Lord Christ you are serving.*

COLOSSIANS 3:23-24

My oldest son Joshua's first job was with Chick-fil-A, serving "Christian chicken" and learning excellent customer service. That was a joke of course, but it seems that all church catering events involve Chick-fil-A at some point. Unless the event is on Sunday of course. When Josh started working, I sat him down and gave him a little speech. It was about how Josh doesn't work for the restaurant, but for himself. Everywhere he goes to work from now on, he'll carry a reputation. I basically told him he was in the "Josh Business" and that he was to build a personal brand of hard work, excellence, and integrity.

I was wrong.

Our verses for today teach that Christians don't work for the company or for themselves, but for the Lord. Everything we do is in service to Him. This is a beautiful paradigm shift. How would your job change if you chose to see it through that filter? How would you view your boss and coworkers? How would your view of customers change?

To work for the Lord means to practice His ways. He is our brand. The byproduct on earth is a great reputation and most likely continual success. After all, the Lord's way is the best way. More than that, today's Scripture points us to our inheritance in heaven. You get eternal retirement benefits when you realize you work for the Lord. You have a new boss. You now serve the King of kings. Go represent the brand well.

*Today I will remember:*

- I work for God. He is my boss.
- To work for the Lord means to practice His ways.
- Heaven's retirement benefits are better than earth's.

*Lord, You are the leader of my life in all things. I pray that everything I do would be for Your namesake and Your glory. Thank You for this honor.*

# SPIRIT OF LEADERSHIP

*So the* L*ORD* *said to Moses, "Take Joshua son of Nun, a man in whom is the spirit of leadership, and lay your hand on him."*
NUMBERS 27:18

I'm not sure that anyone is ever "ready" to lead. I know I wasn't. If my first church just went with my resume and experience, they would have never asked me to lead a large group of teenagers at twenty-two years of age. Fast forward ten years, I wasn't ready to lead a church at thirty-two, either. Yet God in His grace and people in their foresight trusted me with responsibility.

As I get older and I think more and more about giving leadership responsibilities away to others, there are questions that keep coming to mind. Is leadership a gift or can it be taught? The "freshmen get smaller every year." No one ever seems ready. So, how do we choose successors and future leaders? Is leadership something you can identify in others, or is it something that we build into others? Are they born with it, or is it built over time? It's both.

In our verse for today God points out to Moses that Joshua has the "spirit of leadership." Many interpret this as a reference to the Holy Spirit. Leadership is a spiritual gift, and you know it when you see it. But some things about leadership are learned over time and can only be forged in the fire of experience. Not everyone is a natural leader, but anyone can learn leadership principles, and the best way to learn leadership is by leading. The best leaders empower others. Look for the gift in others and invest in it.

*Today I will remember:*
- Leadership is a gift and a skill.
- No one is ever completely prepared to lead.
- I learn leadership by leading.

*Lord, help me to identify those You've gifted around me. I pray that I would invest well in them. Help me continue to grow in leadership.*

# GOOD, PLEASING, AND PERFECT

*Do not conform to the pattern of this world, but be transformed by the renewing of your mind. Then you will be able to test and approve what God's will is—his good, pleasing and perfect will.*

ROMANS 12:2

Sometimes people are afraid to truly surrender to God. We fear that if we were to give God everything, He would somehow ruin our lives. We act as if our dreams, our goals, and our plans are better than His. How about you? Imagine your phone rings, and the Caller ID displays the name "God." Would you pick up the call with eager anticipation? Truth be told, most of us would be afraid and would probably let it go to voicemail. Our verse, however, says that God's will is good, pleasing, and perfect. Let's break it down.

1. Good: His will is best. His goals, His dreams, and His plans are better for us than we can imagine. You and I see with a very limited perspective. He sees it all and He loves us.
2. Pleasing: God's will is not a bummer, but a blessing. When we live out His will, we experience love, joy, and peace in our souls. We start thinking, "You know, God was right!" He always is.
3. Perfect: His will is unstoppable. No one can take any of God's blessings from you as you live for Him. There is no shortage; there is more than enough blessing to go around.

Anything God says is for our benefit. The more our minds are renewed by the truth of the Bible, the more we see that. His will is good, pleasing, and perfect.

*Today I will remember:*

- God's will is better for me than my will.
- Surrendering to His leadership in my life is the best decision.
- His plans are good, pleasing, and perfect.

*God, help me to see what You see so that I might do as You say. Your will is good, pleasing, and perfect. I choose Your ways over mine.*

# IDENTIFYING FUTURE LEADERS

*But the LORD said to Samuel, "Do not consider his appearance or his height, for I have rejected him. The LORD does not look at the things people look at. People look at the outward appearance, but the LORD looks at the heart."*

1 SAMUEL 16:7

One of my mentors says, "The freshmen look smaller every year." He means that the older you are and the more you grow as a leader, the more you are tempted to believe that no one younger is ready to lead. In a sense, that's true. No one is ever ready to lead. We all grow into it. Yes, we must look for talent, but more importantly, we must look for character.

God sends the prophet Samuel to the home of Jesse to reveal His plan to replace Saul as king. As each of Jesse's sons passed before Samuel, the prophet thinks *This is a tall, good-looking man, surely this is the Lord's chosen!* Finally, they bring in David, the smallest and youngest of Jesse's boys. They had to go out to the field and fetch him, as he was a shepherd. Everyone else saw a simple shepherd boy; God saw the future king.

When you're selecting future leaders, ask God to help you see beyond the obvious. Ask for a holy intuition and insight into their gifting and character. God tends to specialize in using diamonds in the rough. The seemingly best and brightest might be the least and the worst. Man looks at the outward appearance while God sees the heart. Ask Him to help you see what He sees.

*Today I will remember:*

- Man looks at the outward appearance while God looks at the heart.
- It is good and wise to pray for God's insight.

*Lord, give me insight beyond the obvious. Help me to see what You see in people. Give me a holy intuition in choosing leaders.*

# LIGHT WORK

*"In the same way, let your light shine before others, that they may see your good deeds and glorify your Father in heaven."*
MATTHEW 5:16

Ministry is not just for professional ministers. It's for everyone who is a follower of Jesus. When I was young and began to believe that God wanted me to be a pastor one day, older pastors would all ask me the same question ... Now let me preface this by saying that I'm from the South, I'm a Texan. I'm telling you this, so that when I give you the question you can hear it in your mind with that sweet, southern, John Wayne-like drawl. They would ask me ... "Son, have you been called to the ministry?" Now what they were asking centered around whether God was leading me in my thinking. That's right and good. However, *all* followers of Jesus are called to the ministry, including you.

God has placed you in your vocation for a reason and it is His desire that you represent Him there. If you're in a place where there are no other Christians and you bemoan that fact, remember that light is most effective in the dark. You are the light of Jesus wherever you go. You are the light of the world. This does not mean that we run around preaching to everyone, but it does mean that we're sensitive to the relationships God has placed in our path. Love people well at your job and represent Him well. Be the best boss or employee you can possibly be. Invite people to church and share your testimony when appropriate. Son, you've been called to the ministry!

*Today I will remember:*

- God has placed me where I am for a reason.
- I am to reflect His light, character, and love to others.
- This includes being the best boss or employee that I can be.

*Father, thank You for the awesome privilege I have in representing You. Use me to draw people to Jesus and to reflect Your love.*

# PERSONNEL

*Do not repay anyone evil for evil. Be careful to do what is right in the eyes of everyone. If it is possible, as far as it depends on you, live at peace with everyone.*

ROMANS 12:17-18

One of my friends is so good at catching largemouth bass that he's made a career out of it. He's won $100,000 fishing boats, he's been in commercials for fishing gear, and he pulls a healthy six-figure income hanging out at the lake. Frankly, I have mixed feelings about it. I don't know if I love it or hate it; jealousy can create such conundrums. He once asked what the hardest part of my job was as a pastor of a large church. I responded without any hesitation, "personnel." He looked at me dumbfounded, "What does that word mean?" I had always been jealous of him, but never more than in that moment.

Managing and leading people is hard. It requires wisdom, patience, humility, tenacity, courage, and boldness. The list of required traits is more than I put in that last sentence, but I'm limited with space here. People are difficult. Wise managers and leaders expect this and know that the hardest part of whatever job they're in is people.

Our verses for today give us wisdom to rise above the fray of personnel problems. Aim to go to bed each night with a clear conscience, knowing you did what was best for the business and right by your people. As far as it depends on you, lead with integrity. Do what is right. Lead in peace.

*Today I will remember:*

- Managing and leading people is hard.
- I will do what is best for the business and right by my people.
- Doing what's best enables me to go to bed with a clear conscience each night.

*God, give me the wisdom, patience, humility, tenacity, and courage to love and lead people well. I pray that I would treat others the way You treat me.*

# PRAYING FOR SUCCESS

*And may the Lord our God show us his approval and make our efforts successful. Yes, make our efforts successful!*

PSALM 90:17 (NLT)

I'm not sure why, but when I was young, I thought it was wrong to pray for success. Perhaps it was because of the church culture I grew up in, but there is this idea out there that success is sinful. For the record, it's not. God loves effectiveness and good fruit. Notice that our verse today involves both effort and prayer. I've met many a man who was willing to pray, but unwilling to work. God does not honor such prayers.

We should pray as if it all depends on God and work as if it all depends on us. God meets us in the middle. Pray for success and do things God's way. But make sure your definition of effectiveness aligns with His. Success is not just about money. It's also about character and how we treat people. God evaluates our hearts more than He does our results. So let's make sure both are aligned with Him. Then with a clear conscience we can pray for success.

*Today I will remember:*

- I should pray as if it all depends on God, and work as if it all depends on me.
- God meets me in the middle.

*Lord, thank You for the ability to work and produce. This is one of life's greatest blessings. Help me be successful in Your sight. This includes my character, honoring You in how I treat others, and being effective with what I've been entrusted.*

# PROSPERING IN DIFFICULTY

*"Also, seek the peace and prosperity of the city to which I have carried you into exile. Pray to the LORD for it, because if it prospers, you too will prosper."*
JEREMIAH 29:7

Do you have a job that you don't want to be in? You dread going into work and find yourself living for the weekend? I've been there. It's hard. In today's verse, God's people are in exile. They're under Babylonian captivity, a place they don't want to be in. God speaks through the prophet Jeremiah and gives a specific command. Babylon is a godless place, and God directs His people to make it peaceful and prosperous. In essence, God is telling them to bloom where they are planted. Why? Because what matters most is not where you are, but who you are. God develops character in difficult places.

Maybe He is doing the same thing in your life. Maybe He is preparing you for something better, or will make a way forward that you can't see yet. He wants you to grow in a challenging situation until He brings about a different one.

You're not here by accident, and instead of griping about it, you could choose to grow through it. If you help your work prosper, then you will prosper. Your attitude is a small thing that can make a big difference, for better or worse. What if you chose to do the best you can, while you can, and where you can, with a great attitude? What difference would that make in your soul and in the environment you work in?

*Today I will remember:*
- What matters most is not where I am, but who I am.
- God develops character in difficult places.

*Father, help me to bloom wherever You plant me. I choose to do my best and to have a great attitude in doing it. Where You lead, I will go.*

# REST IN THE MASTER

*"Come to me, all you who are weary
and burdened, and I will give you rest."*
MATTHEW 11:28

I tend to eat my stress. I'm not proud of it, but there it is. I have this habit when I am stressed, to come home, watch television, and stuff my face. This usually involves salsa and a bag of chips. This is my socially acceptable drug of choice. How do you typically handle stressful days and being overwhelmed? Do you, like me, have any bad habits in the realm of stress management?

There are going to be days when we all feel weary and overwhelmed. But Jesus tells us to come to Him. He is the source of real comfort and only He can replenish an empty soul. But we have a role, too. This requires intentionality and a choice to prioritize margin. No one can pour from an empty cup.

Here are three ways I get rest from the Master. Perhaps they will help you, too:

1. Instead of watching television when I feel overwhelmed, I'll go for a walk. A prayer walk. Usually this involves griping to God for a while, but then moves to prayer and praise, acknowledging that I can trust Him.
2. I also go to a professional Christian counselor. Does that surprise you? Well, I get checkups physically, because it's the wise thing to do. Mental checkups are the same. Strong men deal with their problems instead of avoiding them.
3. I talk with Christian men and get their feedback. Men who love me, will listen, and then tell me the truth.

*Today I will remember:*
- I cannot pour from an empty cup.
- Good habits will help me replenish when I feel empty.

*Jesus, thank You that there is rest in You. I can make better choices than I have been making. I choose to come to You as the Master of life instead of just medicating and getting by.*

# RIGHTEOUS AMBITION

*Do you not know that in a race all the runners run, but only one gets the prize? Run in such a way as to get the prize.*

1 CORINTHIANS 9:24

As a young adult who was getting serious about following Jesus, I had dreams of having a wife and kids and financial success. I wanted to make a large impact and maybe live a little larger too. But I wondered whether thinking like this might not align with my faith. When others talked about Jesus, it didn't seem that He was ambitious. But as I've grown in my faith and become older, I've come to realize that Jesus was very ambitious. He was ambitious about doing the will of the Father and building His kingdom. Our verse highlights such godly ambition. If you're going to run the race of faith, run to win.

Christianity is not a hobby. It's a way of life. Don't do it halfway; go all in. God has given you gifts and abilities. Maximize them for His kingdom. Your family, your career, your station—wherever you are, it is God's will that you give it your all. This includes your aspirations and goals. Remember, your primary ambition is to honor God throughout all of it. Build your net worth and honor God while tithing and being generous. Succeed in your job by honoring God and loving people well. Love your family and work with your wife toward a better future. Live a life of righteous ambition.

*Today I will remember:*

- Running the race of faith means running to win.
- Christianity is not a hobby, but a way of life.

*Lord, give me wisdom to understand what it means to be righteously ambitious. May I be more ambitious about following Your leadership than I am about anything else. Help me run to win.*

# SHARE THE PRAISE

*"This is the one about whom it is written:*
*'I will send my messenger ahead of you, who will*
*prepare your way before you.' Truly I tell you,*
*among those born of women there has not*
*risen anyone greater than John the Baptist."*
MATTHEW 11:10-11

Recently my dad was named employee of the month. Now he retired from his career years ago, and this job is "only" greeting customers. He does it more to keep active and busy than anything else. We had breakfast the other day, and he told me how everyone cheered for him when he won the award. He acted as if it was no big deal, but I could tell it meant a lot. Rightfully so. Public praise is important.

In the workplace, there is nothing more encouraging than public affirmation for a job well done. Celebrating a team member who is doing well before others is good leadership and good business. At the same time, taking credit for someone else's work and receiving personal praise for something they did is demoralizing. It is crucial and, frankly, just right to share the praise.

Jesus was lavish in His praise for John the Baptist. Even when John questions and waffles in his faith, Jesus publicly affirms him. So don't forget to praise those who work with you and for you. Choose to do it publicly and do it often. Teamwork makes the dream work and you want to give credit where credit is due. That's what Jesus did.

*Today I will remember:*

- It honors God when I praise those who work with me and for me.
- Public praise is the best praise.
- Teamwork makes the dream work.

*Lord, forgive me when I forget others and*
*hog the praise. Help me to always give credit where*
*credit is due and to celebrate others' successes.*

# April

## GRACE

For it is by grace you have been saved,
through faith—and this is not from
yourselves, it is the gift of God—not
by works, so that no one can boast.
*Ephesians 2:8-9*

# JESUS CAME TO SAVE

*For God did not send his Son into the world to condemn the world, but to save the world through him.*

JOHN 3:17

Several years ago, our church was picketed on a Sunday morning by the infamous Westboro Baptist Church. This group goes around spewing hate, trying to get attention by carrying signs about how God hates various people. One of their signs was directed at me. It said, "Your Pastor is a Whore." You get the picture. My guess is they picked us because we're a larger church and the Superbowl was in our city that weekend. But, what's most interesting about that day is what happened with the weather. As this group stood outside our church, a thick fog rolled in. No one driving by could see what their signs said. It was amazing! Mostly because we live in the desert where fog is extremely rare. A friend who drove by that day sent me a picture of that thick fog, and the caption said, "Well played, God, well played." I agree.

The message of Jesus is not a message of condemnation, but salvation. This is grace. The shocking thing about Christianity is that God loves sinners like you and me. We deserve condemnation, and yet He brought us salvation. The Bible word for this is *gospel*. The word *gospel* means "good news." The good news is we have a Savior. God made a way for us by offering us the holiness of Jesus through His death and resurrection. We are not condemned because Jesus' salvation covers us with His righteousness if we will receive it. This is amazing grace.

*Today I will remember:*

- Jesus did not come to condemn me.
- He came to save me.
- His righteousness covers me if I receive it.

*Jesus, give me wisdom to understand Your amazing grace. Thank You for desiring good for my life. Make me a man who receives Your grace and gives it to others.*

# A GREAT EXCHANGE

*God made him who had no sin to be sin for us,*
*so that in him we might become the righteousness of God.*
2 CORINTHIANS 5:21

The Christian life is all about a great swap. Jesus swapping His life for ours. The theological word for this is *imputation*. It's Jesus taking on Himself what we deserve and imparting to us what we do not deserve and could never earn. It is the great exchange of our sin for His righteousness. It's shocking! It's the scandalous love of God. It's amazing grace.

John Newton, writer of the famous hymn "Amazing Grace," had been a slave ship captain. After converting to Christianity, he renounced the slave trade and helped to abolish slavery in Great Britain. When Newton wrote Amazing Grace, specifically the line that says, "that saved a wretch like me," he meant it. It is only in understanding how wretched we are that we can understand how amazing God's grace is. Jesus taking on our sin and imparting to us His righteousness is so great an act that there really are no words to describe it. *Amazing* is the best we have. God is that good, and you are that loved.

The proper motivation of a Christian man is not guilt or shame, but love. Understanding God's love for us drives us to love Him in return. Grace motivates obedience and full devotion. Jesus took on all your sin—past, present, and future—and clothed your wretchedness with His righteousness. That's amazing grace!

*Today I will remember:*

- Jesus covers my sin with His righteousness.
- I am made new in Him.
- I should be motivated more by love than by shame.

*Thank You, Jesus, for loving and saving a wretch like me.*
*Help me begin to grasp such profound love. May Your*
*amazing love for me fuel complete obedience to You.*

# HELP FROM THE KING

*Let us then approach God's throne of grace with confidence, so that we may receive mercy and find grace to help us in our time of need.*

HEBREWS 4:16

We have an enemy. He's called the Devil or Satan. The name Satan means "the accuser," and that's what he does. Revelation 12:10 says that he accuses mankind before God both day and night. He accuses you personally too. His goal is to keep you away from God, especially in your time of need.

Our verse for today says that the throne of God is a "throne of grace." We must remember that. Jesus has taken on Himself all our shame. The message of the gospel is not shame on you. Through what Christ has accomplished on our behalf, it's shame *off* you. The Enemy wants you paralyzed in your shame. God wants you to be rid of it. Satan knows that if he can isolate you from God and from others, then he'll keep you trapped in your sin. This is his tactic. He's an accuser, and let's give the Devil his due; his strategy has worked for thousands of years.

The Bible, however, says that we can approach God's throne of grace with confidence. This is the truth. Our Heavenly Father is there to help us in our time of need, and when we approach Him to get help with overcoming our sin, He will give us mercy and grace. Stay close to His throne. Don't run from Him, run to Him with confidence. His mercy and grace are waiting for you.

*Today I will remember:*

- God wants me to confidently come to Him.
- Satan's strategy is to accuse me.
- Jesus has taken my shame.

*Father, my tendency when I feel guilty is to run from You.*
*Thank You for wanting me instead to run to You.*
*Thank You for Your continual grace and mercy in my life.*

# ONLY BY GRACE

*For it is by grace you have been saved,*
*through faith—and this is not from yourselves,*
*it is the gift of God—not by works, so that no one can boast.*

EPHESIANS 2:8-9

Biblically speaking, an "arrogant Christian" is an oxymoron—the two things don't go together. Yes, there are plenty of cocky, self-righteous dudes who call themselves Christians, but we are not saved by our own goodness. Salvation and peace with God do not come from us; they are a gift we receive through faith in Jesus. Therefore, there's no room for boasting. There's no such thing as an arrogant man who follows Jesus.

Grace through faith means we are made right with God not through our trying, but our trusting. The whole thing is about a trusting relationship. Think about it, what does the word *faith* mean? It means, "to believe or trust." To believe someone or to trust someone is relational, which means *faith* is a relational word. We are not trying to earn status through works-oriented transactions; we are trusting in Jesus who loves us. There's no room for arrogance in that. He did all the work through His sacrifice on the cross and through His resurrection, and we trust in what He has done for us. In that trust, we obey Him. Our obedience is not about earning anything. It's simply a relational response to His love, mercy, and grace. There's no boasting in the life of a true believer, just gratitude in response to how we've been blessed.

*Today I will remember:*

- An arrogant Christian is an oxymoron.
- *Faith* is a relational word.
- I am made right with God solely by trusting in Jesus.

*Thank You, Lord, for Your mercy and grace.*
*Forgive me for my pride. I choose to live for*
*You today in gratitude for Your love for me.*

# SINNERS FIRST

*Jesus said to them, "Truly I tell you,
the tax collectors and the prostitutes are
entering the kingdom of God ahead of you."*
MATTHEW 21:31

In our verse today Jesus is telling a parable to some self-righteous religious people. I encourage you to look up the full passage and read it for yourself because He makes an interesting point. Self-righteousness does not help you experience the kingdom of God; it hinders it. In fact, there's a better chance of a prostitute experiencing the joy and power of the Kingdom than a self-righteous pastor. Shocking? Yeah, it was for those people too.

The kingdom of God is accessed through His grace, and His grace only flows to the humble. Self-righteous people are not self-aware of their sin. They are on a self-salvation track, trusting in their good works. People who are unaware of their sin miss the power of grace because they don't really think they need Jesus. They find Him inspirational, but unnecessary.

Pride is the biggest deterrent to real Christianity. Brothers beware of it. It closes the door on the mercy, grace, and power of God. In humility talk to God about your sin. In gratitude, fall to your knees, overwhelmed by the goodness of His grace. We are not made right with God by our own good works but by trusting and receiving the good work of Jesus. Sinners know this. Do you?

*Today I will remember:*

- I am a sinner saved by grace through my trust in Jesus.
- God's grace flows to the humble.
- Pride is the biggest deterrent to my faith.

*Lord, thank You for Your grace. I would be lost
without it. Let me never be proud, but instead
let me always be grateful for Your grace.*

# WHAT MAKES CHRISTIANITY DIFFERENT

*For God so loved the world that he gave*
*his one and only Son, that whoever believes*
*in him shall not perish but have eternal life.*
JOHN 3:16

Our verse for today is the bottom-line message of what God has done for us. Perhaps you've seen this verse on banners at football games, or maybe even painted on players' faces. Tim Tebow might come to mind.

Notice that the verse starts with God and ends with life. This is what God wants for you, eternal life. He wants you to have it so much so that He paid a huge price to give it to you. Christianity in its essence is not a religion. It is about receiving this gift of God. The gift is not rules or precepts; the gift is Jesus.

This is what separates Christianity from every other faith in history. It's about trusting and receiving a person. Religion is advice about how to work your way to God. Christianity is news about how God has worked His way to you. This is the "good news" of the gospel: that Jesus came and died on the cross to cover all sin for all time and then three days later He rose again. This is good news of great joy for all people! We have a Savior, Jesus Christ, who is the Lord.

Religions are about earning. Christianity is about receiving. Grace is unmerited favor. It's getting what you don't deserve. This means that achievers don't go to heaven; receivers do. God's grace comes when you believe and receive Jesus.

*Today I will remember:*

- Grace is what makes Christianity different.
- We receive the righteousness of Jesus as we trust in Him.

*Jesus, I choose to receive You and trust in You.*
*I believe You died on the cross and rose again,*
*and I trust You as the savior and leader of my life.*

# BELOVED SON

*See what great love the Father has lavished on us,*
*that we should be called children of God!*
*And that is what we are! The reason the world*
*does not know us is that it did not know him.*

1 JOHN 3:1

My favorite word in our verse for today is *lavished*. God doesn't just love you; He extravagantly loves you. He's poured out His love on you in great abundance! He loves you so much that He calls you His child. If you've given your life to Jesus, you've been adopted into the family of God. Jesus called God, "Father," and so can you. You're an adopted son of the King of kings and the Lord of lords. Think about that. There's been an identity shift.

If someone were to ask who you are, what would you say? I'm a husband, a dad, a whatever your job is? Some of us would just give our names. Others wouldn't want to be known for the reputation of their last names. Well, in the spiritual realm, you in essence have a brand-new name. There's been a seismic shift in your very existence. Who are you? You're a child of God.

The world may not see it yet. They may not know that you're the product of profound love, but you do. In the love God has for you, there's a humble strength that secures you like a massive anchor in the ebbs and flows of life in a broken world.

*Today I will remember:*

- I am a beloved son of God, the King of kings and the Lord of lords.
- This is who I really am.

*Father, thank You that You have lavished Your great*
*love upon me. Help me to believe it and to walk*
*in it. Who am I? I am Your beloved son.*

# WHAT CAN A DEAD MAN DO?

*But because of his great love for us, God, who is rich in mercy, made us alive with Christ even when we were dead in transgressions—it is by grace you have been saved.*

EPHESIANS 2:4-5

Many men misunderstand what Jesus gives His followers. Some think it's some sort of get-out-of-jail-free card. Like, you can do anything you want because ... you know ... Jesus forgives. This is a gross misunderstanding of the gospel and a very limited grasp of Christianity. Our verses for today say that Jesus does much more than forgive sinners. He makes dead men alive! The problem is not just that we sin; it's that in our sin we are dead.

This reality blows religious thinking right out of the water. Religion is about earning one's way to God. But the Bible says that sinners are dead in their transgressions. Christianity can't be about working one's way to God. After all, what can a dead man do? Nothing.

What we need is life. This is what Jesus gives. It's more than forgiveness. It's waking up to a new reality. We are made spiritually alive through receiving His grace. This life, not religious works, gives us access to God. In this grace we experience fellowship with the triune God, Father, Son, and Spirit. New life in Jesus allows us to call God what Jesus calls Him: Abba Father. We are born into new life with Him.

*Today I will remember:*

- Dead men can't work their way to God.
- Jesus took on my death and has given me His life.
- New life changes my relationship to God.

*Father, thank You for the life You have given me in Jesus.*
*Now I can know You and forever be called Your son.*
*Help me to walk in this new life as You intend.*

# THE WORST SINNER

*Here is a trustworthy saying that deserves full acceptance: Christ Jesus came into the world to save sinners—of whom I am the worst.*

1 TIMOTHY 1:15

The apostle Paul is perhaps the greatest Christian that ever lived. If you're thinking, *what about Jesus?* Jesus is not a Christian; Jesus is the Christ. Meaning He's the promised "anointed one." He is the Savior. Paul is in the running, in my opinion, for greatest Christian who ever lived because of his impact. He wrote much of the New Testament. Much of our theology comes from his writings. He is the first missionary to the Gentiles (anyone who is not Jewish), so if you are reading this and you're not a Jew, then you are experiencing the legacy of Paul's ministry in this very moment.

Paul accomplished many amazing things for the kingdom of God. Yet in our verse for today he describes himself as the worst of sinners. Before Paul's conversion to Christianity, he was a zealot. That's a nice way of saying he was a terrorist. He hated Christianity and Jesus. He was on the march to wipe out the church. One day while he was traveling to Damascus, the resurrected Jesus called him out and changed Paul's life, and Paul changed the world. The Christian killer became a Christian.

The question with Paul, with you, with me, and with all men is not about the greatness of our sin, but the greatness of our Savior. No matter where you've been, what you've done, or what's been done to you, He loves you. His saving grace is for you.

*Today I will remember:*

- Jesus came into the world to save sinners.
- I am deeply flawed and deeply loved.
- This love changes me.

*Jesus, thank You for Your love and sacrifice for sinners like me. Your grace is more powerful than my sin. I do not trust in my goodness. I trust in Your grace.*

# LIFE-CHANGING LOVE

*This is love: not that we loved God,*
*but that he loved us and sent his Son*
*as an atoning sacrifice for our sins.*
1 JOHN 4:10

God made the first move. When we were hopeless and helpless, He had a rescue mission already in place. We are not saved because we love God. We are saved through receiving His love. This love is revealed through the sacrifice of His Son. When we receive that love, we are changed. The root of our love for Him is found in His love for us. If you want to grow in your love for God, then think about and meditate on His love for you. Most of the wrong things we do in life are not because we don't love God enough, but because we do not realize how much He loves us.

If we really grasped the love of God, we would do what He says. He can see what we can't see, He knows what we don't know, and He loves us! So why don't we trust Him? There's something in our sin nature that rebels. We, like Adam and Eve, believe the lie that maybe God is holding out on us. Like a child who rebels against the love of a good father, men reject the love of our good and great God. But if we could see what God sees, then we would do what God says because we would see that it is for our good. The problem is that we can't see what He sees and so must trust His heart.

*Today I will remember:*
- God made the first move while I was helpless.
- I grow in my love for God by thinking about His love for me.
- I will trust God when I can't see what He sees.

*Lord, thank You that You made the first move. Thank You*
*that You loved me first and made a way for me in Jesus.*
*Help me to know Your love so that I might trust You.*

# A SON GIVEN

*He who did not spare his own Son, but gave him up for us all—how will he not also, along with him, graciously give us all things?*

ROMANS 8:32

Have you ever wondered if God really loves you? I have. There have been seasons that were so difficult that I doubted all kinds of things. During one painful time, I doubted if God was real; and, if He *was* real, I wasn't sure He liked me very much.

Listen, doubt is a prerequisite for faith. It's part of the journey. Show me a man who says he never doubts, and I'll show you a man who is not self-aware, is possibly untruthful, or just hasn't thought about it very much. Difficult times can fuel our doubts, but it is in these times that our faith grows the most. Feelings can greatly affect our faith. In times of struggle, we must remember that feelings aren't facts.

When we think about God's love, we must be careful not to measure it in light of our circumstances but in light of the Cross. God has given you His own Son. He has done everything to make a way for you. Consider the bigger picture. Ultimately, everything is going to be all right. Your sin has been covered for all time. Jesus rose again, and in Him you have eternal life. Feelings come and go. The truth remains.

*Today I will remember:*

- God's love for me is most revealed at the Cross.
- Feelings aren't facts.
- When in doubt, I will remember the Cross.

*Father, sometimes my life is hard and my faith falters. Let me always remember Your love for me in Jesus. Help me to focus on who You are.*

# DEATH OR LIFE

*For the wages of sin is death, but the gift of God is eternal life in Christ Jesus our Lord.*

ROMANS 6:23

Today's verse is a matter of life and death. It tells us that the gift of eternal life, or life forever with God, can never be earned or achieved. It can only be received.

But all of us have achieved and earned *something*. Our verse says that our sin has earned us death to God. Have you ever sinned? Yeah, me too. We deserve death—eternal separation from God. That's the bad news. The good news is that God offers us life. The word *eternal* is an adjective that tells us how long the life He offers lasts—forever. If you and I were talking and I died from a heart attack, we couldn't talk anymore. But if you revived me with CPR, our relationship could continue. Death separates. Life restores.

The verse says that this life-saving gift of God comes in Jesus. Jesus died on the cross and then rose again. His resurrection means that He beat death and can give life to anyone He chooses. We receive this life by asking Him to be our Savior and Lord. *Lord* means that we put Him in charge. We make Him the leader of our lives. Death is what we've earned, and life is what He gives.

*Today I will remember:*

- I deserve death and Jesus gives life.
- The only thing I contributed to salvation was my sin.
- Jesus did it all.

*Jesus, thank You for the gift of eternal life that can only be found in You. I am a sinner and deserve death, but I believe in You and trust in You as my Savior and Lord.*

# GOD SERVES

*"For even the Son of Man did not come to be served,
but to serve, and to give his life as a ransom for many."*
MARK 10:45

I'm going to say something that may sound shocking. God loves and serves sinners. Before you go all ballistic on me, think about it.

Jesus is God in the flesh. He left the glory of heaven to be born in a manger, so that He could grow up and die a bloody death on the cross to save sinners like you and me. He healed people, He fed them, He taught them. He allowed people to insult Him, persecute Him, and kill Him. God went through all of this for *sinners*. Know why? Because He loves them. And do you know what love does? Love serves.

God has served you and me. The Almighty, the all-powerful King of the universe, gave up His life to rescue the lawbreakers and rebels of the Kingdom. Why did Jesus come? Because God loves sinners. God hates sin because He is holy and because sin hurts that which He loves, sinners. He came to rescue us from sin, to pay the penalty we deserve, and to conquer death, hell, and the grave, which are the consequences of sin. God loves and serves sinners. This is mercy. This is grace. This is the character and holiness of our great God.

*Today I will remember:*
- God serves because He loves.
- Because God has served me, I choose to serve Him.

*God, help me grasp who You really are. The greatness
of Your character is far beyond my comprehension.
I'm overwhelmed at Your goodness toward me. Thank You.*

# GRACE CHANGES ME

*Therefore, there is now no condemnation for those who are in Christ Jesus, because through Christ Jesus the law of the Spirit who gives life has set you free from the law of sin and death.*

ROMANS 8:1-2

The Christian life is not about rules but about a relationship. Perhaps you've heard that before. It has been said so often that many people see it more as a cliché than as an accepted biblical truth. But if Christianity were just about rules, we would all be condemned, because we all break the rules of God. Yet our verses remind us that there is no condemnation for those who are in Christ Jesus. Why? Because in Jesus there's a change in the system. We are free from the rules of the law because Jesus has covered us with His life, His grace, His Holy Spirit. This relationship changes us.

How do you know an apple tree is an apple tree? Simple, it produces apples. An apple tree couldn't be an orange tree no matter how hard it tried. But what if somehow that apple tree could be supernaturally altered from the inside out? What if it was given new roots? New roots would equal new fruit. The Holy Spirit is Jesus' supernatural presence in us. As we get to know Him and allow Him to lead us, He begins to change us from the inside out. Rules are about the fruit. The Spirit is about the roots, and new roots change everything. In the Christian life, we learn to know and surrender more and more to this new relationship.

*Today I will remember:*

- Rules don't change people's lives. Grace does.
- The more I grow in grace, the more my faith grows.

*Holy Spirit, empower me. Help me to see what You see, so that I might be changed from the inside out. Change the roots in my heart, so that the fruit of my life reflects You.*

# GRACE FOR ALL PEOPLE

*And they sang a new song, saying: "You are worthy to take the scroll and to open its seals, because you were slain, and with your blood you purchased for God persons from every tribe and language and people and nation."*

REVELATION 5:9

Recently in South Africa I was honored to be part of two pastor's gatherings. One was in Mahikeng in the North West Province and the other was in Cape Town. Singing with my African brothers and sisters was a foretaste of heaven. I didn't speak their language, but we were unified in spirit. I wept in gratitude for the worldwide grace of Jesus.

Today's verse is part of a future song to Jesus, sung about the beauty of His salvation. Jesus is worthy because He is without sin. He is the only one worthy! Jesus is fully God and fully man, and in His humanness, He remains without sin. His righteous blood paid for the sin of people from every tribe, tongue, and nation. I'm looking forward to this moment when we all sing this song! We'll be joining thousands upon thousands of angels in the singing.

Christianity celebrates diversity. Christians look different as persons, but we are united in purpose. Our unity is about our mission. The gratitude and worship we share honor our King. God's grace is worldwide.

*Today I will remember:*

- Jesus is worthy of worldwide worship.
- One day, every tribe, tongue, and nation will be represented around His throne.

*Thank You, Jesus, that You love diversity. I look forward to worshiping You with people from all over the world. I pray that even though we all have our differences, we will be united in our purpose and grateful in our worship.*

# GRACE WORKS

*What good is it, my brothers and sisters, if someone claims to have faith but has no deeds? Can such faith save them?*

JAMES 2:14

If I were to ask you what faith is, what would you say? Most people's definition is probably somewhere in the vicinity of mental assent. Meaning faith is acknowledging or agreeing.

Biblical faith, however, is broader and more robust. Yes, mental agreement is involved, but faith also encompasses relational interaction and obedience. In the Bible, *faith* is a trust word, and trust is relational. To have faith in God means that you relationally trust Him. You take Him at His word and therefore do what He says. Here's the flow of biblical faith: to believe is to trust, and to trust is to obey. Trust and obedience are the fruit of faith, showing that the faith is real.

James here is saying that real faith has real fruit. If someone says he trusts God but never does what He says, he doesn't really believe. To be clear, James is not saying that we work our way to God. James is saying that if you have received God's gift of grace, then you will trust Him and do good deeds as the fruit of that trust. See the difference? God's grace is a gift. We can't work for it or earn it. We are saved by grace alone through faith alone, but real faith never stands alone. It is always followed by action.

*Today I will remember:*

- Real faith has real fruit.
- We are saved by grace alone through faith alone, but real faith never stands alone.
- Faith is always followed by action.

*Lord, I pray that my faith is evident. May my beliefs match my actions. I believe in You and trust You, which means I choose to obey You.*

# RESCUED IN ADVANCE

*But God demonstrates his own love for us in this:*
*While we were still sinners, Christ died for us.*

ROMANS 5:8

Sometimes I'll be talking with someone who doesn't believe what I believe. This person will ask me when God began. I understand why he would ask that, but it is not applicable to God, who is eternal and outside of time. He created time, so He transcends it. The question of when He began assumes that the eternal, timeless God is still somehow inside the construct of time. This is logically impossible. Tracking? When we who are finite ask such questions, we show that we are trying to comprehend He who is infinite.

Why am I rambling on about this? Because God made a way for you before you were ever born. He paid in advance for the crimes you would commit in the future. He knew you would need His help. He stepped into time to rescue sinners for all time.

God proved His love for you even though He knew all your sin in advance. Sins past, present, and future. God knew the things you are ashamed of even before you knew them, and He loved you and made a way for you in Jesus. Nothing is hidden from God's sight. He sees all things at once. His love and salvation were there waiting on you. You've never surprised or shocked Him. The question is not whether He will receive you; the question is whether you will receive Him. No matter where you've been, what you've done, or what has been done to you, God loves you. He has already proved His love through what Christ did for you on the cross. Receive it and trust in Him.

*Today I will remember:*

- God has always loved me.
- I have never shocked or surprised Him.
- Grace was there before I knew I needed it.

*Father, help me understand this great salvation.*
*Thank You for making a way for me in advance.*
*When I do wrong, help me not to run from You,*
*but to You. Your grace is always waiting.*

# SEATED WITH JESUS

*And God raised us up with Christ and seated us with him in the heavenly realms in Christ Jesus, in order that in the coming ages he might show the incomparable riches of his grace, expressed in his kindness to us in Christ Jesus.*

EPHESIANS 2:6-7

There's nothing better than going to a game and sitting just behind your home team's dugout or on the fifty-yard line, twenty rows from the field. For me, if you're sitting in the nosebleed section, you might as well stay home. I only want to go if it's a great seat. The Bible says that through the resurrection of Jesus, we have the best seat in all the universe. We can sit with Jesus in the heavenly realms for all eternity.

Not only do we have a great seat. We are raised with Christ through His resurrection, seated in Christ forevermore through His worthiness, and we are trophies of grace by His kindness. If you have given your life to Jesus, then God considers you a prized possession. More than that, He considers you a son. This is what it means to be part of the family of God. Usually when we say that, we're referring to fellow Christians, our brothers and sisters in Christ, but it's more than that. In Jesus, you have been adopted into the family. You have a seat at the table next to Jesus. The Lord is your brother; God is your Father; and your adoption is sealed permanently by the Holy Spirit. God is proud of you because of His grace, and He'll show you off for all eternity.

*Today I will remember:*

- In Jesus, I have a seat in heaven.
- I am now part of the family of God.

*Father, I am amazed that You welcome a sinner like me into Your family. Thank You!*

# MATURING IN LOVE

*I pray that your love will overflow more and more, and that you will keep on growing in knowledge and understanding.*

PHILIPPIANS 1:9 (NLT)

Have you ever met a man who told you he was a "mature Christian" but was kind of a jerk? Yeah, he's still immature. Mature believers are loving and kind because that's what Jesus is. To be a mature Christian is to be more like Christ. You can know a lot of the Bible and still be immature. There's a difference between intellectual knowledge and heart knowledge. Our verse today is more about the heart.

One of the ironies of the Christian faith is that the more you know, the less you're impressed with what you know. Christian maturity is about growing in grace, and grace is about getting what you don't deserve. The more you understand it, the more you realize you don't deserve it. This produces humility, which produces gratitude, which produces love for others. An arrogant Christian is an ignorant one. Such people may know a lot about what the Bible says, but they don't understand what it means. The more the love overflows, the more understanding and knowledge grow.

Think on the love of God today. Ask the Holy Spirit to help you understand His grace and love. The more He opens your eyes to these things, the more you will be changed.

*Today I will remember:*

- The more I understand the grace of God, the more I will grow in my love for others.
- An arrogant Christian is an ignorant one.

*God, help me grasp who You really are. I don't want to just know things about You. I want to know You. Teach me Your grace and love. May it flow in me and through me.*

# MADE NEW

*Therefore, if anyone is in Christ,*
*the new creation has come:*
*The old has gone, the new is here!*
2 CORINTHIANS 5:17

Our church's baptismal services make me cry. They're huge celebrations of God's grace that we do five times a year. Last year we baptized over sixteen hundred men, women, and children. The thing that gets me every time is when we baptize a mom and dad, and they turn and baptize their kids. It's a picture of a changed family and a new legacy. I'm getting choked up right now just thinking about it.

Our verse reminds us that people are made new in Jesus. It's not just that they have a second chance, a new opportunity. They have become a new creation. Something has radically changed. A metamorphosis has taken place. A man who was spiritually dead has awakened and been made alive. He can now understand things about God that were impossible to comprehend before. The Holy Spirit has moved into his inner being. The old has gone and the new has come. Sinners become saints—not through their own goodness, but by the goodness of Jesus entering their lives.

*Today I will remember:*

- Jesus makes all things new.
- He didn't just give me a second chance to do better; He has made me a new person to live a new kind of life.

*Jesus, thank You that in You I am a new creation.*
*You've transformed my inner being by Your Spirit.*
*Give me wisdom to walk in this new way of grace.*
*Thank You that all things are new in You.*

# SINNERS ONLY

*On hearing this, Jesus said to them, "It is not the healthy who need a doctor, but the sick. I have not come to call the righteous, but sinners."*

MARK 2:17

Jesus didn't come for the righteous. He doesn't call saints; He calls sinners. To be rescued by Jesus and to have His call on your life, you must be a sinner—which means we are all overqualified. Congratulations, you made the cut.

Read this account in Mark. Levi threw Jesus a party to celebrate Jesus' invitation to be one of His disciples. Levi is his Hebrew name; most know him by the name of Matthew. Levi was a tax collector. None of us are excited to see the tax man, but Levi was far worse in the eyes of his contemporaries. Jewish tax collectors were considered turncoats, as they worked for the Roman oppressors, even siphoning extra cash for themselves. Think of a Jewish person collecting taxes for the Nazis and getting rich off it and you will see how despised Levi was.

Yet Jesus called Levi. The self-righteous are another matter. Jesus calls them, but they suffer from self-imposed deafness. They do not realize their need for a Savior. Thank God for His grace. Thank God that Jesus came to save sinners like you and me.

*Today I will remember:*

- The only thing I contributed to God's call on my life is my sin.
- Jesus rescued me not because I deserve it, but because He loves me.

*Jesus, thank You that You call people like Levi and me to salvation. When I couldn't work my way to You, You worked Your way to me in love, mercy, and grace. I'm grateful for who You are and for what You have done.*

# HE KNOWS YOU

*"Are not five sparrows sold for two pennies? Yet not one of them is forgotten by God. Indeed, the very hairs of your head are all numbered. Don't be afraid; you are worth more than many sparrows."*

LUKE 12:6-7

Maybe the hair thing here doesn't seem that impressive because you don't have any. Perhaps it would make more sense if Jesus had said that God knows every crease of your shiny, bald head. Regardless, the point is the same. You are loved. God cares for sparrows, but not like He cares for you. Human beings are the most valuable beings on the planet. God loves animals but He loves you more. You are very special to Him.

Notice the rest of the verse. The fact that you are known by God means that you needn't fear. God knows you. This is not meant to be a scary truth, but a hopeful one. He knows you because He created you, and there's no need to fear because He loves you. The Bible does teach us to fear God, but that's about respect and honor, not terror and trepidation. God knowing you and loving you means that you can rest in Him. Whatever trials we face in this broken world, we know that everything ultimately will be made right. You are not forgotten. You are fully known and fully loved. God loves you as you are, not as you should be. This is grace.

*Today I will remember:*

- God knows everything about me and loves me still.
- I am very important to Him.

*Father, it blows my mind that You know and care for me with such detail. I rest in the peace of Your grace today. Thank You that I'm never alone and never out of Your sight. May I live in reverence toward You and in the peace of Your presence.*

# GRACE-FUELED OBEDIENCE

*Or do you show contempt for the riches of his kindness, forbearance and patience, not realizing that God's kindness is intended to lead you to repentance?*

ROMANS 2:4

I'm grateful for my church upbringing, because it gave me a good moral foundation and protected me from a bunch of stupid decisions as I grew older. But I think our pastors hesitated to tell us much about God's love and grace, afraid we might go out and abuse it. So instead they dwelled on guilt and shame, which made me not like God very much. After all, who wants to be with somebody who is constantly mad and disappointed with you? Not me.

Our verse, in contrast, teaches that God's kindness leads us to real repentance. The more you understand God's goodness and grace, the more you will want to spend time with Him and live for Him. Religious leaders throughout the ages have not always understood this truth, fearing that unless they keep the sheep shameful and afraid, the flock might rebel. This verse says that leaders like this are showing contempt for the riches of God's kindness.

Biblical faith is not religiously transactional, but relational. God's grace encourages us to live for Him. When you understand God's love, you want to do what He says. Christian living is grace-fueled obedience.

*Today I will remember:*

- Understanding God's love is the greatest motivation to obey Him.
- I am compelled to live for Him when I think about the love He showed for me on the cross.

*Father, help me to know and understand Your love so that I might trust and obey You. May I keep reverent gratitude foremost and never show contempt for Your kindness. May Your kindness compel me to keep in step with You.*

# FOR US

*What, then, shall we say in response to these things?*
*If God is for us, who can be against us?*
ROMANS 8:31

It was said by A. W. Tozer, "What comes into our minds when we think about God is the most important thing about us." This is true because our thoughts shape everything we do. Today's verse says that God is for us. He wants what is best. Do you believe this? If so, are you doing things that are outside of His will? If He is indeed for you, then those things will be harmful to you. Obedience to Him is always the best choice because it serves both Him and you. And yet we all disobey Him. Why?

Our real problem is not that we don't love God enough, but that we don't realize how much He loves us. If you and I understood God's love for us, we would always do what He says. All decisions are faith decisions. Everybody is trusting somebody. Whether it be us, our culture, our friends, or our God, we are all making faith decisions. We all believe the word of someone.

There will be times when what God says doesn't seem right to our limited view and experience. In those moments, we must remember that He is for us. He sees what we can't see, He knows what we don't know, and He loves us.

*Today I will remember:*
- God is for me, and I can trust Him.
- His words are for my good.

*God, thank You for Your commands. I know that You are not trying to bum me out. Your commands are there to bless my life. Help me to be a man who understands, represents, and lives this truth.*

# GOD SINGS

*"The LORD your God is with you, the Mighty Warrior who saves. He will take great delight in you; in his love he will no longer rebuke you, but will rejoice over you with singing."*

ZEPHANIAH 3:17

I sing when I'm happy. I do it so much that those who are close to me tease me about it; not so much because I start singing, but because I won't stop. My soul must sing, baby! It amazes me that God sings over us as we trust in Him. I'm pretty sure that when He sings over me there's a Johnny Cash vibe to it—because that's what I like.

Our verse today is a word from God through the prophet Zephaniah concerning God's joy for His people and how in His grace, He will restore them. Principally, it's a word to all God's people for all time about how He feels when we repent and trust in Him. He delights in those who trust Him to the extent that He shouts over them with joy and may even break out in song.

How can we be so amazed by God's power, but so lackadaisical about His love? We believe in His anger over sin but doubt the grace we find in Jesus. Perhaps it's our own shame or low self-esteem, but those things are irrelevant when it comes to God's love. He doesn't love us because we're awesome. He loves us because He is awesome. God sings over you in grace.

*Today I will remember:*

- God sings over those who trust in Him.
- He has a song in His heart for me.

*Father, I look forward to hearing Your song for me. I choose to receive and trust in the joy of Your grace. Help me focus on Your love today, that there might be a song in my heart for You.*

# HONEST PRAYER

*Hear me, Lord, my plea is just; listen to my cry.*
*Hear my prayer—it does not rise from deceitful lips.*
PSALM 17:1

When I was younger, I brought an older pastor with me to visit a friend in the hospital. The pastor was in his seventies, and I was twenty-four. I picked him up, and he told me stories of his life and ministry. When we got to the hospital, we visited with my friend, and then it was time to pray. After I prayed, he looked at my friend and said, "Now, are you ready for a real prayer?" I stood there, embarrassed and confused, and he started to pray. It sounded nothing like the man I had just conversed with for over an hour. His voice changed, and not only that, he also started speaking in the King's English, using words like thee and thou. It was so strange and unnecessary.

Prayer is simply communicating and communing with God. We can be ourselves. In fact, He wants us to be ourselves. Think about it. God can't love or connect with the person you're pretending to be because that person does not exist. God is real, and He only operates in the construct of reality. He knows everything. Nothing is hidden from His sight. You can pretend with yourself and others, but you cannot pretend with God. Be yourself. He loves the real you, and He wants to spend time with you.

*Today I will remember:*

- God loves the real me.
- Prayer is simply me talking to my Heavenly Father as His son.

*Father, thank You that I can just be myself*
*when I pray and that You love me as I am.*
*Thank You that my words do not have*
*to be perfect and that You hear my heart.*

# INFINITE GRACE

*From his abundance we have all received one gracious blessing after another. For the law was given through Moses, but God's unfailing love and faithfulness came through Jesus Christ.*

JOHN 1:16-17 (NLT)

When Jackson, my youngest (I call him my "Scottish son" because of his red hair and fair skin), was around four years old, we would play a little game back and forth about our love for each other. I would say, "I love you, Jackson." He would reply, "I love you, Dad, plus a hundred." I would up the ante and say, "Well, I love you plus a thousand." He would say, "I love you plus a million!" Finally, one day, I said, "Jackson, I love you infinity." He thought for a long moment and responded, "Dad, I love you infinity! Plus a hundred." He had me beat.

Our verse says that in Jesus "we have all received one gracious blessing after another." The idea in the original Greek is that we receive grace upon grace upon grace. It means there is more grace in Jesus than there is sin in you. We will never run out of grace! You can't exhaust Him. His kindness remains. When you understand this relationally, you don't abuse it. You surrender to it. His grace for us compels us to live for Him. It is grace infinity! Plus, a hundred.

*Today I will remember:*

- God's grace for me never runs dry.
- There is more grace in Jesus than there is sin in me.

*Father, Your kindness makes me want to live for You. I am so grateful for Your infinite love! Help me to trust in You and to know that You are for me. Thank You that Your grace is infinite.*

# JESUS HEALS

*Great crowds came to him, bringing the lame,*
*the blind, the crippled, the mute and many others,*
*and laid them at his feet; and he healed them.*

MATTHEW 15:30

Why did Jesus heal people? John's Gospel describes miracles as signs that Jesus is the Messiah. He wrote about seven signs or miracles with the seventh being the resurrection. That makes sense. One reason Jesus did miracles was to prove His legitimacy; they were signs that He is the Messiah.

I have always thought that another reason might have been to draw crowds. I guess it's the marketer in me, but doing miracles gets attention. People want to see and experience the spectacular. Miracles would happen, a large crowd would gather, and then Jesus would begin to teach.

Signs and crowds aside, I think the primary reason Jesus heals people is because He loves them. Sickness, lameness, blindness, and other disabilities were not part of God's original plan for us. No one got sick in the Garden of Eden. After the fall, sin entered the world and sin broke things, including our bodies.

One day God will redeem all things, including our bodies. Heaven has no sickness, death, crying, mourning, or pain. Everything is made right. Jesus physically healed people because He was bringing the love of heaven to the world. In Jesus, the kingdom of heaven is at hand, available to all who will trust in Him.

*Today I will remember:*

- There is healing in Jesus.
- Everyone in Jesus will be healed either in this life or the next.

*Jesus, thank You that complete healing*
*will come. Please continue to do miracles in*
*the here and now, while Your church looks*
*forward to total healing in the hereafter.*

# STELLAR LOVE

*For I am convinced that neither death nor life, neither angels nor demons, neither the present nor the future, nor any powers, neither height nor depth, nor anything else in all creation, will be able to separate us from the love of God that is in Christ Jesus our Lord.*

ROMANS 8:38-39

I've been through some difficult seasons. My parents divorced when I was eight. I've been betrayed by friends. I've lost jobs. Years ago, my wife and I were separated for nine months, and I didn't think we were going to make it.

Life is hard. But God loves us through it all. So if you're going through a hard time and wondering if God still loves you, do you know what that makes you? Normal.

We may sometimes feel like our pain, sorrow, and loss distance us from God's affection. But remember, feelings aren't facts. If you're wondering if God still loves you, try to think less about your circumstances and more about what Jesus did for you on the cross. Sometimes we believe the myth that if God really loved us, we wouldn't have any problems. That's not true. The fact is, Jesus taught that in this world we would have trouble, but we have a great hope because He has overcome the world. Jesus didn't promise us immunity; He promised us eternity. Nothing in this life or the next can separate you from the love of God. Eventually, He will make everything right.

*Today I will remember:*

- If it's not good, then God is not done.
- He didn't promise immunity from life's problems.
- He promised eternity with Him.

*Jesus, life is hard. You said that it would be. Help me to remember Your grace in the hard times as well as in the good.*

# WHAT A SAVIOR!

*But when the kindness and love of God our Savior appeared, he saved us, not because of righteous things we had done, but because of his mercy. He saved us through the washing of rebirth and renewal by the Holy Spirit, whom he poured out on us generously through Jesus Christ our Savior, so that, having been justified by his grace, we might become heirs having the hope of eternal life.*

TITUS 3:4-7

Read these verses again slowly. Take it all in. Jesus is the kindness and love of God embodied. If you want to know what God is like, look at Jesus. He saves us not because of our righteousness, but because of His goodness. We are reborn as children of God and cleansed by the Holy Spirit. We are justified and given life forever as fellow heirs with Christ through His amazing grace.

To be justified by the grace of Jesus is to have a clean standing before God. One of the most common ways to explain the doctrine of justification is to say it is "just as if we never sinned." In Jesus, we are holy before God because Jesus has clothed us with His holiness by the Holy Spirit. Our Savior rescues us, clothes us with His goodness, and makes us heirs of an inheritance beyond all imagining. His radical grace compels us to risk living lives of full devotion. This is not a wimpy religion where we are nervous, never knowing where we stand. We don't obey to be loved; we obey because we are loved. What a Savior!

*Today I will remember:*

- I am justified in Jesus.
- I don't obey Him so He will love me; I obey Him because He loves me.

*Jesus, give me a deeper understanding of Your great salvation. Help me to never get used to it but always stand in awe of it. I live each day in gratitude and in wonder because of Your amazing grace.*

# May

## RELATIONSHIP WITH GOD

"Now this is eternal life: that they know you,
the only true God, and Jesus Christ, whom you have sent."
*John 17:3*

# BECOMING A MAN

*When the time drew near for David to die, he gave a charge to Solomon his son. "I am about to go the way of all the earth," he said. "So be strong, act like a man, and observe what the LORD your God requires: Walk in obedience to him, and keep his decrees and commands, his laws and regulations."*

1 KINGS 2:1-3

When does a male go from being a child to becoming a man? Is it when he grows facial hair? No, there are lots of grown-up boys with beards. The question remains, When does a male child step into manhood?

David answers the question. Manhood begins when a male begins to follow the ways of God. God is the one who makes a man, so real manhood will always be found in Him. If you're waiting on your wife, your job, or your muscles to make you feel like a man, then you'll always be chasing masculinity instead of living it out.

Notice in the charge that to step into manhood requires strength, wisdom, and action. Manhood is different than just being male. It's about our actions. David says, "act like a man." How do we act manly? We do what God says. This call to manhood is not for the weak or faint of heart. It is for those who will submit to the marching orders of the King of kings and the Lord of lords. Real manhood begins with an acknowledgment that it is God who makes us men.

*Today I will remember:*

- Manhood is listening to God and doing what He says.
- God is the One who makes males into men.

*Father, help me step into manhood today. Give me wisdom to know Your ways and courage to act accordingly. Let my actions match my beliefs. Help me to act like a man.*

# ONE ELEVEN

*And a voice came from heaven: "You are my Son, whom I love; with you I am well pleased."*

MARK 1:11

I was going through a difficult time. Things at work weren't great. Everything was shut down due to the 2020 pandemic. I had some serious struggles at home too. My prayers were mostly me expressing my frustrations to God, but then something happened. I started seeing the number one hundred eleven everywhere. It was weird. I'd look at the clock at 1:11 p.m. I'd see buildings continuously where the address was 111. Crazy! One night I woke up at 1:11 a.m. and thought, "OK, God. What is it?" At that moment God impressed on my mind the verse above. My phone was next to me, and I looked it up.

This verse is at the baptism of Jesus. God speaks over Him. If you've received Jesus in your life, God speaks this over you, too (Ephesians 1:5). Think on it:

1. You belong. *"You are my Son ..."*
   You're adopted into the family of God through your faith in Jesus. No matter what's happened in your life, God has made a way for you. You belong to Him.
2. You are loved. *"... whom I love; ..."*
   No matter where you've been, what you've done, or what's been done to you, God loves you. He loves you because of who He is. You are His beloved son.
3. You are special. *"... with you I am well pleased."*
   God created you. He knows you better than you know yourself, and He cherishes you. You are special in His eyes.

Now, every time I see one eleven, I just remind myself, *I belong, I am loved, and I am special.* The same is true for you.

*Today I will remember:*

- In Jesus, I am a beloved son of God.
- In Jesus, I belong, I'm loved, and I'm special.

*Father, as Your adopted son, remind me that my place is always with You. Thank You that I don't have to prove myself to You and that I am part of Your family.*

# ALL THAT MATTERS

*"Teacher, which is the greatest commandment in the Law?" Jesus replied: "'Love the LORD your God with all your heart and with all your soul and with all your mind.' This is the first and greatest commandment. And the second is like it: 'Love your neighbor as yourself.' All the Law and the Prophets hang on these two commandments."*

MATTHEW 22:36-40

The mortality rate continues to hover right around one hundred percent. All of us are born and all of us are going to die. When your life comes to an end, your relationship with God and your relationships with people will be the only things that count. You won't care about the type of car you drive, the brand of watch on your wrist, or the square footage of your house. You'll be focused on your wife, your children, and your friends. You'll be stepping into eternity and thinking about your relationship with God. Why? These things are all that matter.

Every day we need to center ourselves on what will matter on our last day. Otherwise, we'll live frivolous lives for frivolous things. Remembering what matters in the end helps us live for what really matters in the present. In the end, all that matters is God and people.

Think about it. Lots of people can do the work you do. Only you can be a dad to your kids. Lots of people can replace you in your job. Only you can be a husband to your wife. You are responsible for your relationship with God. No one else can do that for you. Choose today and every day to live for what matters most. Live for God and people.

*Today I will remember:*

- In the end, all that matters is God and people.
- I must live every day for what will matter most on my last day.

*Father, I don't want to waste my life on frivolous pursuits.*
*Help me to invest my days in that which matters most.*
*Today I choose to focus on love for You and love for others.*

# A RECEPTIVE HEART

*"Still other seed fell on good soil, where it produced a crop—a hundred, sixty or thirty times what was sown."*
MATTHEW 13:8

Preachers are like farmers that scatter the seed of God's Word. The seed lands on all types of soil and the good soil will be receptive. Jesus is illustrating that our hearts, like the good soil, must be receptive to the seed of His teachings.

Have you ever planted anything? I used to plant crops with my Grandad on his farm in Troup, Texas. Before we planted, we always had to prepare the soil. We broke it up. We plowed it. We made the soil soft in advance so that it might be receptive to the seed. Sometimes the rain from the storm would soften it, so that it was more easily broken.

Our hearts are a lot like that. Without brokenness, which usually requires trial and pain, we are unreceptive to what God is saying. His Word just bounces off our hard hearts. But the storms of life loosen us up a bit. They make our hearts tender. Pain is fertile ground for God to work in our lives. After all, who prays when the plane is going down? Everybody.

Could it be that perhaps you are in a difficult season right now because God is tilling the soil of your soul for something new? You and I want soft, receptive souls when it comes to the Word of God. We want His Word to take root, grow in us, and change us, so that we might produce good fruit. Fruit that honors Him and will last. Broken ground is fertile ground. It is necessary for new growth.

*Today I will remember:*

- Pain is fertile ground for God to grow something new in my life.
- Don't waste the pain; be receptive.

*God, give me a soft, receptive soul. May I receive Your Word completely, so that it will grow in me and produce good fruit.*

# ALL-THE-TIME PRAYER

*Pray continually.*

1 THESSALONIANS 5:17

How often do you pray? Once a day? Once a week? Never? Remember the story I told about the guy in my church who was facing a difficult challenge? I had asked if he'd prayed about it. He replied, "Oh, no! Do you think it's come to that?" Dudes, it has always come to that. Why do we think that prayer must be problem oriented? Like we're only supposed to pray when we have a big problem. God wants us to talk to Him throughout the day, every day. God loves you. He wants a relationship with you.

Continual prayer does not mean that you must bow your head, close your eyes, and talk out loud to God all the time. After all, we have jobs, responsibilities, people, and things to take care of. To "pray continually" means that our relationship with God is our primary focus. It's our priority, so we talk to God about everything. We are in constant communication with Him wherever we go. Don't overthink it. Talk to God throughout the day.

Why not memorize this verse? Memorizing verses from the Bible is a great practice. It will make your faith strong and help you in times of need. We get so intimidated by memorizing Scripture, but you don't have to be. You can start here: "Pray continually."

*Today I will remember:*

- God wants me to talk to Him throughout my day about everything.
- My relationship with God should be my focus.

*Father, help me to simply talk to You throughout my day today. I love You and need You in every area of my life. May prayer be an ongoing conversation between us.*

# BEING THE CHURCH

*And let us consider how we may spur one another on toward love and good deeds, not giving up meeting together, as some are in the habit of doing, but encouraging one another—and all the more as you see the Day approaching.*

HEBREWS 10:24-25

My parents divorced when I was eight. I love my dad and saw him every other weekend, but the men in my church had a far greater impact on me. My fourth grade Bible study leader would take us camping. My eighth-grade leader took us to play basketball. These men had a profound effect on my life, and I wouldn't be where I am today without them. The church is where I learned about what it means to be a godly man.

Church is one of the main ways God communicates and directs our lives. God's will is that we be part of a local church family. To neglect church is to choose to be an orphan. The church needs you, and you need the church. Church is part of what it means to be a follower of Jesus.

Yes, you can experience God on the lake fishing or on a golf course. I've had those experiences. But church is where we put our faith into action. The truth is if you're a believer in Jesus, you don't *go to* church, you *are* the church. To neglect gathering with other believers is to neglect God's call on your life. It's to ignore part of God's will for manhood. My point? Get involved in a Bible-believing church. Commit yourself to it with your time and your money. Don't just live your life; invest it in the church.

*Today I will remember:*

- The church needs me, and I need the church.
- Church is not just something I attend; it's part of my core identity.

*Lord, I commit myself to a local church. Direct me in how You want me to give and serve. This is part of Your will for me as a man. I choose to play my part.*

# BRAIN CHANGE

*Do not conform to the pattern of this world,*
*but be transformed by the renewing of your mind.*
*Then you will be able to test and approve what*
*God's will is—his good, pleasing and perfect will.*
ROMANS 12:2

God wills that we grow and change. The word translated as "transformed" in the verse above comes from the Greek word from which we get the word *metamorphosis*. Think about that. We're to go through a metamorphosis, completely changed and set apart from the world around us—like transforming from a caterpillar to a butterfly. It reminds me of something Winston Churchill once said: "We are all worms, but I do believe that I'm a glowworm."

How is this possible? If we're honest, all of us have things in our lives that need to change. This happens by the renewing of our minds. What do we choose to think about? God transforms our lives not from the outside in, but from the inside out. God desires that we start thinking differently. In fact, that's the very definition of the word *repent*. It is to do a one-eighty in your thinking. What do you think about most of the time? Where is your focus? Choose today to think about godly things. Make thinking about what you think about a habit. The more we think on God, the more the character of God will show up in our lives.

*Today I will remember:*

- It is important to be aware of what I'm thinking about.
- The more I think on God, the more the things of God begin to show up in my life.

*Holy Spirit, fill me today. I give You my mind. Help me to focus on You today, so that Your transforming power can work in me and through me. Transform me however You wish.*

# A GOOD FOUNDATION

*And I pray that you, being rooted and established in love ...*
EPHESIANS 3:17

Foundations are important. Roots matter. In our verse, the apostle Paul uses two metaphors. The first is botanical. We're to be rooted in love. Everything in our lives should be firmly planted in the love of God. The second is architectural. Love is the foundation of our life. That's "established." Love is also the source. That's being "rooted."

What we believe about God is the foundation or the roots. Paul here in his prayer for the church in Ephesus, and ultimately his prayer for all of us, is that we would understand God's love for us. That we would know it in its full dimensions. If His love is the foundation or roots of our lives, our actions will reveal it. A Christian man's life and good works are not established in willpower, but in love.

One of my daily prayers is "God, help me to know Your love for me so that I might trust You." I want to know God's love for me because love is the proper motivation for trust and obedience. Do you believe that God loves you? The truth is, if we knew God's love for us, we would always do what He says because we would really know that His will is for our good.

*Today I will remember:*

- God loves me and is for me.
- Fruit begins with roots, and God wants me rooted in His love.

*Jesus, help me to know Your love for me. Root me and establish me in Your love. May my life be built on it and may You grow good fruit from it.*

# COUNSELOR, COMFORTER, AND FRIEND

*"But when he, the Spirit of truth, comes, he will guide you into all the truth. He will not speak on his own; he will speak only what he hears, and he will tell you what is yet to come."*

JOHN 16:13

Jesus says it is good that He is going away so the Holy Spirit can come. Have you ever wished that you could have a face-to-face conversation with Jesus? What question would you like to ask Him? Some piece of advice that you would inquire of Him?

The Holy Spirit continues Jesus' ministry on the earth. He is our Counselor, Comforter, and Friend. He wants to lead and guide us just as Jesus did with the disciples. If you've given your life to Jesus, then His Spirit is with you wherever you go. He speaks to us through words of knowledge and gives us wisdom beyond ourselves. He helps us better understand the Bible and gives us specific direction.

Unfortunately, most of us do not know how to listen to Him. Usually when we pray, we're doing all the talking. Rarely do we ask the Holy Spirit to guide us. So consider changing how you regularly pray. Ask the Spirit to guide you in prayer, clear your mind of distractions, and wait. When thoughts, ideas, or pictures come to mind, ask Him about those things. Check it out with Scripture. If a verse comes to mind, look it up and pray over it. If He brings people to mind, then text them and let them know you prayed for them. Involve the Holy Spirit in your prayers. He wants to guide you.

*Today I will remember:*

- The Holy Spirit is Counselor, Comforter, and Friend.
- He wants to guide me.

*Holy Spirit, give me wisdom about who You are.*
*Help me to know You better and to allow You to guide my steps.*
*Fill me and lead me today. Help me to know Your voice.*

# GOD FOR ME

*If God is for us, who can be against us?*
ROMANS 8:31

God is for you, not against you. This does not mean that He agrees with everything you do and say, of course. But it does mean that He wants what's best for you. All of His laws, precepts, and commands are for your good.

There were days when I would ask my sons to do something or not to do something. When they asked why, most of the time I would just tell them to trust me. But occasionally I would answer: "Are you smarter now, or were you smarter when you were younger?" They would answer "now," and explain to me that they had more life experience. They knew they were much smarter at six years old than when they were three! I would tell them that's why they should trust me. I would point out, "I'm thirty years older than you are. I can see what you can't see, and I know what you don't know. I've got thirty years on you, and most importantly, I love you. So just do what I say. Trust me!"

God is for us. He is infinitely smarter than we are. He loves us. There is no reason not to trust Him and do what He says in everything.

*Today I will remember:*

- God is for me.
- All His commands are for my benefit.
- I disobey Him to my own detriment.

*Father, forgive me for not trusting You at times. That's not about Your character, but mine. I'm sorry. Help me to understand Your love for me so that I might trust You in all things.*

# HEARING GOD'S WORD

*All Scripture is God-breathed and is useful for teaching, rebuking, correcting and training in righteousness, so that the servant of God may be thoroughly equipped for every good work.*

2 TIMOTHY 3:16-17

If you want to know someone, you must listen to him. The same is true with God. If you want to know His voice, then listen to His Word. His Word is the Bible. The primary way God speaks to men is through the Bible.

Notice that the verse says that Scripture is "God-breathed." This is the language used in Genesis 2:7 when God created Adam: "Then the LORD God formed a man from the dust of the ground and breathed into his nostrils the breath of life, and the man became a living being." This means that the life of God is found in the Scriptures. If you want to know God, then get to know your Bible.

Most people are intimidated by the Bible, which is why devotionals like this one are so important. Don't overcomplicate it. Just commit to reading, remembering the bottom line, and praying the prayer each day. The compounding effect over time will help you know God better. Consistency and commitment are what counts. In fact, knowing God is just like any other relationship. It's up close and over time. That's why the apostle Paul uses the word *training* in this verse. As we train each day in the Word of God, over time we will be more spiritually fit in the knowledge of God.

*Today I will remember:*

- If I want to know God and hear from Him, then I must know His Word.
- Instead of looking for a sign, I will look for a verse.

*God, give me the grace to know the Bible. I want to know You, so give me wisdom from Your Word. Help me to spend time with You each day.*

# A BETTER LIFE

*After John was put in prison, Jesus went into Galilee, proclaiming the good news of God. "The time has come," he said. "The kingdom of God has come near. Repent and believe the good news!"*

MARK 1:14-15

When Jesus tells us to repent and believe the good news, it's not a threat. It's an invitation to a better way of life. Everything Jesus commands is for our good. To reject or to disobey His teachings is to say no to greater joy. His way is better.

The word *repent* here comes from the Greek word *metanoia*, which means to do a one-eighty in our thinking. How we think or see the world can lead us in the wrong direction. Decisions come from perspective. Jesus' invitation is to stop thinking our way and to start thinking and practicing His way.

Most of us think that what really needs to change is on the outside of us. Jesus taught that the problem is actually what we believe and how we process things on the inside. He teaches us to repent and begin to see what He sees and gain His perspective. In essence, if you change your thinking to be in line with Jesus, it will change your life. If we could see what Jesus sees, then we would always do what Jesus says.

*Today I will remember:*

- If I could see what Jesus sees, I would always do what He says.
- Jesus is the author of life, and He knows how life works best.

*Jesus, help me see things through Your eyes.*
*Give me insight and wisdom, so that*
*I might follow You. Your way is best.*

# FREEDOM PATH

*"Then you will know the truth, and the truth will set you free."*

JOHN 8:32

What is the opposite of truth? A lie. What is the opposite of freedom? Bondage. If truth sets people free, then lies enslave us. Any sin that has taken ahold of us and entrapped us comes from believing a lie. Lies lead to bondage.

Following Jesus and experiencing His freedom are not just matters of intellectual assent or general agreement. Following Jesus is about obedience. Jesus commands things that are hard to swallow. For example, He commands us in Matthew 5 to love our enemies and bless them. There's nothing in a man that wants to do that. In fact, that goes against my very nature. I don't want to love my enemies; I want to destroy them.

This is where the brilliance and life-giving freedom of Jesus come in. To love and bless your enemies is to make them your friends. Haven't you actually defeated your enemy when you make him a friend? That friendship avoids war and brings peace, resulting in freedom for both of you. Smart! When we do what Jesus says, freedom follows. Notice, the freedom is not just in the knowing but in the doing. Do what Jesus says. He is the truth, and He will set you free.

*Today I will remember:*

- When we do what Jesus says, freedom follows.
- Jesus is brilliant.
- Trusting His counsel is always best.

*Lord, help me to remember Your commands and to obey them. My way leads to captivity; Your way sets me free. Protect me from lies, and help me to walk in the truth.*

# JESUS SERVES

*"For even the Son of Man did not come to be served, but to serve, and to give his life as a ransom for many."*
MARK 10:45

In this verse, Jesus says He came to serve and to give His life away for you, for me, and for all of mankind. You're never more mature, nor more like Jesus, than when you give and serve. The very essence of the Christian life requires action. Men of God courageously serve!

Most people who have been going to church for a while think being a mature follower of Jesus is about information. It includes knowing the teachings of Jesus, of course, but real discipleship is primarily about doing something. Jesus didn't just say, "Listen to me"; He said, "Follow me." This is action oriented. It's about what we choose to do and not do. If you really break down what discipleship is, it can be summed up in one word: obedience. Discipleship is as simple as your next step of obedience. This will always include giving and serving in some way, shape, or form.

*Today I will remember:*

- Jesus didn't just say, "Listen to me"; He said, "Follow me."
- Faith is action oriented.
- I am most like Jesus when I give and serve.

*Jesus, teach me Your ways. Instead of thinking about how people can serve me or give to me, help me to reverse that. How can I serve today? How do You want me to give today? Help me to courageously and kindly represent You.*

# KEEPING IT REAL

*All of you, clothe yourselves with humility toward one another, because, "God opposes the proud but shows favor to the humble."*
1 PETER 5:5

What does it mean to be humble? I used to think (like most men) that humility implies being weak and frail, allowing yourself to be a doormat. But I've since learned that humility is reserved for the strong. Simply put, humility is about reality, while pride is about pretending. Most people don't want to face reality because it requires courage. In fear, people hide in their pride. Thus, proud people are too weak to face the truth.

*Humility* is a trust word in this verse. It's about trusting God with who you really are. After all, God cannot help who you are pretending to be. That person doesn't exist! You can't play poker with God; He knows what's in your hand. God is real. He only operates in reality. He loves the real you, so let Him. To proudly fake it is to live in opposition to reality. To be humble is to get real. In the reality of who you are, God shows His favor and grace.

The only way to experience the real love of God is to be courageous enough to be the real you. Will you practice this type of courage? Be honest with God about all things. This is where you find His favor and grace.

*Today I will remember:*

- Pride is about pretending, while humility is about reality.
- To experience the real love of God, I have to be courageous enough to be the real me.

*Father, forgive me for faking it sometimes.*
*Thank You that I don't have to pretend with You.*
*You love me as I am, and You want to help me.*
*I need You today in every area of my life.*

# KNOWING GOD

*"Now this is eternal life: that they know you, the only true God, and Jesus Christ, whom you have sent."*
JOHN 17:3

This verse changed my life. I grew up in church and knew lots of Bible stories and things about God. I'm grateful for the great foundation I received. But when I was nineteen, a friend showed me this verse, and it changed everything. The light bulb came on! I thought the whole purpose of Christianity was to try and not sin. Yes, certainly we need to fight sin, but there's so much more. Jesus says that He came to give us eternal life, and eternal life is knowing God.

Eternal life therefore is not about a destination but a state of being. It is a relationship with God. This is your purpose. It's why you were born—why you're breathing in and out right now. You were created to know God.

There is a difference between knowing about someone and knowing him. I'm a huge Theodore Roosevelt fan. I know a lot about him, but I never actually met him. When Jesus defines eternal life as knowing God, He is speaking personally, not academically. Eternal life is a relationship with God, and He wants you to know Him! Ask God today and every day to give you knowledge of who He really is.

*Today I will remember:*

- Eternal life is a relationship with God.
- The purpose of life is to know Him and walk with Him.

*God, help me to know You and walk with You. This is why You created me. There is nothing greater, and nothing matters more, than knowing You. This is what life is all about.*

# ONE THING

*"Blessed are the pure in heart, for they will see God."*
MATTHEW 5:8

In the movie *City Slickers*, Billy Crystal plays a confused character who thinks that the best in life has already passed him by. He's having a classic midlife moment. Jack Palance plays an old, leathery cowboy who is wise to the ways of the world. He advises Billy that the secret of life is pursuing "one thing." The movie doesn't spell out what it is, but the one thing is always what we are building our life on. Everyone has chosen their one thing.

For some, it's their job. Their identity, hope, and meaning are all wrapped in their work. But your job doesn't love you. You will leave it one day, or it might leave you. For some, it's a relationship. If you build your life and identity on relationships, as important and satisfying as they can be, you will always be on shaky ground. In fact, if a person is your "one thing," it will be impossible to truly love them. You'll just use him or her to validate yourself. Even then, at some point, this person is going to die. What then?

To be pure in heart is to build your life on God. You love your wife, family, and others out of your love for Him. He is the "one thing," the eternally secure foundation.

*Today I will remember:*
- Life is ultimately about one thing.
- God is the secure foundation.
- I must build my life around Him because He is the right thing.

*Lord, I choose to build my life upon You, and everything else on this firm foundation. I have nothing to prove and only You to please. You are my one thing.*

# KNOWING GOD'S LOVE

*... and to know this love that surpasses knowledge—*
*that you may be filled to the measure of all the fullness of God.*

EPHESIANS 3:19

The apostle Paul is praying for the church in Ephesus and for the church at large, which includes you and me. He prays that we would know the love of God, "this love that surpasses knowledge." How do we do that? How can we know something that surpasses our ability to know it?

There's no book we could read or class we could take that would teach us the love of God. It's too vast. God's love is larger than our brains can comprehend. Well, we can't learn it, but it can be supernaturally revealed to us. Thus, the need for the prayer. God's love is something He gives, and which we supernaturally receive. The love of God is not informational, but relational. Like all relationships, it requires experience.

Paul prays the Holy Spirit would relationally reveal the love the Father has for us in Christ Jesus. One of the most powerful prayers you can pray is for God to empower you to know how great His love is for you. It's a relational exchange that requires the work of the Spirit in your life. Pray regularly that you would know the love of God that surpasses knowledge.

*Today I will remember:*

- God's love for me is greater than my ability to understand.
- I am profoundly loved, and I need the Holy Spirit to understand this.

*Holy Spirit, help me to grasp the greatness of God's love for me.*
*Help me know this love that surpasses knowledge. I cannot*
*understand it on my own. I need You to reveal it to me.*

# HIGH FLEX

*This is what the Lord says: "Let not the wise boast of their wisdom or the strong boast of their strength or the rich boast of their riches, but let the one who boasts boast about this: that they have the understanding to know me, that I am the Lord, who exercises kindness, justice and righteousness on earth, for in these I delight," declares the Lord.*

JEREMIAH 9:23-24

My son Jackson gave me a compliment the other day. Anytime your teenage boy says something good about you, you remember it and take it to heart. He told me I was "low flex." When I asked him to explain, he taught me that when someone is low flex, they're not trying to impress anyone. There's no showing off or bragging. No talk of money, success, or accomplishments. He said that low flex is being chill. I later wondered if perhaps I'm low flex because I'm older and don't care as much. There is one area of my life, of course, where I want to be high flex, that's in my relationship with God.

Speaking through Jeremiah, God says if you're going to flex, then flex about Him. The more we know the Lord, the more secure we become. There is a humble, bold, and strong kindness among men who know God. Think today on His justice, righteousness, and kindness. God takes pleasure in our seeking Him, knowing Him, and declaring the truth about Him.

*Today I will remember:*

- It is right and good to boast about the goodness of God.
- If I'm going to brag, I'm going to brag about the Lord.

*Lord, thank You for Your kindness, righteousness, and justice. Help me know You more that I might gratefully brag on Your goodness. May I be slow to honor myself and quick to honor You.*

# LOVING GOD

*"Whoever has my commands and keeps them is the one who loves me. The one who loves me will be loved by my Father, and I too will love them and show myself to them."*

JOHN 14:21

Loving God is as simple as doing what He says. How do we know if we really love God? Jesus answers the question here; we obey Him. This is what real faith does. It takes God at His Word and reveals itself in our actions.

Jesus equates obedience with love because obedience is about our faith. Faith is about what we believe, but it's more than that. Think about it. To believe is to trust, and to trust is to obey. We tend to overthink the word *faith*. It's not really a mystery. Faith is about trust. Trust is a relational word, an act of love. How do we know if we really love God? We trust Him. We do what He says.

What does God want you to do today? Do that; it's love for Him. What do you think God does *not* want you to do today? Don't do that. Not doing it is love for Him. The more we do what God says, the more we will understand Him and see what He sees. The more we see what God sees, the more we will know Him and do what He says. Obedience to God will grow as you trust Him. The more your trust grows, the more your love grows.

*Today I will remember:*

- Loving God is as simple as doing what He says.
- The more we obey God, the more we will understand Him.

*Father, I choose to trust You today because I love You. Love is not just about my beliefs but about my actions. Today I will trust You by doing what You say.*

# SEARCHING TRUTH

*Now the Berean Jews were of more noble character than those in Thessalonica, for they received the message with great eagerness and examined the Scriptures every day to see if what Paul said was true.*

ACTS 17:11

A wise man knows it's good to test things. Not everything we see and hear is the truth. This seems especially applicable these days. We live in the information age, but there seems to be very little wisdom.

Facts, figures, and opinions are dumped on us constantly through television, social media, and various news outlets. People's personal "truths" are coming at us constantly. We are inundated with propaganda. Carefully crafted narratives are marketed and hyped at us all the time. It's enough to make anyone scratch his head in wonder. I have a hard time even knowing what the actual news is. So how do we know *the* truth?

We do what the Bereans did. We search the Scriptures. We test things against the Bible. There is no such thing as "my truth"; there's just truth. Truth exists outside of my feelings, opinions, experiences, and preferences. In fact, truth is ultimately a person whose name is Jesus. We get into trouble when we allow our sinful behaviors to adjust our beliefs. This places us outside of truth. So let's follow the Bereans' example and search the Scriptures.

*Today I will remember:*

- In the information age, I must seek wisdom.
- God's ways are found in God's Word.
- This is where we find truth.

*Lord, help me to know the truth of Your Word and to walk in it. Help me to discern between truth and fiction. May I study the Scriptures and evaluate things in the light of Your Word.*

# SHARPEN UP

*As iron sharpens iron, so one person sharpens another.*
PROVERBS 27:17

While God primarily speaks to us through the Bible, He also speaks to us through godly friends—that is, other men who are trying to follow Jesus and live out His will. We all need friends like that. Being part of a Bible-teaching church is important. I get information when I read the Bible, but I experience transformation when I do what it says. This requires help from good friends.

I have found an old saying, "The eye cannot see the I," to be true. When examining someone else's life, I can spot the real issue almost every time. It seems obvious. In fact, I don't understand why the other person can't see it! But when I try to examine my own life, I realize "the eye cannot see the I." I need good friends to help me.

If you've ever played football, golf, or any other sport where you watch game film to improve, you know what I'm talking about. You can't see yourself on the field. Good, godly friends coach us to adjust our lives to fit what the Bible teaches. Here's an important question. Do you have real, godly friends to help you listen to God and live out His Word?

*Today I will remember:*

- I need good friends to help me see what I can't see.
- The eye cannot see the I.
- Godly friends help me follow Jesus.

*Father, give me good, godly friends who help me understand Your Word and live it out. Help me to be that kind of friend to others. Help me to sharpen other men in truth as they in turn sharpen me.*

# THE GOD-MAN

*The Son is the image of the invisible God,*
*the firstborn over all creation.*
COLOSSIANS 1:15

A few years ago, a British man I was talking with assumed that I thought God was an old man up in the sky with a long, white beard. I told him, "That's not God; that's Gandalf the Grey from Lord of the Rings." God is not like us. In his book *Know What You Believe*, theologian Paul Little describes God as an infinite, eternal spirit without any external limitations who has an intellect, personality, feelings and a will.

I don't know that God can be defined, but if He can, then that's close. God is big, infinite in every way. We are very small, and yet God wants us to know Him. How could we who are finite understand the personality, intellect, feelings, and will of the One who is infinite? Well, for us to best understand the one who is infinite, He would need to wrap Himself up in flesh and walk among us. That's Jesus. If you want to know what God is like, then look at Jesus. Jesus is God incarnate, God made flesh. Jesus is God with a bod. When you read Matthew, Mark, Luke, and John, you're reading the biographies of Jesus. More than that, you're doing a case study on the personality and character of God. You want to know what God is really like? Look at Jesus. He is the image of the invisible God.

*Today I will remember:*

- If I want to know what God is like, I look at Jesus.
- Jesus reveals the character and personality of God.

*Jesus, I want to know You. Thank You for stepping into humanity, so that I might understand who You are. The more I understand You, the more I understand the personality, intellect, feelings, and will of God.*

# LISTENING TO GOD

*"My sheep listen to my voice;*
*I know them, and they follow me."*
JOHN 10:27

Why is it that if someone talks to God, he's considered spiritual, but if someone hears from God, we think he might be crazy? Jesus says that His followers will know His voice. Knowing God through faith in Jesus means we'll know when He speaks to us. We usually overcomplicate this. If you have an impression and believe God has spoken to you, ask three questions:

1. *Does it fall in line with Scripture?* God will not contradict His Word. If He is speaking to you, it will be in line with what the Bible teaches. For example, the Bible does not instruct you to marry a specific person giving their specific name. However, the Bible does talk about the type of woman we're to look for. (Proverbs 31 or 2 Corinthians 6:14-15, for example)
2. *What do my godly friends say about it?* Seek counsel from others who are striving to follow Jesus. What do they say about what you're sensing? Bounce it off other believers and see what comes back.
3. *What do the authorities in my life have to say?* Seeking counsel from a Bible-teaching pastor, your wife, your parents, or Bible study leader is also a good idea. Wise people are humble and listen to the counsel of godly authority.

Jesus says that His men will know His voice. One of the best practices of prayer is not just talking, but listening. Ask Jesus to speak to you today. Clear your mind of distractions and wait. See what the Holy Spirit impresses upon you and use the three questions above as a guide.

*Today I will remember:*

- Jesus says that His followers will know His voice.
- God speaks to me and wants me to listen.

*God, what do You want to say to me today? Please speak*
*to me by Your Spirit, through Your Word, through my*
*Christian friends, and through the godly authorities in my life.*

# THE HEROES

*Praise be to the God and Father of our Lord Jesus Christ! In his great mercy he has given us new birth into a living hope through the resurrection of Jesus Christ from the dead.*

1 PETER 1:3

We sometimes forget that the great heroes of the Bible were just like us. Abraham, the patriarch of our faith, pretended Sarah wasn't his wife, afraid that stronger men would kill him and take her for themselves. David, who is famous for killing Goliath, committed adultery with Bathsheba and had her husband Uriah killed on the front lines in battle. Peter, who was martyred for his faith in Jesus, also betrayed the Lord three times. These "heroes" were not always heroic. God makes heroes out of men who know they need His help.

Because Jesus died on the cross and rose again, there is always hope. We have a second chance times infinity. We can't regain time and make better past decisions, but we can redeem our time by making better decisions today and in the future. God specializes in using messed up men. After all, that's all He has had to work with. Jesus is alive and well, and He loves you. Make the right decisions today. Take courage!

*Today I will remember:*

- God makes heroes out of men who know they need His help.
- We can't regain time and make better past decisions.
- We can redeem our time by making better decisions today and in the future.

*Thank You, Father, for the hope and courage I find in Jesus. The only hero in the Bible is You. Everyone else who acted heroically did so through Your work in their lives. Please work through me.*

# SHOW UP TO GROW UP

*Very early in the morning, while it was still dark, Jesus got up, left the house and went off to a solitary place, where he prayed.*

MARK 1:35

Years ago, I heard Brennan Manning give a talk about his relationship with God. Perhaps you've heard of his book, *The Ragamuffin Gospel*. I recommend it. Brennan talked about going out in the woods to meet with God. When people asked him about his agenda for that special time, Brennan said, "I don't really know. I just know the Father likes it when I show up." I always think of that when I read the verse above.

Jesus made it a practice to get up early and spend time alone with God. It would make sense for us to practice this as well. Why? In solitary places we can focus. It's letting God know that we really desire time with Him. We don't have to overcomplicate it; we just have to do it. I live in the Phoenix area, where desert mountains surround the city. I hike and talk to God. Sometimes I sing worship songs in my head as I walk. Other times, I just walk quietly and ask Him to speak and put His thoughts and direction in my mind. It's a solitary place to focus on my relationship with Him.

*Today I will remember:*

- I need times of solitude with God to hear from Him.
- God likes it when I show up.

*Father, help me to set time aside just to be in Your presence. Teach me Your ways, and give me direction. I want to know You more.*

# SMELLING GOOD

*Follow God's example, therefore, as dearly loved children and walk in the way of love, just as Christ loved us and gave himself up for us as a fragrant offering and sacrifice to God.*

EPHESIANS 5:1-2

Every year, my wife buys me cologne. She always asks if I like it, but to me that's irrelevant. I don't wear cologne for me; I wear it for her. It's about her and what she likes, and my preference is whatever she prefers.

Our verses say that when we walk in love, it smells good to God. Reflecting the love of Jesus is a fragrant offering to Him. So how do we smell? Are our lives a fragrant reflection of the love of Christ? Or do we reek of selfishness?

Most people think that love is a feeling, but the Bible teaches it's more than that. Love is about action, how we behave with people. People we agree with and people we disagree with. Whenever we reflect the love of Jesus, it's like a potpourri shot to heaven right up the nostrils of God. Love is a fragrant offering, a sacrifice, which means it's an act of worship.

Let's choose to love God today by loving people well. God doesn't love us because we deserve it. He loves us because of who He is. Think about God's love for you. Express your gratitude and then give love to others. This smells good to God and to others.

*Today I will remember:*

- One of the ways I love God is by loving people.
- Loving people is an offering to God that He enjoys.

*Father, I want my life to be a fragrant offering. Help me to love You well by loving others well. May I reflect the love of Jesus in a way that pleases You.*

# WORD AND WISDOM

*If any of you lacks wisdom, you should ask God, who gives generously to all without finding fault, and it will be given to you.*

JAMES 1:5

Pastoring the same church now for over twenty years has been one of my life's greatest privileges. As the church has grown, my responsibilities have increased. With increased size and responsibility comes increased pressure to make good decisions.

I'm sure you can relate. If you're younger, maybe you're feeling the weight of big decisions about marriage and career. If you're a little older, you might feel the increased responsibility of caring for your life plus the lives of others. How do we make good decisions? Think through the "Word or Wisdom" grid.

"Word" is when you pray about it, and you sense God speaking to you. When you believe this has happened, make sure it aligns with the Bible. Also run it by mature Christian friends. If you don't get a direct "word," then rely on wisdom.

The "Wisdom" part is simply asking, "What is the wise thing to do?" Think through it, pray through it, write out the pros and cons, and then check what you're thinking with godly friends and mentors. A word from God is specific. All wisdom comes from God, but it will be more principled.

*Today I will remember:*

- God speaks through specific words or through the gift of wisdom.
- Both will track with what the Bible says.

*Lord, give me wisdom to know and do the right things. Help me to discern Your voice. Let me receive Your word and Your wisdom in all things.*

# HE KNOWS YOUR NAME

*"Do not fear, for I have redeemed you;*
*I have summoned you by name; you are mine."*
ISAIAH 43:1

I am better at remembering faces than names. For a pastor, sometimes this gets awkward. The other day I asked a couple for their names, and they reminded me that I had performed their wedding. They were gracious, but I felt a bit foolish. The good news is that God always knows your name. It's not just that He has a good memory. You are His, and He has called you by name.

Remember this as you go throughout your day. God knows everything about you, and He cares for you. Sometimes we men can feel all alone under the weight of various responsibilities that no one understands. Brother, feelings aren't facts. The truth is, God is with you. He has a plan for you, and He calls you by your name. You are never forgotten, never alone. So today involve God in everything you do. Talk to Him continuously in your heart and mind. In a world of a billion faces, He looks at you, calls you out of the crowd by name, and in Jesus you are His beloved son.

*Today I will remember:*

- God calls me by my name.
- He knows everything about me and loves me.
- I am never alone.

*Father, thank You for calling me Your own and adopting me into Your family. Help me to focus less on my fickle feelings and more on Your Word that is always true. Thank You that I am never alone, that You are always with me and love me.*

# WHO HE IS

*The Lord is compassionate and gracious,*
*slow to anger, abounding in love.*
PSALM 103:8

I used to think God was always mad at me. In the church I grew up in, it wasn't a good service unless you felt guilt, shame, and fear. My mom says that when I was little, I would line up the stuffed animals on my bed and yell at them about their sin and how they were going to hell. People thought that was cute. Now that I'm older, I find it sad. God is compassionate, gracious, slow to anger, and abounding in love. To not know this is to not know the Bible.

You and I will reflect in our lives what we believe about God, and it is His love that changes men. The more you see Him for who He really is, the more compassionate, gracious, and slow to anger you will become. But if you see Him as continually angry and unforgiving, then you will be quick to anger, full of self-righteousness, and abounding in pride. Your life will be full of fear and deep insecurity.

God is better than we can possibly imagine, and His love changes men. Think today about His goodness. He loves you as you are, not as you should be, because none of us are as we should be. Thank God that He is gracious and kind.

*Today I will remember:*

- I will reflect what I believe about God.
- He is gracious, kind, and slow to anger.
- He abounds in love.

*God, help me to know who You really are.*
*As I learn more about Your character,*
*let Your character be reflected in me.*

# MIRACLE MAN

*"'For in him we live and move and have our being.'*
*As some of your own poets have said, 'We are his offspring.'"*
ACTS 17:28

The wonder about us is that we don't wonder more about us. Every person you see is a miracle. There before your eyes is a living, breathing life-form who thinks, learns, creates, and, at times, ponders the meaning and purpose of it all. We are living beings, inhabiting a ball of dust that is suspended in nothingness. Everything is dialed in, tuned just right to make life on this planet possible. Life is a miracle, and we forget. It gets lost in our going to work, paying our bills, and vainly trying to keep up with the Joneses.

There is no life without the One who makes it possible. In Him we live, move, and have our being. Any time you see a corpse, you see the reality. Even with animals. The body is just the suit that contains the life, which is mysterious because it's connected to God. Even people who say they don't believe are aware of a miracle. They just come up with other reasons.

You were created by God, the author of life. In Him, you are not a human *doing* but a human *being*. You were created to know Him and walk with Him. Your soul longs for this. See your life and the lives of others today for what they are. Miracles. You are a miracle, man!

*Today I will remember:*

- Life is a miraculous gift.
- Everyone I see is alive because of God.
- Every person is a miracle.

*Father, thank You for the gift of life. It pulsates in*
*nature and in human beings. Help me to remember*
*that all of it is a miraculous gift from Your loving hand.*
*Help me to remember the miracle in the mundane.*

# June

## FATHERHOOD

See what great love the Father has lavished on us,
that we should be called children of God!
And that is what we are!
*1 John 3:1*

# PLAYING FAVORITES

*As the boys grew up, Esau became a skillful hunter. He was an outdoorsman, but Jacob had a quiet temperament, preferring to stay at home. Isaac loved Esau because he enjoyed eating the wild game Esau brought home, but Rebekah loved Jacob.*

GENESIS 25:26-28 (NLT)

I love both my sons dearly, and it amazes me how different they are. Same father, same mother, same household—great differences. My oldest, Josh, was a skateboarder. He thrives on risk, is the life of the party, and is a successful salesman, but he didn't think much of school. My youngest, Jackson, is into sporting statistics, likes to know the plan, displays an intelligent smirk when he's being funny, and is an excellent student. Both are talented and gifted, but they are very different.

The twins Jacob and Esau were different, too. Esau, an avid outdoorsman, loved to hunt and fish and smelled like the woods. Jacob, an avid indoors-man, loved to hang out with Mom and smelled like soaps and lotions. Isaac, their father, favored Esau, and Jacob knew it. This caused years of dysfunction and pain. You might relate to one of your children more than the other, but beware playing favorites. It does great harm.

I tell each of my sons that he is my favorite—and it's true. I love Josh's charm and courage, and I love Jackson's logic and dry wit. There are a lot of things about love that are not logical. Love is a mystery, and both my boys are my favorite.

*Today I will remember:*

- Each of my children can be my favorite.
- Celebrate and enjoy their unique differences.

*Father, thank You for the varying gifts in each of my children. Each one is special to You, and to me. They are my favorites.*

# A GOOD FATHER

*"Which of you, if your son asks for bread, will give him a stone? Or if he asks for a fish, will give him a snake? If you, then, though you are evil, know how to give good gifts to your children, how much more will your Father in heaven give good gifts to those who ask him!"*

MATTHEW 7:9-11

God has not promised to give us all our greed, but He will provide for all our needs. Sometimes we say that God did not answer a certain prayer. We think that if we didn't get what we wanted, prayer must be ineffective. But prayer is not about getting what we want from God. He's not our fairy godfather who is there to grant wishes. He is the Kings of kings and Lord of lords who in His grace and love is there to guide as our Heavenly Father. It could be that He *did* answer your prayer. He just said no.

Loving fathers give good gifts to their children, but they do not give their children everything for which they ask. Why? Because children ask for things that are not good for them. Love does not always do what is wanted. Love chooses to do what is best. I want my boys to be happy and have what they desire. But giving them everything they desire would not be healthy. It would make them spoiled and ungrateful. The human heart is never satisfied with the simple solution of "more." Loving fathers practice wisdom and give their children good gifts that are for their good. Our Heavenly Father does the same. He can see what we can't see; He knows what we don't know. We can trust Him.

*Today I will remember:*

- Love does not always do what is wanted but chooses to do what is best.
- The human heart is never satisfied with "more."

*Thank You, Father, that You give good gifts.
Sometimes You say yes and sometimes no. At times
You want me to wait. All of this is for my good.
Thank You for these answers to prayer.*

# A MAN OF CHARACTER

*Now the overseer is to be above reproach, faithful to his wife, temperate, self-controlled, respectable, hospitable, able to teach, not given to drunkenness, not violent but gentle, not quarrelsome, not a lover of money.*

1 TIMOTHY 3:2-3

In many ways, our children will either become who we are, or they will rebel against who we are. Be a man worth emulating. One of the greatest compliments a child could ever give a father is wanting to be like him. Our verse today is for overseers in the church, but it can be applied to an overseer of a family.

It begins with faithfulness. Love your wife well. Your boys are learning their role, and your girls are learning what a husband is from watching you. The verse then moves to being temperate and self-controlled. You don't fly off the handle. A respectable man is both tough and tender. He's wise enough to know what is needed. A hospitable man is kind to outsiders. A man able to teach has some wisdom to pass on. We are to handle alcohol appropriately or not at all. We're to be gentle and to avoid picking fights. Finally, we are not to be greedy. A man worth following manages money well.

These verses are the standard for pastors and leaders, so pray for them. This is also a model worth chasing in your family. You don't have to be perfect at it, but you should pursue it. Be a man worth following.

*Today I will remember:*

- When a young adult says he wants to be like his dad, it's a great compliment.
- I should be a man worth emulating.

*Father, I know I'll never be perfect this side of heaven, but please help me to be a man of character for You and for my family. I choose today to humbly follow You, so that Your character qualities might live in me.*

# A WAY OF LIFE

*These commandments that I give you today are to be on your hearts. Impress them on your children. Talk about them when you sit at home and when you walk along the road, when you lie down and when you get up.*

DEUTERONOMY 6:6-7

Of all the verses in the Bible, these two are the clearest on how to be a good parent and pass on your faith. How? You make faith a way of life. It's not a hobby. It's not a weekend activity. It's who you are, and as you lead, you model. It's who we are as a family.

Notice the rhythm. We first keep God's Word on our hearts. We think about God and His will continually. More is caught than taught. As it's on our hearts, we impress it on our kids' hearts. This is both natural and intentional. Our kids will learn from us more by what we do consistently than by what we say occasionally. We live it, and we talk about it. We talk about it as we go about our daily lives while living it.

My boys and I didn't "walk along the road" much, but I did drive them to school each day. On the way, I would pray for them, or they would pray for me. Sometimes, they would memorize verses, and I would give them a reward. As they got older, I would look for teachable moments about God. These are natural, unforced, yet intentional ways to live out our faith with our children.

*Today I will remember:*

- Talking about my faith and living it out is a model to my kids.
- My faith is a way of life.

*Lord, help me to live out my faith with my family. Help me love and lead in such a way that my kids know You and want to follow You. Help me to be a man who intentionally talks about his faith and walks through his life in faith.*

# ABBA FATHER

*The Spirit you received does not make you slaves,*
*so that you live in fear again; rather, the Spirit*
*you received brought about your adoption*
*to sonship. And by him we cry, "Abba, Father."*

ROMANS 8:15

One of my friends has a hard time addressing God as "Father." It makes perfect sense. She was abused by her biological father and winces at the thought of calling God the same. Perhaps you struggle with this too. Maybe your father was apathetic, absent, or abusive. Many have struggled with deep, lifelong father wounds. The apostle Paul teaches us here that through our faith in Jesus, we have received His Spirit, and by the Holy Spirit we have become adopted sons of God. We can call Him "Abba, Father."

If using the word "Father" is difficult, then maybe go with Abba. This is an Aramaic word. The closest translation would be "Daddy" or "Papa." It is an intimate term and one a young child would call their father. My guess is you've never called anyone Abba, so it could be a special term between you and God. Or maybe go with Papa if that feels better. The point is, God wants an intimate relationship with His children—and with you, His son. Abba is everything you wish your earthly father would have or could have been. He will always love you perfectly. He will never leave you nor forsake you, and He is always there.

*Today I will remember:*

- In Jesus, I am an adopted son of God.
- He is everything I wish my earthly father would have or could have been.

*Abba, I am so grateful to be part of Your family.*
*Help me to see You for who You really are.*
*I want to know and receive Your love.*
*Thank You that You are always there for me.*

# AFFECTION

*"So he returned home to his father. And while he was still a long way off, his father saw him coming. Filled with love and compassion, he ran to his son, embraced him, and kissed him."*

LUKE 15:20 (NLT)

This is from the famous story that Jesus told, often referred to as the "Prodigal Son." It's a story that reveals to us the love of the Father and how the irreligious have a greater capacity in repentance and humility to understand His love more than the pious and pridefully religious do. It is a beautiful teaching in story form that reveals the heart of God for His children. Notice the affection of the father upon his son's return. He doesn't shake his hand. He doesn't give him a fist bump or a friendly, light punch to the shoulder. The father is filled with love and compassion. He embraces and kisses his son. It's passionate, masculine, appropriate, and safe fatherly affection.

I intentionally hug my boys. The oldest is twenty-two and has his own house. Any time we see each other, I make a point to get up and hug him. Why? That affection communicates how I feel more than my words ever could. My youngest is sixteen. He gets hugs too, especially in front of his friends. I'm teasing him, but he and his buddies also know how I feel about my son. If you have a daughter, hug her. Give her safe masculine, fatherly affection. Sometimes guys feel weird about that as their daughters grow older. Dude! She needs affection. She'll either get it from you in a healthy way, or from the football player down the street in an unhealthy way. Let's hug our kids. They need it, and so do we.

*Today I will remember:*

- I will give my children intentional, appropriate affection often.
- My children need affection, and so do I.

*Jesus, thank You for the story of the Prodigal Son and its depiction of the love of the father. Help me love my children well, with great compassion and appropriate affection.*

# CELEBRATE THE TRUTH

*Love does not delight in evil but rejoices with the truth. It always protects, always trusts, always hopes, always perseveres.*

1 CORINTHIANS 13:6-7

In our house, you are loved more, not less, for telling the truth. When you admit something you're not proud of, or might even get in trouble for, we celebrate and affirm the honesty. Love can only be exchanged in the context of truth, because the fake does not really exist. Love only operates in reality.

If one of my sons is honest with me about something, and I'm disappointed in what he did, I choose not to freak out. Otherwise, I just taught him to lie next time because I can't handle the truth. So I thank him for his honesty, perhaps share a time when I did something similar when I was young, and then we move on to whatever discipline is needed. Love rejoices with the truth because that's the only way it can be experienced.

Our kids aren't perfect, and neither are we. Let's be fathers who build an environment of grace where love is exchanged. Otherwise, our children will always go around lying and hiding from us. Yes, rules are necessary, but without relationship, rules will foster rebellion. Rejoice in the truth. Love and guide your kids in the reality of what's actually happening in their lives.

*Today I will remember:*

- Love rejoices with the truth because that's the only way it can be experienced.
- Rules are necessary, but rules without relationship will foster rebellion.
- I can rejoice in the truth.

*Lord, help me to build a home of grace.*
*Let my children feel safe with me, knowing that*
*whatever they share, I will still love them.*
*Help me to rejoice in truth and discipline with love.*

# CHILDREN'S CHILDREN

*But from everlasting to everlasting the LORD's love is with those who fear him, and his righteousness with their children's children—with those who keep his covenant and remember to obey his precepts.*

PSALM 103:17-18

Some of my best memories as a kid come from spending time with my grandfathers. I called my paternal grandfather "Paw Paw." He had a house on Cedar Creek Lake in Malakoff, Texas. Paw Paw and I would fish and work in the yard or in his shop. After dinner, he would take me out in the boat to water ski. At night we would sit on the deck and listen to the lake and talk about life, current events, and the Bible. On my mother's side, I called my grandfather "Granddaddy." He had a little farm outside Troup, Texas. We would work in the garden, tend to a little store he owned, and drink iced tea while eating tomatoes under the big pecan tree on his property. He would pray for me sometimes. Both men made a lasting impact.

It's funny what you remember as a kid. It's not the words so much as the walk. I admired these men, and I picked up their traits by watching them, for better or for worse. They helped shape my thoughts on marriage, parenting, work, and God. Not by what was said so much as by what was lived. Some things I learned were wonderful, while others I've had to unlearn or rethink. In all of it, I'm grateful. It's less about what we say and more about what we do. Let's model well.

*Today I will remember:*

- More is caught than taught.
- It's less about what we say and more about what we do.

*God, help me to be a good role model for my children and my children's children. I know they are watching me and picking up both the good and the bad.*

# FAITH IN THE FATHER

*Everyone who believes that Jesus is the Christ has become a child of God. And everyone who loves the Father loves his children, too. We know we love God's children if we love God and obey his commandments. Loving God means keeping his commandments, and his commandments are not burdensome.*

1 JOHN 5:1-3 (NLT)

Most people misunderstand faith, so let's break it down. *Faith* is a relational word. It's much more than just mental assent or agreement with certain doctrines. For example, the Devil believes, but he does not have faith in God. Faith means you trust God and take Him at His Word. Christianity is trusting the Word of the Father because of what He has done through Christ the Son. In that trust, we become a child of God. The more we understand His love for us, the more we love Him in return by obeying His commands. His commands also increase our love for others. It is all relational.

His commands become less and less burdensome for two reasons: You see the benefit and you want to bless Him. You increasingly trust that His commands are for your good—that's the benefit to you. And because you understand His grace, you want to bless Him with your obedience. My father loves me, and I want to please Him.

*Today I will remember:*

- Faith is relational, because it's about trusting God.
- The more that I understand God's love for me, the more I will do what He says.

*Father, help me to understand Your love for me,*
*so that I might trust and obey You. This is real faith.*

# FAMILY RESEMBLANCE

*"Therefore, come out from among unbelievers,*
*and separate yourselves from them, says the LORD.*
*Don't touch their filthy things, and I will welcome you.*
*And I will be your Father, and you will be my*
*sons and daughters, says the LORD Almighty."*

2 CORINTHIANS 6:17-18 (NLT)

A friend recently got a tattoo on his arm of the family crest. There's a lion, two swords, some Latin meaning "honor and faithfulness," and his last name inscribed on a shield. Pretty cool. Once you become a child of God, you bear the Father's name, and your life is a symbol to the world of what the family and His kingdom represent. Your character is the crest.

When it comes to character, our verses talk about separating ourselves from the things of the world. Particularly the filthy things—pornography, sexual immorality, or basically anything that is not of God. Things like bitterness, slander, gossip, selfishness, false pride, hypocrisy, and self-righteousness would also be on the list. None of these things represent the family, the Father, or His kingdom. As men of God, let's bear His name with honor. Let's shed ourselves of the marks of darkness and walk humbly in the light as representatives of His kingdom.

*Today I will remember:*

- As a child of God, I bear the Father's name.
- My life is a symbol to the world of what God's kingdom represents.
- My character is the crest.

*Father, I am Your servant and Your son.*
*Keep me from filthy things. Help me represent*
*the family well. May my character represent Yours.*

# FATHER KNOWS BEST

*And, "I will be a Father to you, and you will be my sons and daughters, says the LORD Almighty."*

2 CORINTHIANS 6:18

Great fathers learn from the greatest Father how to raise their children. God's love is not always understood, but it is always perfect. After all, we can't see what He sees, but we can trust that He is holy and good. God's love is both tough and tender. He is compassionate and gracious, and He disciplines His children to help them grow morally for their good.

At times, when I was a teenager, I hated my parents. It wasn't about them, but about me. I hated that they had the power, and I didn't. I hated that I had to answer to someone and couldn't do whatever I wanted. After all, at sixteen I pretty much knew everything. How could these neophytes have the gall to correct me, discipline me, and control me? Such is the mind of a rebellious teenager. Of course, as teens get older, they start to realize that maybe Mom and Dad did know a thing or two.

Our biggest problem with God usually centers around the fact that we're not Him. He has the power, and we don't. We must answer to someone. God nurtures us in both grace and truth. We are His sons whom He loves. He gives, He serves, He corrects, and He's compassionate. He's the perfect Father. Wise dads learn from Him.

*Today I will remember:*

- My biggest problem with God is usually that I'm not Him.
- God's love is not always understood, but it is always perfect.
- Great fathers learn how to raise their children from watching the greatest Father.

*Father, I want to reflect Your love and Your ways to my children. Teach me how to be a better father. Forgive me when I rebel against You. You know best.*

# FATHER TO THE FATHERLESS

*Sing praises to God and to his name! Sing loud praises to him who rides the clouds. His name is the LORD—rejoice in his presence! Father to the fatherless, defender of widows—this is God, whose dwelling is holy.*

PSALM 68:4-5 (NLT)

Two things stand out to me in this description of God: His power and His personal presence. His power in that He rides the clouds and His name is Lord. His personal presence in that He cares for the orphan and defends the widow. God is powerful and personal. He is not distant in His authority, letting the earth spin while He stands off, aloof. He knows your name. He cares for you. He is a compassionate Father to those in need.

It could be that you are fatherless. Maybe you never knew your biological father, or perhaps your dad is in heaven. Or maybe you know your dad, but he has neglected the role. The wounds of earthly fathers can be great. Whatever your situation, God wants to father you.

Be encouraged today, brother. The Lord knows your name. You don't have to walk through this day, or this life, alone. God is a father to the fatherless. He wants to guide you in wisdom, love you in strong compassion, and speak a new identity and security into your soul. Let Him. You bear His name. You are His son. One day, you too will ride the clouds with Him in Jesus' name.

*Today I will remember:*

- God is powerful and personal.
- I don't have to walk through this day, or this life, alone.

*Lord, thank You for being a Father to me. Please help me know You and walk with You. Thank You that I am part of Your family and am never alone.*

# FATHERING IN THE TENSION

*Fathers do not embitter your children,*
*or they will become discouraged.*
COLOSSIANS 3:21

Good fathers want their children to work hard, fulfill their God-given potential, and accomplish more than they ever did. This motivation can be a good thing, but don't overdo it. Instead of helping our kids, we can damage them, embitter them, and cause them to resent us. This is especially true when they become older preteens and teenagers. How do we manage the tension of motivating but not embittering?

The simple answer is that we make it about the relationship. As others have said, no one cares how much you know until they know how much you care. A good dad's goal is to have a lifelong relationship with his son or daughter. Great relationships are not built on intensity, but on love. Real love reflects the tension of grace and truth. When your kids screw up, hug them first. Tell them you love them. Humbly share a story of something dumb you did when you were their ages. Consequences and discipline will come next, but you begin with love.

Instead of coming down on our kids, let's come beside them. We embitter when we're all truth. We empower when we're grace and truth. As our kids get older, they'll trust us if we have loved and led them well. Relax. Be wise in the season of fatherhood that you're in. Choose to love first and then lead.

*Today I will remember:*

- Great relationships live in the tension of grace and truth.
- It takes practice to love and lead.

*Father, thank You for being gracious and truthful.*
*Help me to love my children as You love me. Make me*
*a source of comfort and strength for my children.*

# A FATHER'S SACRIFICE

*By faith Abraham, when God tested him, offered Isaac as a sacrifice. He who had embraced the promises was about to sacrifice his one and only son, even though God had said to him, "It is through Isaac that your offspring will be reckoned." Abraham reasoned that God could even raise the dead, and so in a manner of speaking he did receive Isaac back from death.*

HEBREWS 11:17-19

When I was young, hearing the account of Abraham being commanded to sacrifice his only son freaked me out. Why would God demand such a thing? Later, when I had sons of my own, it still bothered me. Eventually, however, I realized that God spared Isaac; He provided a ram in Isaac's place. But God did not spare His own Son. Years later, on that same mountain, Jesus suffered an agonizing death on the cross so that you and I might be saved. God sacrificed His Son so that you and I might be His sons.

God's encounter with Abraham and Isaac foreshadowed His encounter with you and me. As you put yourself in Abraham's shoes, you see great faith and obedience. You see the agonizing march up the mountain and relate to all the wonderings Abraham must have wrestled with. Then you better understand the love of God, who loved us sinners so much that He provided not a ram but Jesus to die in our place. The only begotten Son of God died so that we could be called the sons of God and forever live.

*Today I will remember:*

- The only begotten Son of God died so that we could be called the sons of God.
- In Him we will live forever.

*Lord God, thank You for Your sacrifice.*
*Thank You for the provision of the ram for*
*Abraham and of the provision of Jesus for me.*

# FINISH LINE

*Why, you do not even know what will happen tomorrow. What is your life? You are a mist that appears for a little while and then vanishes.*

JAMES 4:14

Life is fleeting. As you get older, the days seem long, the years short. So make the most of them for those you love. A mentor once taught me what is called the "Finish Line Principle." It's for people whose job is never done. For a pastor, there is always someone else in need, another problem to solve, and, frankly, everyone everywhere needs Jesus. It never stops. If your job is like that, you must choose each day when to be finished. Pick a time when you no longer look at email, you let your phone go to voicemail, and you cross the finish line for work to focus on your family.

Every man will wrestle with this on some level. The pull of work and busyness is always there. You must choose when to focus on what. Otherwise, you're thinking about your family while you're at work and about your work while you're with your family. The "finish line" is about focus.

One way to practice this is to make appointments with your kids. Let your children see you putting them into your schedule. If possible, cancel something else and put their names down instead. This communicates priority and makes them feel special. At times I would hand my boys my phone and let them reserve our time on the calendar. They knew when I crossed the finish line.

*Today I will remember:*

- My schedule communicates my priorities.
- It is important to pick a time each day to be done with work to focus on my family.

*Lord, life is short, and I do not know what tomorrow will bring. Help me love my family well each day. Let me communicate their value not just with my words, but with my actions.*

# GIFT OF GOD

*Children are a heritage from the* Lord*,*
*offspring a reward from him.*
PSALM 127:3

I'll never forget the day I first saw our firstborn. I'm not talking about the day when he was born, although I'll never forget that either, I'm talking about that very first sonogram. It revealed what looked like a little blob, but in the middle of the blob, we saw a beating heart. Josh's heart. The heart of our firstborn. I cried tears of joy and gratitude. Twenty-three years later, I can still see that little beating heart on the monitor. I have learned so much from my sons, Josh and Jackson. Perhaps the greatest lessons come from my better understanding of God's love for me.

At first, all kids do is take. They wake you in the middle of night. They cry, eat, poop their pants, and disrupt your entire world. They don't give you anything but the poopy diaper and interrupted sleep, and yet you adore them. Your love isn't about what they deserve or have earned; you just love them because they're your children.

This is how God loves you. It's not because you're so great, but because He is. You, His son through your faith in Jesus, are the apple of His eye. You might complain a lot and make a mess of things on occasion, and yet He adores you. This is the love of a father for his child, and this is how God loves you.

*Today I will remember:*

- God loves me as His son.
- His love for me is not based on my goodness, but on His.

*Father, thank You for adopting me into Your family*
*and for loving me as You do. I am grateful for Your grace*
*and truth. Help me to love my children as You love me.*

# GOOD DADS DISCIPLINE

*My child, don't reject the LORD's discipline,*
*and don't be upset when he corrects you.*
*For the LORD corrects those he loves, just as*
*a father corrects a child in whom he delights.*

PROVERBS 3:11-12 (NLT)

I recently read an article about bull elephants. A bunch of young, orphaned male bull elephants were separated from the older bulls, taken to Pilanesberg National Park in South Africa, and left on their own as a group. Not long after, these adolescent males began acting hyper-aggressively. They became so out of control that they even started killing rhinos, which is highly unusual for an elephant. The solution? The park brought in older males, and the aggressive behavior immediately dissipated and soon vanished. The lesson: Young male elephants need the strength and guidance of older males. The same is true with teenage boys.

A testosterone-fueled teenage boy needs the strength and guidance of an older man. God wills that we lovingly discipline our children. Not out of anger or selfishness, but with a desire to guide and lead. A child who has not been kindly disciplined has not been loved. Good fathers provide good guardrails for their sons and daughters. Dads, they need our leadership, and we are modeling what manhood looks like.

*Today I will remember:*

- It is God's will that I lovingly discipline my children.
- Discipline should never be done out of anger or selfishness, but with a desire to guide.

*Lord, give me the wisdom and grace to lovingly discipline my children. Let it never be out of anger, but out of a desire to help them be the best they can be.*

# LAVISH LOVE

*See what great love the Father has lavished on us,
that we should be called children of God!
And that is what we are! The reason the world
does not know us is that it did not know him.*

1 JOHN 3:1

One of my best childhood memories is of my grandparents taking me to the airport to pick up my dad. I was somewhere around six years old. My dad was an electrician, and he had gone on a day trip to serve a client and was returning in the early evening. I remember him rounding a corner and heading in our direction. When I saw him, I took off running toward him as fast as I could and jumped into his arms. I can still smell the mix of sweat, flannel, and Old Spice. He hugged me and kissed me on the cheek, and I held him tight. It's one of the best moments of my childhood that I can recall. It was an exchange of healthy, safe, lavish love.

This is the way God loves you. You need the love of the Father in your life, and it's yours if you'll receive it. He doesn't just love you; He *lavishly* loves you. You never have to wonder about it; His arms are always open wide to you. You are His son. One day He will return, and you will be with Him forever.

*Today I will remember:*

- I am lavishly loved by my Heavenly Father.
- He calls me His son, and I am His.

*Father, thank You for Your overwhelming love. Holy Spirit, please fill me with this love today. Help me to not just know it in my head, but to experience it deep in my heart.*

# MINI ME

*The godly walk with integrity;*
*blessed are their children who follow them.*
PROVERBS 20:7

When my oldest son was in the fifth grade, his teacher invited the class members to dress up as their favorite superheroes and give a short speech about why they admired their hero. On the morning of the presentation, Josh came downstairs wearing glasses and carrying my briefcase. Slow to catch the obvious, I asked, "Now who are you supposed to be?" He responded, "I'm you, Dad!" He completed the look with Nike tennis shoes and a plaid, button-up Western shirt. Nailed it!

While my son's gesture understandably flattered and blessed me, at the same time I felt a healthy burden. Josh looked at me as someone to emulate. This is normal between fathers and sons; children watch and mimic us. This is playfully true when they are younger, and practically true in how they live when they are older. Like computers, their little brains are being programmed by watching us. May God help us all.

Living with integrity is the best blessing we can give our kids. To be men of God who are not perfect, but who are honest in our pursuit of Him. Integrity is the integration of the public and the private. Simply put, a real man is a man who is real. Our kids are watching. May we be godly men who walk with integrity.

*Today I will remember:*
- The best blessing I can give my kids is to live with integrity before them.
- A real man is honest in his pursuit of God.

*Lord, help me live a life of integrity.*
*I know I won't be perfect, but let*
*me be honest as I follow You.*

# PEACE IN PARENTING

*Do not be anxious about anything, but in every situation, by prayer and petition, with thanksgiving, present your requests to God. And the peace of God, which transcends all understanding, will guard your hearts and your minds in Christ Jesus.*

PHILIPPIANS 4:6-7

There's a season in parenting that I call the "blessed bubble," between the ages of four and twelve. The kids, in small ways, begin to take care of themselves, you're still their favorite person, and they want to spend as much time with you as they can. I love this season! Most do. It's usually lots of fun, and then something happens at around age thirteen. The bubble bursts. They want to be around friends more, they're not telling you everything, they start speaking in a language you don't understand, and you begin to realize how little control you have. The teenage and young adult years usually increase the anxiety and worry.

One of my most freeing moments was when I realized that my sons don't really belong to me. They belong to God. God is better at parenting than I am. He is a better father than I am and has my children in the palm of His hand. I can choose to trust Him with the children He has entrusted to me. Yes, there are going to be highs and lows, good decisions and dumb ones. My guess is the same was true for your life, and yet here you are, reading a Christian book. Do the best you can and parent in peace.

*Today I will remember:*

- I can trust God with the children He has entrusted to me.
- I can make my requests to God with a heart of gratitude.
- God's peace will guard my feelings and thoughts.

*God, thank You for my children.*
*I know that I can trust You with them.*
*Please guard my feelings and thoughts.*

# PROVISION

*Anyone who does not provide for their relatives,
and especially for their own household, has denied
the faith and is worse than an unbeliever.*

1 TIMOTHY 5:8

I desire to provide financially for my wife and family. I want my sons to have things and opportunities that I didn't have growing up. I don't want my wife to ever worry about money but to feel a sense of financial safety and stability. I want her to have nice things and to live a comfortable life. Today's verse includes the financial, but the application is even broader and more profound.

We're to provide for our families in three ways:

1. *Physically*. This one is obvious. Unless you are lazy, you are probably already striving to provide financially for the physical welfare of your family. If you're not, then you need to grow up and become a man. Allow this verse to convict you. Even if your wife makes more money than you, it's still your responsibility to make sure the necessities of life are covered.
2. *Emotionally*. You may not be thinking as much about emotional provision. Your wife may have emotional needs that only you can provide. Know her and how she needs you to love her. Also, there are some things that only a dad can give to his kids. Bless them, express your pride in them, and tell them often that you love them—regardless of their ages.
3. *Spiritually*. You are the spiritual leader of your family. Lead your wife and children to attend church, pray, give, serve, and know the Scriptures. Provide direction and leadership in your family's relationship with God.

*Today I will remember:*

- I'm called to be a provider for my family.
- I am to care for them physically, emotionally, and spiritually.

*Lord, help me to provide well physically, emotionally,
and spiritually. Give me wisdom, let me be more intentional,
and help me to be what You've called me to be for my wife and kids.*

# QUALITY TIMES

*There is a time for everything, and a season*
*for every activity under the heavens.*
ECCLESIASTES 3:1

How do our families spell love? T-I-M-E. Our kids are, on some level, keeping score with how much time you spend with them. Why? The value of importance is measured by time. They think, "If Dad never spends time with me, then I must not be important to him." When I give a talk along these lines, usually from the book of James, I will state, "There is no such thing as quality time." It always gets me in trouble and bothers people, so yes, I'm planning to stick with it.

Think about it. Time is just time. It passes regardless of what we are doing. There is no such thing as quality time, just quality choices. You can't make time better, but you can make better decisions within time. Semantics? Maybe, but how we speak about things shapes us. When we say something like, "There's never enough time," we're deceived. To blame time for a problem is to abdicate personal responsibility. Time is not going to change. Therefore, we must.

Make quality decisions with your children. Give them a piece of your day, every day. Set appointments with them. Individually take them on daddy dates. Make quality choices each day that communicate their value to you. Choose to love in the time you've been given.

*Today I will remember:*

- There is no such thing as quality time, only quality choices.
- For children, time measures how important they are to me.

*God, help me to make the most of the time*
*You have given. I can't control time, but I can*
*control my choices. May I choose well for my family.*

# SEEING WHAT THE LORD SEES

*Jesse had seven of his sons pass before Samuel, but Samuel said to him, "The LORD has not chosen these." So he asked Jesse, "Are these all the sons you have?" "There is still the youngest," Jesse answered. "He is tending the sheep." Samuel said, "Send for him; we will not sit down until he arrives."*

1 SAMUEL 16:10-11

God has revealed that the new king will be one of Jesse's sons. As each one passes before Samuel, the prophet thinks, "This is a tall, good-looking man—surely this is the Lord's chosen!" Finally, they bring in David, the smallest and youngest of Jesse's boys. They had to go out to the field and fetch him. While the family saw just a simple shepherd boy, God saw the future king.

It's hard for us to see what God might do through our children. We're aware of their shortcomings. It probably doesn't help matters that we used to change their diapers. Even Jesus spoke of how hard it is for a prophet to have honor in his hometown. We see the obvious of what they are and who they were instead of who they are becoming.

Dads play a powerful role in seeing the potential of their children and calling out the best in them. We must manage the tension of affirming and encouraging as well as guiding and correcting. Teach them to be an overcomer without being overbearing. This requires the Lord's wisdom and insight.

*Today I will remember:*

- God sees in my kids what I can't see.
- I need His insight to affirm them and point them to His calling.

*Father, help me see what You see in my children.
Give me grace to live in the tension of loving, leading,
and partnering with You in preparing them for the future.*

# TEACH AND LEAD

*Children, obey your parents in the Lord, for this is right. "Honor your father and mother"—which is the first commandment with a promise—"so that it may go well with you and that you may enjoy long life on the earth."*

EPHESIANS 6:1-3

At first glance, our verses seem to be written only for children. But there is an insight for fathers too. Simply put, children must be taught to obey. Especially when they are young. Good parents do not let their young kids "figure out" right and wrong. Children must be led, taught, and shown proper behavior. Of course, we are never to do this in an aggressive way, but with a heart of compassion and discipline in training up a child in the way he or she should go.

Notice that when a parent leads effectively, and a child follows, a promise appears. The goal of good parenting is to equip our children to live a life that goes well and is both enjoyable and long. Kids need intentional fathers. We're disciplinarians, yes, but we're also coaches called to equip our kids for life. You're not just raising a child; you're training a future adult. Think about what each of your kids needs from you and how he or she needs it. Kids are different in their personalities, in the varying seasons of life, and in their temperaments. Watch them and invest in them what is personally best for them. Boys need the leadership of their dad, and so do girls. How can you equip them to live a long, enjoyable, healthy life?

*Today I will remember:*

- By watching, learning, and investing, I can help my kids experience the best.
- Kids need intentional fathers.

*Lord, give me the wisdom to be a great dad. Help me to equip my kids to enjoy a long life that goes well. Help me lead them in Your ways.*

# THE BLESSING

*"The LORD bless you and keep you; the LORD make his face shine on you and be gracious to you; the LORD turn his face toward you and give you peace."*

NUMBERS 6:24-26

When my boys were younger, I would bless them at bedtime with today's verses. I'd place my hand on their heads and speak these words over their lives. It didn't seem like a big deal at the time, but it was, and they remember. If I forgot one night, Jackson would yell down the stairs, "Dad, you forgot to bless me!" On his sixth birthday, he spoke the blessing over me. I had no idea he had memorized it, but the repetition of speaking it each night made it stick. It was special to him, and he wanted to give something special to me.

Children need words of affirmation from their fathers. Moms are great sources of comfort while Dads are sources of security and identity. Moms let you know you're cared for. Dads tell you who you are. The blessing is a statement of affirmation and affection. It communicates your child's specialness to you. It doesn't have to be these exact verses, but every kid needs regular fatherly encouragement. It is love wrapped up in the confirmation that they are yours and that you are proud of them. Speak blessings over your children.

*Today I will remember:*

- I will speak words of affirmation and affection over my children.
- I will regularly let them know how special and important they are to me.

*Father, thank You for the way You bless me. Help me regularly bless my children. Let me be intentional and consistent with words of blessing.*

# THE POTTER

*Yet you, LORD, are our Father. We are the clay,*
*you are the potter; we are all the work of your hand.*
ISAIAH 64:8

If you could, what would you change about yourself? I'm going to keep it real with you. I'd rather be taller. I am five feet nine, which supposedly is the national average in America, but it seems where I live most men are over six feet. I'd also prefer less body fat and more muscle. I've prayed for that, but apparently God wants me to eat right and work out. Besides these shallow changes, I'd like to be less selfish and more serving. I would think less of me and more of others. God is working with me on these things, and we still have a long way to go.

God shapes us as a potter shapes clay. Have you ever seen that process? It's gentle and slow, not aggressive or quick. As a loving father trains his son for life, so our Heavenly Father trains, shapes, and molds us for holiness. He is less concerned about the outside and focused more on the inside. Less concerned about our comfort and more concerned about our character. We are the work of His hands, and I am grateful that He is still working on us. Let Him guide you and shape you today as a loving Father.

*Today I will remember:*

- Like a loving father trains his son for life, so God cares for us.
- Our Heavenly Father trains, shapes, and molds us for holiness.
- He is less concerned about our comfort and more concerned about our character.

*Father, thank You for Your patience and kindness.*
*Help me participate in the changes You want to make*
*in my life. You are the potter, and I am the clay.*

# THE SMART CHOICE

*A fool spurns a parent's discipline,*
*but whoever heeds correction shows prudence.*
PROVERBS 15:5

God loves you no matter what. There is nothing you can do to make Him love you more, and there is nothing you can do to make Him love you less. He loves you because of who He is, and His love is not based on your performance. His love and forgiveness are infinite. This is one of the things that is so amazing about grace. Now the fool hears this and thinks to himself, "God loves me and forgives me no matter what? Great! I'm going to go do whatever I want regardless of what He says." Yeah, that's dumb. When you realize that God loves you, you also realize that His commands are for your good. Sin is stupid because it will harm you. Trust God.

Question: Do your kids understand that your commands are for their good? Especially as they get older, be sure to explain why you say what you say—at least occasionally. My parents often simply answered my questions with the classic "Because I said so." I get it. I have told my boys the same thing at times. But at the end of the day, I want them to understand that my rules are for their benefit. Talk about why. If they know the rules are for them, then they are more likely to obey them. Have regular conversations about the why behind the rules.

*Today I will remember:*

- Sin is stupid because it will harm me and others.
- It is wise to talk about the "why."
- I will have regular conversations with my children about the why behind the rules.

*Lord, help me to help my kids understand that*
*rules are there to help them and not hinder them.*
*Give me insight to recognize good, teachable*
*moments to discuss the why behind the rules.*

# TRAINING AND TRUSTING

*Start children off on the way they should go,*
*and even when they are old they will not turn from it.*
PROVERBS 22:6

I thought parenting my now young adult boys would get easier as they got older. In some ways, it has, but in many ways, it's more challenging. One of the clearest lessons I've learned is how little control I have. My wife and I do our best and trust the rest to God. Those boys are their own persons and will make their own decisions.

Our verse for today is a proverb, not a promise. This is an important distinction. Promises from God always come to pass, while a proverb is a statement of how life generally works. A proverb is an observed principle, not a guaranteed promise. Here's my point: God is the perfect parent. He put two of His kids, Adam and Eve, in the perfect environment. God couldn't have done any better with the Garden of Eden and the way He loved those two—and you know what they did? They rebelled. As dads, we are to train our children in the way they should go. Then in time we let them go and make their own choices. So as we raise our kids, we're raising future adults. We are preparing them for adulthood, so we do our best and trust God with the rest.

It could be that your son has strayed from the faith. My encouragement would be to continue to love and pray for him as he makes his own choices. Play the long game. The win is a lifelong relationship where you may not have control, but you still have influence. You can trust God with your kids.

*Today I will remember:*

- I will do my best and trust God with the rest.
- My goal is a lifelong relationship of love and influence.

*God, I love my children and pray that Your hand*
*would be on their lives. Help me to train them*
*well and to trust You. May my heart reflect Yours.*

# TRUTH WALK

*I could have no greater joy than to hear*
*that my children are following the truth.*
3 JOHN 4 (NLT)

One of my dreams for my two sons is that they would do better than I have. Occasionally, I meet parents who are jealous of their adult children's lives, almost insecure in the fact that their kids have succeeded. I don't understand that. I want my boys to do better than I have in every category of life. In fact, I see their success as mine, so to see them win means I have won. There is no greater category where I long to see them outshine me than in their faith. I want them to walk closer with God than I have. To know Him better than I do. More than the money they make or their achievements at work, I want them to walk with God. There is no greater joy than that.

Here are a few things dads can do to help:

1. *Pray*. Pray that the Holy Spirit would draw them to Jesus and give them insight into the love of the Father. It is the Holy Spirit who makes faith real. Pray for His work in their lives.
2. *Model*. How you live out your faith matters. More than anything else, they're watching how you treat them and their mother. They know if your faith is legit. Be humble. When you make mistakes, apologize. They're not expecting perfection, but they do know whether you are pursuing the Lord.
3. *Celebrate*. Cheer them on in the realm of faith. Ask them how their walk with God is going and celebrate the small victories. Express your pride in their decisions to follow Jesus and how you admire those decisions.

*Today I will remember:*

- To see my kids win means I have won.
- There is no greater joy than seeing my children know God and walk with Him.

*Holy Spirit, please draw my children to Jesus.*
*Help them to know the love of the Father and reveal*
*His truth to them. Let them know You and walk with You.*

# YOU CAN COUNT ON ME

*Every good and perfect gift is from above,*
*coming down from the Father of the heavenly lights,*
*who does not change like shifting shadows.*
JAMES 1:17

One of the best things a father can give his children is the gift of consistency. Fathers bring stability. When a child lacks a good, strong, kind, and consistent presence, he or she will be fearful and insecure. Consistency brings stability. Do your children know that you will be there for them? Can they count on it? Can they count on you?

I have a friend whose dad always sat in the same seat at our football games. My friend never wondered if his father was going to make the game, or where he would be. They wouldn't even talk about it ahead of time. My buddy would just look up in the stands, in the direction of that seat, and his dad would be there. Awesome. That is an example of consistent, stable love. It communicates importance and an "if you need me, you know where I'll be" type of security. Consistency builds trust, and all great relationships require it.

Be a man of your word with your children. It is one of the best gifts you can give them. If you must adjust, call them ahead of time, apologize, and make that type of adjustment extremely rare. Don't be like a shifting shadow. Be a "you can count on me" type of dad.

*Today I will remember:*

- Consistency brings stability.
- It builds trust, and all great relationships require it.
- I will be a man of my word with my children.

*Lord, I want to be a source of stability and strength*
*for my children. May I give them the gift of*
*stability and security through consistent presence.*
*Help them to know that they can count on me.*

# July

## LEGACY

Therefore, since we are surrounded by such a huge crowd
of witnesses to the life of faith, let us strip off every weight
that slows us down, especially the sin that so easily trips us up.
And let us run with endurance the race God has set before us.
*Hebrews 12:1 (NLT)*

# NUMBERED DAYS

*Teach us to number our days,*
*that we may gain a heart of wisdom.*
PSALM 90:12

I turned fifty a couple of years ago. My wife and some friends threw me a party and invited my closest friends and colleagues. We had barbecue from my favorite place. My friends hosted the gathering at their place. They have a beautiful home, and they decorated it with a cool Texas vibe, since I'm from Texas. We laughed, told stories, and reminisced. For the first time in my life as we left that party, I was sobered to realize that my shot clock on this earth was counting down. I have more time behind me than in front of me. And something shifted in my soul. I stopped thinking so much about what I was building and started thinking more about what I will be leaving behind.

How about you? Do you think about your legacy? This life is not a dress rehearsal. There are no do-overs. It's a one-shot gig. Our verse tells us to remember this in order to be wise. Our decisions today will be the legacy that we leave tomorrow. Choose wisely.

This month, we're looking at the lives of various people in the Bible and at the legacy they left behind for better or worse. There is a lot we can learn from them. Friend, your days are numbered. Such is life. Let's choose to live well.

*Today I will remember:*
- The decisions we make today will be the legacy we leave tomorrow.
- This life is not a dress rehearsal.
- There are no do-overs; it's a one-shot gig.

*Lord, my days are numbered.*
*Help me to remember this and live wisely.*
*Help me to invest in the things that matter most.*
*I want to leave a legacy that honors You.*

# THE LEGACY OF DAVID

*"Now when David had served God's purpose in his own generation, he fell asleep; he was buried with his ancestors and his body decayed."*

ACTS 13:36

What will your legacy be? The mortality rate of every man on the earth is still hovering right around one hundred percent. All of us are born and all of us will die. Your legacy is what you leave behind. The memories people have of you, the impact you made or didn't make, and your contribution to the family tree. Your legacy is that little dash on the tombstone between birth and death. What will yours be?

David is known for many things. He killed Goliath with a slingshot. He would go on to become king and lay the groundwork for his son Solomon to build the temple. David also had an affair with Solomon's mother, Bathsheba, and had her husband killed in battle to cover it up. David wrote most of the Psalms, and people have been edified by his prayers, poems, and songs for generations. We know lots of things about David's life, the good, the bad, and the ugly. This is his legacy.

Our verse says that David "served God's purpose in his own generation." When all was said and done, David fulfilled his mission for God. Now that's a good legacy. David was not perfect. He made some horrible mistakes and hurt his family. David had regrets. But he strived to live for God.

How about you? What is your driving purpose? The only thing that will matter in the end is how you served God and people. Fulfill God's purpose in your generation. Make God and His ways the driving ambition of your life.

*Today I will remember:*

- I will prioritize serving God and others.
- I will make God and His ways my driving ambition.

*Lord, help me to live out Your purposes.*
*Success is doing what You created me to do.*
*To love and glorify You is my purpose.*

# THE LEGACY OF ABRAHAM

*And the scripture was fulfilled that says,*
*"Abraham believed God, and it was credited to him*
*as righteousness," and he was called God's friend.*
JAMES 2:23

The three largest faiths on the planet—Judaism, Christianity, and Islam—trace their roots back to Abraham. Jews and Christians look to Abraham's son Isaac, and Muslims revere Ishmael. Abraham believed God, and his faith made a huge impact on the world. If you read about him in Genesis, however, you'll see that this "father of faith" didn't always practice it very well. He doubted, disobeyed, and did some things that he regretted. Yet, in the end, his imperfect, wavering faith was credited to him by God as righteousness.

What is faith? In America, most people believe that faith is just mental assent. It's the belief that something happened. A person believes that Jesus really did die on the cross and rise again. Yes, such mental assent is necessary, but it's only the beginning. Faith in the Bible is relational and action oriented.

The Christian life is about you and me trusting God. When you trust someone, you count on them and take them at their word. I love that our verse today says Abraham was called "God's friend." That's relational; that's biblical faith. It's a relational exchange of trust that leads to actions. Abraham's legacy is not one of perfection, but one of faith. God did the work, and Abraham walked the road of God's work in his life. This is real faith.

*Today I will remember:*

- To believe is to trust and to trust is to obey.
- To believe God is to do what He says.
- Faith is action oriented.

*Father, help me to know You, trust You,*
*and do what You say. Help me be a man of faith.*
*Let my actions reflect my belief in You.*

# THE PARENTS OF MOSES

*By faith Moses' parents hid him for three months after he was born, because they saw he was no ordinary child, and they were not afraid of the king's edict.*

HEBREWS 11:23

God's hand was on Moses from the beginning. His parents recognized it and lived by faith. If it weren't for the actions of his parents, specifically his mother, there would have been no account of his life. Yet God used this man to free a people, establish a religion, and lead a nation. This all began with the courageous actions of his parents, Amram and Jochebed.

The Israelites were growing in number, so to maintain control, Pharaoh issued a decree for the midwives to kill the boys at birth. Then the order expanded to throwing all the baby boys into the Nile. Jochebed, Moses' mother, hid him for three months and then placed him in a basket close to where Pharaoh's daughter bathed and sent Moses afloat. The daughter rescues this child, raises him in the palace, and the rest is history. This was God's providence at work through these parents. Moses' legacy is their legacy.

Our church's ministry to children and students is our most important and impactful ministry. You never know what God might do with someone. That inattentive, troublemaking seventh grader most likely has some leadership gifts, which is why he questions everything you say. The seeds of faith you plant in his life may one day grow into an orchard. A good, appropriate, and wholesome investment in a child is always valuable. After all, their legacy will be yours.

*Today I will remember:*

- Investing faith in a child is always a good investment.
- Children need safe men who will speak love and encouragement into their lives.

*God, work in and through my life. I look forward to You doing above and beyond what I could ask or imagine through the people in whom I invest. Help me to be a source of life and encouragement to the next generation.*

# THE LEGACY OF JUDAS ISCARIOT

*Going at once to Jesus, Judas said,*
*"Greetings, Rabbi!" and kissed him.*
MATTHEW 26:49

Not all legacies are positive. We all stand at a crossroads each day deciding various paths to take. Some lead to good things and others to destruction. Our legacy is simply the decisions we make each day. Which begs the question, where are your decisions leading you?

The legacy of Judas Iscariot is one of betrayal, regret, and infamy. He betrayed Jesus for thirty pieces of silver. Perhaps the worst moment of all was when he sealed this betrayal with a kiss. That decision has made his name, and his legacy, synonymous with greed, hypocrisy, disloyalty, and treachery.

And yet Judas saw the miracles, the healings, the supernatural multiplication of food to feed thousands, the calming of storms and walking on water. In the end, he understood the evil he had done and returned the money to the complicit religious leaders, who used it to buy a parcel called Akeldama, or the Field of Blood. Ultimately, Judas committed suicide. This is his legacy. Let's remember to consider the consequences of our decisions before we make them. We all leave a legacy. What do you want yours to be?

*Today I will remember:*
- My life will be summed up by the decisions I make.
- Every decision has a ripple effect.
- Thinking about the consequences helps me choose wisely.

*Father, every decision I make is*
*leading somewhere. Help me to choose wisely.*
*Let my legacy be one of loyalty and faith.*

# THE LEGACY OF DANIEL

*So the king gave the order, and they brought Daniel and threw him into the lions' den. The king said to Daniel, "May your God, whom you serve continually, rescue you!"*

DANIEL 6:16

Daniel's legacy is profound. You might know the Bible stories if you went to Sunday school. Perhaps you know of the prophecies spoken through him about the end times. If you went to Bible college and if you've ever done a deep dive on the Christmas account, then you know that Daniel had an impact there as well. In our verse for today, Daniel is thrown into the lion's den for committing the crime of praying to God in public. If you go on reading, and I hope you will, then you'll find (spoiler alert) that God shuts the mouths of the lions, does a miracle, and Daniel is spared.

Daniel stands out to me as an excellent example of what it means to follow God in a godless culture. Jerusalem is sacked by Babylon. King Nebuchadnezzar brings the best and brightest Jews to serve him in his court. Daniel's name is changed, he's made to study the occult, and he was most likely castrated. (They probably didn't teach you that last part in Sunday school!) Daniel was stripped of his dignity and faith, at least seemingly. Yet he continued to trust God and serve Him amid occult practices to the extent that, years later, the magi would read his prophecies, make the connection in the constellations, and journey to worship the newborn King.

*Today I will remember:*

- I can worship God anywhere.
- I can follow God in a godless culture.
- This requires wisdom, humility, and strength.

*Lord, make me faithful no matter what life brings. Make me wise, humble, and strong.*

# THE LEGACY OF JOSEPH

*"You intended to harm me, but God intended it for good to accomplish what is now being done, the saving of many lives."*

GENESIS 50:20

Just before my time to speak at a men's conference in Texas, a guy shared his testimony. This guy was a former Navy SEAL and was now volunteering as the head of his church's safety team. As he shared about his life, he told us about becoming a SEAL, facing battles, and the challenges he had faced growing up. As he spoke about his father, he broke down and began to cry. This formidable warrior talked about how forgiveness was the hardest and most freeing thing he'd ever done.

Joseph's legacy is complex, but perhaps the most profound part was when he forgave his brothers, who had sold him into slavery, left him for dead, and told their father that he was dead. Joseph's life is a story of grit, hope, and God's hand being on his life. By the grace of God's providence, Joseph became Pharaoh's right-hand administrator. He could have destroyed them in revenge. Instead he chose to forgive. It is through the line of his brother Judah that, years and years later, the Messiah, Jesus Christ, would be born. Joseph saved his people, and, without knowing it, helped save the world through his decision to forgive.

*Today I will remember:*

- The most formidable of men choose to forgive.
- To forgive is to trust and agree with God.

*Father, give me the grace to reflect Your character and practice forgiveness. Bitterness never made anyone better. May Your forgiveness flow in me and through me.*

# THE LEGACY OF JOSHUA

*"But if serving the Lord seems undesirable to you,*
*then choose for yourselves this day whom you will serve,*
*whether the gods your ancestors served beyond the Euphrates,*
*or the gods of the Amorites, in whose land you are living.*
*But as for me and my household, we will serve the Lord."*

JOSHUA 24:15

Joshua's legacy of God working in and through his life is impressive. He replaced Moses to lead God's people into the Promised Land. He led the army to march around the walls of Jericho seven times and saw those walls come tumbling down. But I think his greatest legacy is found here in our verse for today. He is known for leading some amazing exploits, but I think his greatest leadership was at home.

In high school, I worked for my dad's company as an electrician's apprentice. We served the wealthy of Dallas, and I remember this one occasion of being in a very nice home where we were changing out light switches in the owner's office. There was a picture hanging over the fireplace that said, "No success at work can compensate for failure at home." That stuck with me. Of all the things we accomplish, our greatest legacy is what happens in our houses. You are leaving some type of legacy to your children and your children's children. The emotional and spiritual investments we make ripple out over time, for better or worse. Invest wisely. It could be that you want to carry on what was handed down to you, or that you want to change the family tree. It's your time now. What type of legacy will you leave?

*Today I will remember:*

- No success at work can compensate for failure at home.
- My greatest legacy is the one I leave with my family.

*Father, help me to invest wisely in*
*my family. These loved ones are my highest*
*priority next to my relationship with You.*

# THE LEGACY OF NOAH

*By faith Noah, when warned about things not yet seen, in holy fear built an ark to save his family. By his faith he condemned the world and became heir of the righteousness that is in keeping with faith.*

HEBREWS 11:7

Church people can be weird. Sometimes we get so familiar with something that we become, in a way, unfamiliar with it. Take the account of Noah for example. There's a church in America somewhere right now that has decorated the children's area with a picture of Noah's Ark. Animals of all kinds are lining up two by two in perfect harmony while a rain cloud is forming in the distance. Noah and his family are smiling, and so are the animals. Week in and week out, visitors comment on how lovely and picturesque it all is.

The problem is that the account of Noah is about God destroying all of mankind with a flood. God spares Noah and his family in His grace but destroys the rest because of wickedness. It's a great big do-over because of the evil of men. There's nothing cute in the biblical account. Sometimes we get so familiar with things that we forget the context.

Noah trusted God. That's his legacy. To believe is to trust and to trust is to obey. Noah did what God said, crazy as it seemed at the time. As a result, humans and all the land animals lived on. Without the faith of Noah, the human story would have been over. Obeying God is not always easy, but it is always worth it. You never know what God might be doing in and through your obedience.

*Today I will remember:*

- We never know what God might do through our obedience.
- Obeying God is not always easy, but it is always worth it.

*Lord, I want to be familiar with Your Word. Help me to take it in and apply its lessons. May I trust You by doing what You say.*

# THE LEGACY OF ENOCH

*Enoch walked faithfully with God; then he was no more, because God took him away.*

GENESIS 5:24

The Bible does not tell us a lot about Enoch, but what it does say is powerful and profound. Our verse seems to foreshadow the New Testament verse in 1 Thessalonians 4:17, which says that future believers will be "caught up" with the Lord in the air. Enoch seems to have had such an experience long ago. It appears that he never tasted death. He was walking with God so closely that he just stepped from this dimension of life into the spiritual realm of the next.

The phrase "walked faithfully with God" implies that Enoch lived a life of such deep faith and obedience that his fellowship with God was continuous. I wonder what my children will say of my walk with God. When they think of me after I'm dead and gone, will my obedience and fellowship with the Father be the first things that comes to mind? I pray so.

It appears that Enoch so pleased the heart of God that God just decided to bring him home to heaven. Almost as if God couldn't wait that long to be with him, so his time on earth was cut short. Brothers, the purpose of life is to know God and walk with God. This is why you were born. It's why you're breathing in and out and reading this book right now. God wants you to know Him and to walk faithfully with Him. There is no greater legacy.

*Today I will remember:*

- The purpose of life is to know God and walk with God.
- There is no greater legacy.

*Father, help me to know You and walk faithfully with You. I choose to focus on You throughout my day today, and every day.*

# THE LEGACY OF PAUL

*For I am already being poured out like a drink offering, and the time for my departure is near. I have fought the good fight, I have finished the race, I have kept the faith.*

2 TIMOTHY 4:6-7

Writing to a young pastor named Timothy, Paul knows that soon he will leave this life and go on to the next and be forever with Jesus. Notice how he describes his journey of faith. It's a temporary "race" that we run. It's a "fight" that is good, necessary, and right. It's a charge we must keep to the end. The wording here tells us that there must have been times when he wanted to give up.

I'm not a natural runner but have been made to run at various times. The self-talk in a long run can be interesting. You gripe, you complain. You encourage yourself. You tell yourself you got this (and to stop being such a whiney wimp). The best feeling is when you finally see the finish line. You begin to feel a healthy pride, your head lifts in triumph, you cross the finish line in pure joy. This is Paul's expression to Timothy here. The end is near. He did it. He was faithful.

In the words of William Wallace in the movie *Braveheart*, "Every man dies, not every man really lives." Fight the good fight of the faith. If you've fallen, get up and keep going. Run the race God has for you. Be faithful to the end. This is the stuff of a great legacy.

*Today I will remember:*

- We must fight the good fight and keep the faith.
- Anyone can start a race; only a faithful and strong man will finish.

*Lord, thank You that You are with me in this race of life. Help me to run Your race and to finish well. I choose to fight for faithfulness.*

# THE LEGACY OF SOLOMON

*God gave Solomon wisdom and very great insight, and a breadth of understanding as measureless as the sand on the seashore.*

1 KINGS 4:29

The Bible calls Solomon the wisest man who ever lived. He was a gifted leader and businessman. In fact, some scholars say that if you were to measure Solomon's net worth according to current value, he would have been a trillionaire. Israel experienced tremendous blessing during his reign. He wrote the book of Ecclesiastes and most of the Proverbs. He also built the Temple. Solomon's legacy is one of great success and blessing. At the same time, it's one of deep regret.

Solomon liked women. A lot of women. Over time, despite all his success, he assembled a large harem of wives and concubines. He pursued the pleasures of wine, women, and song, and my guess is he didn't have time to drink that much. It was hundreds of women! Not surprisingly, he allowed some of these women to lead him astray. Despite all the blessings of God, Solomon chose to honor their foreign gods and betray the Lord God and the calling on his life.

Sometimes the greatest test of faith comes not in times of trial, but in times of success. Everyone prays when the plane is going down, but we tend to forget God when things are going well. Success can breed arrogance, and arrogance brings prayerlessness. Don't let the good seasons of life cause you to forget God. Remain faithful and stay humble. Let's choose to honor God in all things.

*Today I will remember:*

- Sometimes the greatest test of faith comes not in trial, but in success.
- I won't let the good seasons of life cause me to forget God.

*God, let me honor You in every season. Forgive me when I forget You. I am grateful for Your blessings and know that they come from You.*

# THE LEGACY OF THE BOY

*"Here is a boy with five small barley loaves and two small fish, but how far will they go among so many?" ... Jesus then took the loaves, gave thanks, and distributed to those who were seated as much as they wanted. He did the same with the fish.*

JOHN 6:9, 11

Jesus multiplies. This account is often referred to as the feeding of the five thousand. However, if you go back and read it, you'll notice that this number only includes the men. There were also women and children present, so there's a good chance it was the feeding of at least twelve thousand. It all begins with the generosity of one young boy. We don't know his name, age, or any other details about him, other than he gave five small barley loaves and two small fish to Jesus. Yet here we are talking about him thousands of years later. You never know what God might do through a simple act of generosity.

When I was young, I received a scholarship to attend youth camp. I was raised by a single mom. Camp was expensive, and it was only through the generosity of someone I didn't know that I got to go. Sitting by a campfire that week, God spoke to me and called me into ministry. I have been a pastor now for over twenty years and have been blessed to see thousands of people come to faith and millions of dollars given to the poor.

The legacy of the boy and the legacy of the one who gave the camp scholarship is one of simple generosity. When we give what we have, Jesus multiplies it into considerably more. What does God want you to give? The legacy of that gift might astound you!

*Today I will remember:*

- We never know what God might do through a simple act of generosity.
- The legacy of a simple gift may be astounding.

*Father, let me give generously, knowing that You will multiply exponentially. You are generous. Make my life reflect Your generosity.*

# THE LEGACY OF SIMON THE CYRENE

*As they were going out, they met a man from Cyrene,*
*named Simon, and they forced him to carry the cross.*
MATTHEW 27:32

I believe the Bible is true in part because of the details it provides: who was ruling at the time, where an event took place, what time of day it happened, and other specifics. Our verse today, for example, tells us that Simon, who was drafted to help carry the cross of Christ, was from Cyrene, a city in North Africa (in modern-day Libya).

Many travel to Jerusalem to walk this path of Jesus known as the Via Dolorosa, which is Latin for "Way of Suffering." There are fourteen stations on the path, starting with where Jesus was condemned by Pilate and ending at the presumed location of His tomb. As Jesus walked this way of suffering, Roman soldiers grabbed this man, Simon, and had him carry the cross. As I've walked this path, I have often wondered what Simon was thinking. Had he heard of Jesus? Was he a distant follower? Did he have any idea how big this moment was?

Helping Jesus accomplish His mission is Simon's legacy. Jesus was born to die on an old rugged cross to pay the penalty of your sin and mine. Simon helped Him get there. I want to help fulfill the mission of Jesus too. He calls us to live for something greater than ourselves and to join Him in ushering in the love, mercy, grace, and truth of His kingdom. This is a legacy that will last forever.

*Today I will remember:*

- I have a part to play in the mission of Jesus.
- I, too, carry a cross each day to die to myself and live for Him.

*Father, give me wisdom to do my part. I choose*
*to partner with You today to bring love, mercy,*
*grace, and truth to a world that desperately needs it.*

# THE LEGACY OF JOB

*As you know, we count as blessed those who have persevered. You have heard of Job's perseverance and have seen what the Lord finally brought about. The Lord is full of compassion and mercy.*

JAMES 5:11

Job's life was characterized by faithfulness and perseverance amid tremendous suffering. Job continued to trust God even when he lost his wealth, health, and family. His story asks the question of why the righteous suffer. It also shows his questioning of God, praying out his frustrations, and yet choosing to continue walking by faith. Although, in the end, he is blessed tremendously, his life included a long road of suffering.

If you're suffering right now, some of what I'm about to share may seem trite and emotionally unsatisfying. If that's you, I get it. I've been there. Theology, at times, is more interesting than comforting. But when we really begin to understand it and rest in it, the comfort starts to flow. So when you don't understand what God is doing, trust His heart.

God is infinite. He knows all things. He can see what we can't see, He knows what we don't know, and we can trust Him. While we can be tempted to shake our little bitty fists in the face of an almighty God who loves us, remember that it's OK to pray out your frustrations. He understands. But it's not OK to walk away. Choose to grow through whatever you're going through. Feelings aren't facts. Your loving Heavenly Father is still there. Walk on with Him.

*Today I will remember:*

- I will pray out my frustrations and stay with God.
- Feelings aren't facts, and God is still there.

*Lord, there are many times I don't understand what's happening, but I choose to trust Your heart. Help me to push through and persevere.*

# THE LEGACY OF SAMSON

*One day Samson went to Gaza, where he saw a prostitute. He went in to spend the night with her.*

JUDGES 16:1

The journey into darkness is a path, not a light switch. Nobody wakes up one day and decides to blow up his life, ruin his marriage and reputation with his kids, and destroy his legacy. The bombs that blow up people's lives start with a fuse that was lit dozens of decisions earlier. This is the story of many a man. This is the story of Samson.

God made Samson a superhero. He was blessed with supernatural strength. Judges 15:15 says that on one occasion he killed a thousand Philistines with the jawbone of a donkey. Samson was strong physically, but weak in mind and character. Our verse is just another link in the chain of his demise. One compromise after another. Each step down a disobedient path. He is eventually enslaved by the very enemy that he so easily had defeated. The Philistines plucked out his eyes, but he had been blind with lust most of his life. He chose a prostitute over the power of God.

God would grant Samson mercy, but his life is a sad legacy of foolishness. He wasted an amazing gift from God because of his lusts. What a travesty! So let's choose to guard our hearts and watch our steps. Be careful of little compromises. Our legacies are determined decision by decision and step by step.

*Today I will remember:*

- The journey into darkness is a path, not a light switch.
- Legacies are determined decision by decision and step by step.

*Father, help me to guard my steps each day and walk the road You have for me. The little choices matter. Protect me from the temptation of little compromises.*

# THE LEGACY OF PETER

*Then Peter stood up with the Eleven, raised his voice and addressed the crowd: "Fellow Jews and all of you who live in Jerusalem, let me explain this to you; listen carefully to what I say."*

ACTS 2:14

I love the apostle Peter. I relate to him in so many ways. If you read the biographies of Jesus in the New Testament—Matthew, Mark, Luke, and John—it seems that Peter has foot in mouth disease. He's constantly saying the wrong thing at the wrong time. He's reckless and impulsive. Yet God does amazing things in and through his life. Our verse records how Peter starts the sermon that launches the church, with three thousand people receiving Jesus on that day.

Prior to this moment, Peter had denied Jesus not once, not twice, but three times when his Lord was going to the cross. Peter loved Jesus, yet when Jesus needed him most, this wavering disciple abandoned Him. It seemed at that moment that his legacy would be one of denial and failure. God, however, had something else in mind. Jesus rose from the dead, conquering death, hell, and the grave. He appeared many times to Peter and the other disciples after the resurrection and in His grace restored their friendship and Peter's place of leadership.

Your legacy is not established. How do I know? You're still breathing. God is not done with you. He still has a purpose for your life. If you have fallen, choose to get back up and walk on!

*Today I will remember:*

- Saints are just sinners who fall and choose to get back up.
- God is not done with me yet.
- He calls me to move forward with Him.

*Jesus, I choose today to get up and walk on with You. Thank You for forgiveness and grace. Even when I fall, help me get back up and continue on in faith.*

# THE LEGACY OF BARNABAS

*But Barnabas took him and brought him to the apostles. He told them how Saul on his journey had seen the Lord and that the Lord had spoken to him, and how in Damascus he had preached fearlessly in the name of Jesus.*

ACTS 9:27

Barnabas is one of the unsung heroes of the New Testament. His name means "son of encouragement," and he lived up to his name. His actual name was Joseph, a Levite from Cyprus. He's mentioned here and there in the Scriptures, but his fingerprints are everywhere.

Look again at our verse. Saul was a Christian killer who became a Christian. He would go on to become the apostle Paul, write much of the New Testament, and take the gospel to the Gentile world. Here's my point: no Barnabas, no apostle Paul. When Saul converted, no one believed him. People thought he was pulling a fast one, spying on them to destroy them. But Barnabas stood in the gap and vouched for Saul, who would become the apostle Paul, who would go on to change the world.

The church needs more people like Barnabas. We are quick to judge, and he was quick to encourage. Barnabas was full of grace and knew that the power of God changes people's lives. He was a behind the scenes champion who changed the world through his optimism and belief in the new life found in Christ. Who needs encouragement from you today? Let's carry on the legacy of Barnabas.

*Today I will remember:*

- A word of courage can change people's lives.
- Everyone needs encouragement.

*Father, thank You for men like Barnabas.*
*Help me to encourage others.*

# THE LEGACY OF JETHRO

*Jethro was delighted to hear about all the good things the Lord had done for Israel in rescuing them from the hand of the Egyptians. He said, "Praise be to the Lord, who rescued you from the hand of the Egyptians and of Pharaoh, and who rescued the people from the hand of the Egyptians. Now I know that the Lord is greater than all other gods, for he did this to those who had treated Israel arrogantly."*

EXODUS 18:9-11

Jethro, Moses' father-in-law, was a source of encouragement and wisdom. Moses married Jethro's daughter Zipporah. A Midianite, Jethro served his gods and his people as a priest. Yet when he hears of all that God has done for the Israelites, he puts his faith in the Lord God. He's a supportive father-in-law, a priest from another faith who converts to worshiping Yahweh, and a model of wisdom for Moses. While lots of people believe that all in-laws are a pain, it isn't necessarily so.

With two boys, most likely I'll be a father-in-law one of these days. I'm praying that regardless of our differences, I will be a source of encouragement and wisdom for them. Let's bust the negative generalizations of in-law relationships. Let's learn to keep our mouths shut in wisdom and speak with humility at the right times. Moses was blessed by Jethro, and Jethro in turn was blessed by Moses. Be the father-in-law or son-in-law that you would like to have. Your sons, daughters, and wife will be grateful. Your grandchildren will be, too.

*Today I will remember:*

- I should be an in-law of blessing.
- My children are blessed when I choose to bless those they love.

*Lord, thank You for the example of Jethro. Give me wisdom to be a blessing to my in-laws and the grace to love them well.*

# THE LEGACY OF PONTIUS PILATE

*When Pilate saw that he was getting nowhere, but that instead an uproar was starting, he took water and washed his hands in front of the crowd. "I am innocent of this man's blood," he said. "It is your responsibility!" All the people answered, "His blood is on us and on our children!"*

MATTHEW 27:24-25

Pontius Pilate governed Judea under Emperor Tiberius. He was responsible for maintaining order and upholding Roman law. Historical sources outside the Bible, including Josephus and Tacitus, report that at times he used excessive force to suppress dissent. Of course, Pilate is most known for his role in the crucifixion of Jesus.

Our verses describe his craven abdication of leadership. Pilate says that he is not responsible, and yet this cosmic injustice is his responsibility. Pilate handed over Jesus to be flogged and crucified; humanly speaking, only he possessed the power to do so. Instead of going with his conscience (he earlier had stated, "I find no fault with this man"), he goes with the crowd. In Matthew 27:19, we learn that his wife had had a terrible dream and sent Pilate a message to have nothing to do with Jesus. Despite all this, Pilate gives in. This is his legacy.

There will be times when we know the right thing to do, but doing so will require going against the crowd. Will we have the requisite wisdom and courage in those moments? Let's live as men of conviction, not as men of the crowd.

*Today I will remember:*

- I must listen to my conscience.
- This means living by my personal convictions and not the fickle opinions of the crowd.

*Holy Spirit, make me sensitive to Your leadership. Let me follow You over the crowd. Give me strength to do what's right even when all others are doing wrong.*

# THE LEGACY OF THOMAS

*Then he said to Thomas, "Put your finger here; see my hands. Reach out your hand and put it into my side. Stop doubting and believe." Thomas said to him, "My Lord and my God!"*

JOHN 20:27-28

After Jesus is resurrected, the apostle Thomas famously says in John 20:25, "Unless I see the nail marks in his hands and put my finger where the nails were, and put my hand into his side, I will not believe."

Before we get too critical of "Doubting Thomas," let's put our feet in his shoes. Jesus was crucified. He was dead. Talk of resurrection is something to be skeptical about. I love how the Lord responds in our verses. Read them again. Jesus knew exactly what Thomas had said and met him right at the place of his doubts.

Doubt is a prerequisite for faith. You cannot have one without the other. Real faith is simply believing more than you doubt. It's based on convincing evidence without conclusive proof. I believe in the resurrection of Jesus because of the evidence. One day, I too will see the nail-scarred hands and the side that was pierced. In that moment, faith will no longer be necessary because I'll have proof. In the meantime, I'll go with the evidence. Thomas would go on to be a missionary to India. He would be martyred there for his testimony that he had seen the risen Jesus.

*Today I will remember:*

- Faith is about convincing evidence without conclusive proof.
- Doubt is a prerequisite to faith.

*Lord, I believe, and I doubt. Help me to walk this journey of faith with You as I examine the convincing evidence of Jesus.*

# THE LEGACY OF ESTHER

*"For if you remain silent at this time, relief and deliverance for the Jews will arise from another place, but you and your father's family will perish. And who knows but that you have come to your royal position for such a time as this?"*

ESTHER 4:14

If you've never read the account of Esther, I encourage you to do so. It's an amazing story of God's providence, and the twists and turns in the stranger-than-fiction account of Esther make for an amazing page-turner. Read it in one sitting; you'll be glad you did. One of the amazing things about the account is that God is never mentioned, yet you see Him working behind the scenes all the way through.

The legacy of Esther is one of wisdom and courage. In our verses for today, Esther's Uncle Mordecai is challenging her to seize her moment of destiny. God has put her in a place to influence the king to rescue the Jewish people. As always, God is the hero. Esther plays a part.

God places you and me in places of destiny each day. We must recognize and seize this reality. While the lives of an entire people group may not be on the line for us, individual lives certainly are. It could be that He has put you in the path of lost people all around you. You never know what God might do through an intentional friendship, an invitation to a church service, or even a kind word at the right time. God has placed you in various spaces "for such a time as this."

*Today I will remember:*

- God is always working behind the scenes.
- He has me where I am and doing what I'm doing for a reason.

*Father, give me eyes to see where You're working so that I might work with You. Help me to bloom where You've planted me for Your purposes.*

# THE LEGACY OF JONAH

*But to Jonah this seemed very wrong, and he became angry.
He prayed to the Lord, "Isn't this what I said, Lord,
when I was still at home? That is what I tried to forestall
by fleeing to Tarshish. I knew that you are a gracious
and compassionate God, slow to anger and abounding in love,
a God who relents from sending calamity. Now, Lord,
take away my life, for it is better for me to die than to live."*

JONAH 4:1-3

God tells Jonah to go preach repentance in Nineveh. Jonah instead boards a ship and heads in the opposite direction. A storm comes up and is about to capsize the ship. Jonah tells the sailors that he's the problem, they throw him overboard, and he is swallowed by a great fish. The next three days, he's being slowly digested. Of course his prayer life increases substantially. He is now ready to do whatever God says.

Here's the question, why doesn't he want to go to Nineveh? The blunt answer: he's bigoted and hates the Ninevites. As sad as it is, this is his legacy. He is a man filled with racism.

Jonah is angry because God doesn't destroy the city. The people receive the message, repent from their evil, and turn to God. Most missionaries would be ecstatic, but Jonah is furious. He wanted them to be destroyed, and he is mad at God because God is gracious and compassionate. So mad that he wants to die. That's some serious hatred. The book ends revealing the dark heart of Jonah and the amazing grace of God.

*Today I will remember:*

- God's grace is offered to everyone who will receive it.
- He is slow to anger and abounding in love.

*Father, may my heart reflect Yours. Cleanse me
from any bigotry. I pray Your grace over all peoples
and desire that everyone would come to repentance.*

# THE LEGACY OF THE CENTURION

*The centurion replied, "Lord, I do not deserve to have you come under my roof. But just say the word, and my servant will be healed. For I myself am a man under authority, with soldiers under me. I tell this one, 'Go,' and he goes; and that one, 'Come,' and he comes. I say to my servant, 'Do this,' and he does it." When Jesus heard this, he was amazed and said to those following him, "Truly I tell you, I have not found anyone in Israel with such great faith."*

MATTHEW 8:8-10

The centurion was a professional officer who would have commanded a *centuria*, which was typically eighty to a hundred soldiers. Centurions were the backbone of the Roman military and were responsible for disciplining, training, and leading troops into battle. Centurions led from the front and demanded loyalty and respect. This one is known for his compassion for his servant and for his faith. Faith to the extent that Jesus was amazed by it!

He recognized Jesus' authority over creation and His power to heal. The root of the word *authority* is "author." The centurion sees Jesus for who He is, the author of all things. In other words, this soldier recognizes Jesus' rank. This gentile Roman soldier believed in Jesus more than the Israelites who were waiting for the coming Messiah.

Do we recognize Jesus as the King of kings and the Lord of lords who loves us and has power over all things? Do we recognize His authority? If you are a follower of Jesus, then you are a man who serves the author of life.

*Today I will remember:*

- Jesus is all powerful and loves me.
- I serve the author of life and humbly walk under His authority.

*Jesus, may I see You for who You really are. Let me know Your love for me that I would boldly pray. I choose to practice big faith because You are a big God.*

# THE LEGACY OF ONESIPHORUS

*May the Lord show mercy to the household of Onesiphorus, because he often refreshed me and was not ashamed of my chains. On the contrary, when he was in Rome, he searched hard for me until he found me. May the Lord grant that he will find mercy from the Lord on that day! You know very well in how many ways he helped me in Ephesus.*

2 TIMOTHY 1:16-18

I have a friend in ministry who has written lots of books and, at one time, was the lead pastor of one of the largest churches in America and a highly sought-after conference speaker. Now serving mostly behind the scenes, he mentors younger pastors. Most people in the pews would not know his name, but my guess is their pastors do. His face is not everywhere, but his fingerprints are. His influence is much greater than his fame. I have deep respect for this man. He told me that in all his years of service, these recent ones have been his favorite.

The legacy of Onesiphorus is kind of like that. Most people don't know his name, but they have felt his impact because of his ministry and influence on the apostle Paul. He ministered to Paul while Paul was in prison and helped him in times of need. The fame of his name is not large, but his impact is. Would you rather have great fame, or great impact? I know a few famous people, and fame is not all it's cracked up to be. God doesn't care about us being famous; He cares about us being faithful.

*Today I will remember:*

- Impact and influence are more important than fame and recognition.
- God isn't impressed with fame, but with faithfulness.

*Lord, help me be faithful. Help me to serve*
*Your cause in the world however I can.*
*May my life be marked by faithfulness.*

# THE LEGACY OF PHOEBE

*I commend to you our sister Phoebe, a deacon of the church in Cenchreae. I ask you to receive her in the Lord in a way worthy of his people and to give her any help she may need from you, for she has been the benefactor of many people, including me.*

ROMANS 16:1-2

Phoebe was an influential deacon and generous participant in the early church. She financially supported the apostle Paul and the spread of the gospel. Many scholars believe that Phoebe was entrusted to deliver Paul's letter to the church in Rome. The book of Romans is that letter, and it is considered to be one of the most theologically rich books in all the Bible. If she did, she likely explained Paul's message to the Roman Christians, as letter carriers often served as interpreters. The word *deacon* in Greek is *diakonos,* meaning "servant." Deacons did not necessarily teach, but they served and supported those who did.

In Mark 10, Jesus taught His disciples that serving is the path to greatness. If you want a great legacy, then choose to serve. You can live for yourself and have a small life, or you can live for God in service to others and have a great life.

When I come home each day, my wife Katrina will ask me how my day was. How do we evaluate a day? What determines if it was lousy, fine, good, or great? The Bible teaches that it is great if we choose to serve. Phoebe did just that. She chose to give and to serve. She chose greatness.

*Today I will remember:*

- Greatness is found in serving.
- When I choose to serve my family, my friends, and my church, I am also serving God.
- Great days are full of great service.

*Jesus, thank You for people such as Phoebe,*
*who gave and served to spread Your message.*
*Help me also choose to live a great life each day.*

# THE LEGACY OF TIMOTHY

*Timothy, guard what has been entrusted to your care. Turn away from godless chatter and the opposing ideas of what is falsely called knowledge, which some have professed and in so doing have departed from the faith. Grace be with you all.*

1 TIMOTHY 6:20-21

When Katrina was pregnant with our firstborn, overwhelming waves of responsibility would occasionally wash over me. I had just turned thirty, still felt like a kid, and now I was going to be raising a kid. That son is now a young adult, and I also have a teenager. I'm in my fifties and still feel those waves. The weight of being a husband and father is both a blessing and a burden. God's call on a man's life is to guard and guide those He has entrusted to him.

Timothy was a key disciple, pastor, and companion to the apostle Paul. He played a crucial role in the early Christian church. Paul wrote two letters to Timothy in the New Testament. I have turned to these letters often as Paul speaks courage and gives instruction to a young pastor. I've also turned to these letters for guidance as a father and husband. As you read these letters, it is obvious that Timothy at times felt unworthy and inadequate. If you've ever felt that way, then you are normal. Timothy went on to be a very effective leader. He grew into his calling, and so will you.

*Today I will remember:*

- God calls me to guard and guide those entrusted to my care.
- To feel inadequate is normal.
- Legacy is not about how I feel, but what I choose to do.

*Father, help me to guard and guide well those You have put in my care. It is a blessing and at times a burden, so please give me wisdom and courage. Thank You that You are always with me.*

# THE LEGACY OF CALEB

*Then Caleb silenced the people before Moses and said,*
*"We should go up and take possession of the land, for we can*
*certainly do it." But the men who had gone up with him said,*
*"We can't attack those people; they are stronger than we are."*

NUMBERS 13:30-31

Any time I'm feeling inadequate or intimidated by the challenges of life and leadership, I go back and read the words of Caleb. Caleb is a "can" man. He saw God do miracles and believed that with God anything is possible.

God's people had been delivered from Egyptian bondage. They had witnessed amazing miracles, such as God parting the Red Sea. They saw the physical manifestation of God's presence in a pillar of cloud by day and fire at night. God was leading them across the desert and into the Promised Land. As they are standing on the border of this blessing, they send out twelve spies. Ten come back saying, "There's no way we can cross over." Two come back saying, "Let's trust God and go; He is the way." Caleb is half of the two.

The one who says, "I can" and the one who says "I can't" are both right. I want to be a man who says we *can*, in my own life and in the lives of others. The people, however, decide not to listen to Caleb. Instead of trusting God, they wander around the desert for the next forty years. Fear is a killer, and it screams "can't" to all of us. Eventually, God's people would believe and take possession of the land. Caleb was forty when he first spied it out, and eighty-five when they finally took possession. He always knew they could.

*Today I will remember:*

- The one who says, "I can" and the one who says "I can't" are both right.
- Trusting God is about choosing action and moving forward with Him.

*Lord, thank You for the legacy of Caleb.*
*Forgive me for being negative at times and for*
*not trusting You. Help me be a man of the "can."*

# THE LEGACY OF MARY

*"I am the Lord's servant," Mary answered.*
*"May your word to me be fulfilled." Then the angel left her.*
LUKE 1:38

Mary gave birth to the Savior of the world, and it's the only virgin birth ever recorded in history. She is remembered and honored as the mother of Jesus, holding a unique place in the legacy of Christianity. What impresses me most is her humility and courage.

When the angel tells Mary she is going to be miraculously pregnant, Mary responds with faith. Despite the risk of shame and rejection, she trusts God fully. Knowing she will have to tell Joseph and her family. Knowing that the town she lives in will be full of gossip. Living in the Middle East two thousand years ago, Mary knows she will face significant shame and condemnation. Yet she simply obeys.

This is the call on every Christian man's life, to simply obey. This is what it means to be mature in the faith. Maturity is not measured by your ability to pontificate on the mysteries of unexplainable things. It is measured simply by your obedience, and you never know what God might do through a simple act of obedience. Mary was a young woman, from a small town, seemingly insignificant in every way, but she obeyed God. The Savior of the world would be born. The Messiah, the fulfillment of prophecy, the Anointed One, would be nourished and raised through her obedience. That is a legacy of faith.

*Today I will remember:*

- God does big things through obedience.
- A legacy of faith comes from the simple decision to obey.

*Father, thank You for the faith of Mary.*
*Faith is followed by obedience. May I too live as*
*Your servant and may Your Word be fulfilled in me.*

# THE LEGACY OF JONATHAN

*And Saul's son Jonathan went to David at Horesh and helped him find strength in God. "Don't be afraid," he said. "My father Saul will not lay a hand on you. You will be king over Israel, and I will be second to you. Even my father Saul knows this." The two of them made a covenant before the LORD. Then Jonathan went home, but David remained at Horesh.*

1 SAMUEL 23:16-18

Real friendships can be hard to come by. I'm not talking about guys who are your acquaintances and that you occasionally shoot the proverbial bull with. I'm talking about real friends. Men committed to seeing you fulfill your God-given potential, who are loyal and will love you through thick and thin. This is the type of friend that Jonathan was to David. This is his legacy.

Jonathan's father, Saul, was extremely jealous of David. He knew that David would one day be the king and that this was God's will. Saul tried to murder David, but Jonathan rescued David several times, unashamed in his loyalty. He would speak courage into David and remind him of God's purposes. Their friendship was one of commitment and covenant.

One of the most valuable things in a man's life is the loyalty of a few good friends. Trusted confidants who care more about your future than your feelings. The only way to have this is to be this. Do you have a Jonathan in your life? Are you like Jonathan to someone else? Commit to this. Build a legacy of real friendship.

*Today I will remember:*

- Real friendships require commitment and covenant.
- The only way to have a real friend is to be one.
- A real friend cares more about your future than your feelings.

*Father, please give me a couple of real friends. Men who I fully trust and who will help me through life. Make me this type of friend. May I build a friendship of commitment and covenant.*

# A NO-FIB FUNERAL

*It is better to go to a house of mourning than to go to a house of feasting, for death is the destiny of everyone; the living should take this to heart.*
ECCLESIASTES 7:2

I don't get to do many funerals these days. But any time I have the honor of performing a memorial service, I always share today's verse. Solomon, who is called the wisest man who ever lived, says that attending a funeral is better for us than attending a party. Why? Because we need to remember that one day people will be attending *our* funeral.

Live in such a way that no one has to lie at your funeral. Some of the saddest moments in my pastoral career have been when I've met with family members to plan a memorial service. When I ask them to share good memories of the departed, they can't think of any. It's tragic. On the other hand, some of my greatest moments of laughter and joy have come when the family can't stop talking about the memories, the precious times, and the love they felt and feel for the person who has passed on.

It is good to think about how we will be remembered. This is your one and only life. As others have said, all that matters is God and people. Choose to invest in what matters most. My prayer for you is that you have a no-fib funeral.

*Today I will remember:*
- We should live in such a way that no one must lie at our funeral.
- I will choose to invest my life in the things that matter most.

*Father, help me to live a life of love for You and for other people. Help me be a blessing to my family, friends, and You.*

# August

## FRIENDSHIP

As iron sharpens iron,
so one person sharpens another.
*Proverbs 27:17*

# COMMIT

*A friend loves at all times, and a*
*brother is born for a time of adversity.*
PROVERBS 17:17

Sometimes people get on my nerves. How about you? If I'm honest, I'll admit that sometimes I get on my *own* nerves. Such is life. We all must learn that real friendship requires commitment. True friendships are not about convenience, but a commitment to love at all times. You're not going to have very many friends like that. Partly because men don't do this well and partly because it requires time and energy, and there's only so much of that to go around.

Who are a couple of guys that you can commit to as a true friend? These are men that you choose to regularly spend time with. You choose to work out your differences when they come along, and you stick it out over the long haul. If you have two friends like that over a span of decades, you are very blessed. Most men get irritated and bail easily. If you do that, you'll never have a real friend. You'll just have acquaintances.

Most guys start a friendship over a common bond. Golf, hunting, cigars, fishing, or whatever. But friendship builds the more time you spend together and get to know each other. Inevitably, difficulties will come. It is in those times that a friendship is cemented. Difficulties will change the conversation from hobbies to matters of the heart. You start talking about the real stuff of life. You pray for each other. You become brothers. Friendship like this is part of God's will for all of us.

*Today I will remember:*

- Real friendships require a commitment.
- Inevitably, difficulties will come, and that is when a friendship is cemented.

*Lord, give me the grace to be a real*
*friend in the highs and lows of life.*
*I choose to commit to a few friendships.*

# CAREFUL WHO YOU LISTEN TO

*If your very own brother, or your son or daughter,*
*or the wife you love, or your closest friend secretly entices*
*you, saying, "Let us go and worship other gods" (gods that*
*neither you nor your ancestors have known, gods of the*
*peoples around you, whether near or far, from one end of the*
*land to the other), do not yield to them or listen to them.*

DEUTERONOMY 13:6-8

We become like those we hang out with. It is right and good to be friends with people outside the faith, with the goal of seeing them come to know Jesus. At the same time, we must be careful who we listen to. Any time we're in a conversation, reading a book, or watching television, let's be aware of what we're taking in, and choose to leave some things out. I used to naively assume the author of anything I read knew what he was talking about. But now I know that media of all kinds are full of false information. When we watch, read, or listen, let's learn to take in the meat of the good things and spit out the bones of the bad. We must be careful who we choose to listen to.

This is true in our friendships and families as well. Just because Mama said it don't make it true. Run things through the Bible. Not "What do my friends and family say?" but "What does the Bible say?" God's will is found in God's Word. Everything else is opinion. Be intentional with what you take in and who you listen to.

*Today I will remember:*

- I must be careful who I listen to.
- I become like those I spend time with.

*Father, help me to listen with discernment*
*and wisdom. May I know Your Word, so that*
*I might filter things well and walk in truth.*

# STAY AWAKE

*When he came back, he again found them sleeping, because their eyes were heavy.*

MATTHEW 26:43

Has a friend ever disappointed you? You trusted, needed, and had reasonable expectations of this person, and he let you down. Yeah, me too. Welcome to the disappointment of humanity. Every relationship you ever have will have disappointments. At some point, you will hurt the other person. At some point, he will hurt you. In today's verse, Jesus is at the most difficult crossroad of His life. He'll soon be going to the cross. The Bible says that He is sorrowful, even to the point of death. His heart is breaking. All He asks of His closest friends is that they sit with Him and pray. What do they do? They fall asleep.

What do we do when our friends disappoint? It's not a matter of if but when. We all must learn forgiveness. We must learn to ask for it and to give it. If we don't, we'll never have real friends. True friendship requires a commitment to work through difficult times. Far too many of us give up too easily. We're quick to write someone off if he hurts us. Or we choose to stay on the surface of things. We talk about trivial things, but never real life. What would it mean to awaken to a real friendship? To commit ourselves to some other guys to be brothers, come what may? True friendship is not for the weak, but the strong. Who do you need to forgive? Who do you need to ask forgiveness from? Forgiveness is part of friendship.

*Today I will remember:*

- True friendship is not for the weak, but the strong.
- Far too many of us give up too easily.

*Lord, help me to be a better friend. Let me be quick to forgive and quick to apologize. Teach me real friendship.*

# BECOMING ONE

*"My prayer is not for them alone. I pray also for those who will believe in me through their message, that all of them may be one, Father, just as you are in me and I am in you. May they also be in us so that the world may believe that you have sent me."*

JOHN 17:20-21

There was diversity in the small group of disciples. Many believe that prior to following Jesus, Simon the Zealot was part of a group known as the knife-wielding "dagger men" or the Sicarii. They were passionately opposed to Roman rule over the Jews and would stab their oppressors. The title of the movie *Sicario*, about a Mexican assassin, comes from them.

Matthew the tax collector, however, worked for the Romans. Prior to following Jesus, he collected taxes from his fellow Jews, would add his own fees to the collection, and got rich serving the enemy. This would be like a Jew collecting taxes for the Nazis during World War II and getting wealthy off it.

These guys would have been mortal enemies. Yet Jesus chose them for His close group of disciples; in time, they became friends. I often wonder if Jesus had to break up an occasional altercation. Becoming one is His prayer in our verses today. Oneness is about a group of people who have individually decided to put Jesus on the throne of their hearts. The group is unified in its allegiance to Him first. Jesus prays for this type of unity, and it changes everything.

*Today I will remember:*

- My allegiance is to Jesus first.
- Oneness is about a group of people who have individually decided to put Jesus on the throne of their hearts.

*Jesus, I too pray that all believers would be one and unified in You. Help me to keep You, and You alone, on the throne of my heart.*

# STAY SHARP

*As iron sharpens iron,*
*so one person sharpens another.*
PROVERBS 27:17

Proverbs is full of advice that has stood the test of time. The book has thirty-one chapters, so I read the chapter that coincides with the day of the month I'm in and mark what stands out to me. I don't want to be foolish, so I read Proverbs. Today's counsel is about the importance of having men in our lives who can sharpen us.

Sharpening only emerges from real conversation. Iron must strike iron. There will be good questions, disagreement, challenges, and healthy confrontation in real conversations. When iron strikes iron, there will be sparks. Do you have any men in your life who are allowed to challenge you? To question you? To disagree with you? If not, then you're probably dull. You've most likely stopped growing. To grow, you must get uncomfortable. You must move beyond just talking about sports to talking about your real life. It can be a bit awkward, and you'll have to set aside your pride, but it's the only way to stay sharp.

Here's one other thing to consider. A great temptation is to just hang around men who think like us, look like us, feel like us, and act like us. That too can be a dull environment where there's not much sharpening going on. A sharpening environment is a diverse one. Diversity helps us see what we can't see. A healthy, diverse environment encourages growth. Diversity can mean different ages, different cultural backgrounds, or just men who think differently. Who do you need in your life to stay sharp? How can you help sharpen others?

*Today I will remember:*
- Real conversations about real life help keep me sharp.
- Iron must strike iron.
- Real conversations will have good questions, disagreement, challenges, and healthy confrontation.

*God, help me to find some men that I can*
*sharpen and that will help sharpen me.*

# THE POWER OF A FRIEND'S PRESENCE

*Then he said to them, "My soul is overwhelmed with sorrow to the point of death. Stay here and keep watch with me."*

MATTHEW 26:38

If you've ever been heartbroken, deeply sad, or troubled to the point of hardly being able to function, then know that Jesus understands. In the Garden of Gethsemane, Jesus was so overwhelmed with the knowledge of going to the cross that His sorrow was deadly. It wasn't the physical suffering to come that was breaking Him. It was the reality of being separated from the Father and bearing the sin of the world. Jesus is sorrowful to the core of His being and all He wants is for His friends to sit and pray with Him.

When a friend is going through a difficult time and you don't know what to say, don't say anything. Just sitting and being there is real love and true friendship. Placing your hand on his shoulder and praying is what is needed. Silence and presence are best in those moments.

I sometimes feel alone. Sometimes there are moments as a husband, father, and leader when no one around me understands the burden I carry. I try to explain it to my wife, but she doesn't understand—nor should I expect her to. It's not her burden; it's mine. Men often share common burdens. When a brother is experiencing a dark night of the soul, the best we can do is just sit with him. Having a friend just be there in a time of distress brings comfort and strength. Jesus knows in a much more profound way what it is to carry a burden alone. He understands.

*Today I will remember:*

- When a friend is hurting, my presence and silence are enough.
- To just sit and be there is real love and true friendship.

*Jesus, thank You for carrying the burden of the cross. When I feel like no one understands or relates to my difficult times, I know You do. I'm never alone. Thank You.*

# A FRIEND'S PRAYER

*Dear friend, I pray that you may enjoy good health and that all may go well with you, even as your soul is getting along well.*

3 JOHN 2

Years ago after a church service, Paul asked if I liked Cajun food and wanted to grab lunch with him. I do and we did, and Paul has become one of my closest friends. We meet most Fridays for lunch, perhaps enjoying a cigar afterwards, or maybe riding our Harleys. Paul is a former counselor. If you've ever seen the movie *Good Will Hunting*, you'll understand when I say he's the Robin Williams character in my life. I'm grateful for our friendship and for the regular sounding board he has been. Paul helps me see things I otherwise can't see.

Every Saturday morning, I receive the same text from Paul. Usually around eight in the morning my phone will buzz, and I'll get a text: "Praying for you, Chad." That's it. I used to think he meant he was praying for me about the sermon I would preach that weekend. We have Saturday and Sunday services in our church, so I always assumed he was praying over my final preparation and delivery. People pray for their pastors. But he is not praying for his pastor on those days; he is just praying for me. I can't put into words how much the consistent prayers of a friend mean to me. And he doesn't just keep it between him and God. He encourages me every week at the same time, letting me know I'm prayed for. Who is someone you can pray for consistently? Do it regularly and let him or her know you are doing it. That's friendship.

*Today I will remember:*

- I can find someone to pray for.
- I can pray for him regularly and let him know about it.
- Consistent prayer is caring for a friend.

*Father, thank You for friendship. Please put someone on my heart who You want me to pray for consistently.*

# WHAT FRIENDS DO

*And we urge you, brothers and sisters, warn those who are idle and disruptive, encourage the disheartened, help the weak, be patient with everyone.*

1 THESSALONIANS 5:14

We all need friends. I don't just mean guys who talk with us about the game or offer the obligatory "What's up?" when we go down the hall. We all need other men who help us become better men. We not only need that, but we all need to be that for someone else. But men usually suck at friendship. I don't know that we know how to be friends. We all want it, but most of us don't know how to do it. Fortunately, our verse gives some direction. What do real friends do? Four things are listed in the verse. Let's break it down.

1. True friends care more about our futures than they do our feelings. They love us enough to warn us when they see us going down the wrong path.
2. Friends also encourage. We don't just need guys who will kick our butts when we're being stupid. We also need men who encourage us when we're feeling weak.
3. Friends help friends. There is an exchange of giving and serving in true friendship. We meet needs when others need our help.
4. Lastly, friends are patient with one another. Any true friend will eventually bug you or hurt you. You'll find him irritating at times. When he hurts you, you will question the friendship. This is normal. Real friendships require patience because human beings are involved, and human beings make mistakes.

Bottom line, friendships require time and commitment, and we all need a couple of real friends.

*Today I will remember:*

- Friends warn, encourage, help, and show patience with one another.
- True friends care more about our futures than they do our feelings.

*Lord, help me to make friends and to be a good friend. This is an important part of Your will for me.*

# HELP BEAR THE BURDEN

*Carry each other's burdens, and in*
*this way, you will fulfill the law of Christ.*
GALATIANS 6:2

Years ago, my marriage was falling apart. A friend named Chris asked me if I wanted to get out of the house and play a round of golf. I'm not a golfer and would have rather stayed home and wallowed in a pity party, but I said yes. On the ninth hole, I fell apart. I collapsed on the green and started to cry. We were a foursome, and the other two guys were strangers. My buddy came over and picked me up, looked at them, and said, "He's having a bad day," and walked me back to the cart. I was so embarrassed. I apologized, but Chris said he was proud that I made it nine holes. He was helping me carry the burden.

Many people gave me marriage books and offered advice. They meant well and thought they were helping, but I didn't need advice. I needed the love and presence of friends. Sometimes the most spiritual thing you can do is shut your mouth and just be there. You need not have an answer. You just say, "This really sucks, and I love you."

Over twenty years have passed. My wife and I are still married and are doing great. I don't remember any of the advice that my friends gave me during that season. But I do remember those who were simply there for me. That is enough.

*Today I will remember:*

- To carry a burden with someone is to be a listening presence.
- Sometimes the most spiritual thing I do is shut my mouth and just be there.

*Father, help me to love my friends well.*
*Especially in difficult times. Help me*
*simply be a strong and stable presence.*

# A FRIEND OF GOD

*The LORD would speak to Moses face to face, as one speaks to a friend.*

EXODUS 33:11

If you read the book of Exodus, you'll see that the people had seen God do miraculous works through Moses. They saw the Red Sea part when he lifted his staff, they saw the plagues that God brought on Egypt so they would be set free, they saw Moses go up a mountainside to meet with God, and when he came down forty days later, his face glowed from the glory he had witnessed. The people knew God was with Moses. In this amazing verse, we learn that Moses would meet with God for the purpose of simply talking with Him.

To speak with God as one speaks to a friend would be terrific and terrifying all at the same time. Terrific because the ruler of the universe cared about you enough to have a conversation. He trusted you with His friendship and presence. What an honor! At the same time, it would be terrifying to be face to face with infinite, awesome power. You would be as reverent and respectful as humanly possible. The sheer magnitude of the moment would require it.

The Bible teaches that through our faith in Jesus, we too can speak to God. Not just as a friend, but as a Father (Romans 8:15). In fact, we have in us the same Spirit Jesus had, the Holy Spirit. God wants to be close to you, and I encourage you to speak with Him today. Share what's on your heart the way a boy would talk to his dad. There's honor, reverence, and intimacy. Be quiet and listen to Him. As things come to mind in that quiet, talk to Him about them. His Spirit will connect with your spirit.

*Today I will remember:*

- I can talk to God as a boy talks to his dad.
- There's honor, reverence, and intimacy.

*Father, I want to have conversations with You. Please give me wisdom to know Your voice and to talk with You about everything.*

# A FRIEND OF JESUS

*"I no longer call you servants, because a servant does not know his master's business. Instead, I have called you friends, for everything that I learned from my Father I have made known to you."*

JOHN 15:15

I recently watched a video in which the host was randomly asking people on the street, "Who is Jesus?" The answers were all over the place. One said, "That dude in the Bible"; another responded, "My Savior"; and then another said, "Oh! He's the guy that cuts my lawn." How about you? Who would you say Jesus is? Perhaps the best answer was from a five-year-old boy: "Jesus is my friend."

Jesus wants to be your friend. While we see Him in different ways because of movies, paintings, and church culture, the reality is that He meets us where we are. God left heaven, wrapped Himself up in flesh, and walked among us. That's not a power move but a relational one. God wants people to know Him and to be close to Him, and He has revealed Himself in Jesus. If you want to know what God is like, then look to Jesus. To know Jesus is to know God. Talk to Jesus as you would a friend today. Yes, we are His servants, and He is Lord, but He wants the relationship to be closer than that. He calls you a friend.

*Today I will remember:*

- If I want to know what God is like, I will look to Jesus.
- God left heaven, wrapped Himself up in flesh, and walked among us.
- That's not a power move but a relational one.

*Jesus, thank You for all that You have done so that I might know You. Help me to walk and talk with You as a friend.*

# A FRIEND OF SINNERS

*All the people saw this and began to mutter,*
*"He has gone to be the guest of a sinner."*
LUKE 19:7

Of all the things for which the religious criticized Jesus, the most common one was that He was a "friend of sinners." I often wonder what the problem was. After all, if you can't be a friend of a sinner, you can't have any friends. You can't even be friends with yourself. The irony is that the only one in history who was sinless intentionally befriended sinners. Further, Jesus seemed to go out of His way to eat with the obvious kind of sinners. I'm so glad He did.

In the church in which I grew up, I was taught that people in the world were the enemy. But that is not how Jesus lived. He spent time with people who were far from God and who thought they could never be good enough for God. People outside the church are not the enemy; they're the mission. We are to impact the world with the love of God. If you're going to make an impact, then you must have contact. Our closest friends ought to be fellow brothers in Christ, but we also need friends in that outer circle who don't know Jesus yet. You can be friends with obvious sinners and not sin. Jesus did it all the time. Be wise, don't go in environments where you are weak, but hang out with people outside the faith. Religious people might criticize you, but this puts you in good company. The company of Jesus.

*Today I will remember:*

- If I'm going to make an impact, I must have contact.
- Jesus intentionally spent time with people who were far from God and thought they could never be good enough for God.

*Holy Spirit, please guide me in making*
*some friends who don't know Jesus.*

# ABRAHAM AND LOT

*When Abram heard that his relative had been taken captive, he called out the 318 trained men born in his household and went in pursuit as far as Dan. During the night Abram divided his men to attack them and he routed them, pursuing them as far as Hobah, north of Damascus. He recovered all the goods and brought back his relative Lot and his possessions, together with the women and the other people.*

GENESIS 14:14-16

Abraham is Lot's uncle and a good friend. Lot is in trouble, so Abraham puts together this team of trained men and goes and rescues him. Friends do not sit idly by when their friends are in trouble. A godly man chooses action to help his friends and come to the rescue. There is nothing more powerful and affirming than knowing you're not alone. That you have friends who will have your back and come to your aid when you need it.

At one time in my life, everything was falling apart. My marriage was struggling, things were difficult at work, and on top of that, the housing market crashed. I was upside down in almost every category of life. I was desperate. When you're in survival mode, things slip, such as your yard or the aesthetics of your home; you're just surviving. My friends didn't know what to do for me, so you know what they did? Something. They gathered, cleaned up my yard, and let me know that I was not alone. That's friendship. Who needs your help? Grab some guys and do something.

*Today I will remember:*

- When you don't know what to do, do something.
- There is nothing more powerful and affirming than showing someone that he is not alone.

*Lord, help me to be a friend who chooses action when my friends are hurting or in trouble. Forgive me for apathy at times. Let me be a man who takes action on behalf of my friends.*

# AQUILA AND PRISCILLA

*Then Paul left Athens and went to Corinth. There he became acquainted with a Jew named Aquila, born in Pontus, who had recently arrived from Italy with his wife, Priscilla. They had left Italy when Claudius Caesar deported all Jews from Rome. Paul lived and worked with them, for they were tentmakers just as he was.*

ACTS 18:1-3 (NLT)

Aquila and Priscilla were not only married but were partners in business and ministry. In their extensive travels throughout the Roman Empire, they made disciples and supported ministry in Rome, Corinth, and Ephesus. They were heroes behind the scenes, but heroes, nonetheless. Their marriage was strong, and their friendship ran deep.

I hope your wife is your closest friend. We need male friends for sure, but we should be closest to our wives. Our male friends are there, among other reasons, to support us in this most important of friendships. This is why they stand with us when we get married. Do you see your wife as your partner? This is God's will. She is not there to support your life; she is there as an equal partner in the building of your lives together. Have a few very close male friends, but make your closest friend your wife.

*Today I will remember:*

- I should have close male friends, but my wife should be my closest friend.
- She is an equal partner in the building of our lives together.

*Father, thank You for my wife and for how she differs from me. She is the partner You gave me. You knew what I needed. Of all my friends, she is the most treasured.*

# BE THE ONE

*My friends and companions avoid me because of my wounds; my neighbors stay far away.*

PSALM 38:11

Everything was falling apart for a man in my church. There were financial troubles, marital troubles, and sickness. No one wanted to hang around him because he was no longer fun. He only talked about his troubles because troubles were all he had. In my office, he broke into a full episode of sobs. He was lonely and broken. His friends had abandoned him.

Do you know anyone like that right now? Someone who is going through all kinds of difficulties? Friendship is not just about fun. Instead of avoiding these people, draw near to them. If there was ever a time they needed a friend, it's now. Be the one. I am grateful that Jesus is long-suffering. He sticks with me when I'm a disappointing bummer. He loves me through thick and thin. Be the kind of friend who stays when the going gets rough.

Maybe you're the one who feels abandoned. If so, I want to encourage you to choose not to be alone. Set a meeting with a pastor. Tell your friends you need them; they may not know. See a counselor. Get some coaching. Seek help and receive it when it comes. That's not weak; it's right and good.

*Today I will remember:*

- Friendship is not just about fun.
- I should be the kind of friend who stays when the going gets rough.
- I can be the one.

*Lord, thank You that You*
*will never leave me nor forsake me.*
*Help me be the kind of friend You are to me.*

# BETRAYAL OF A FRIEND

*But even as Jesus said this, a crowd approached, led by Judas, one of the twelve disciples. Judas walked over to Jesus to greet him with a kiss. But Jesus said, "Judas, would you betray the Son of Man with a kiss?"*

LUKE 22:47-48 (NLT)

There is nothing that stings quite so much as betrayal. Especially when it's someone you are close to. It breaks the heart and can leave lifelong scars. What do we do when a friend betrays us? Do we go on a rampage like Clint Eastwood in the movie *Unforgiven*? That's probably what we feel like doing. Jesus was betrayed by one of His disciples. To make matters worse, it came with a kiss.

The path to healing from the wounds of betrayal is filled not with revenge, but with forgiveness. Revenge never fully satisfies. It may feel good for a moment, but it does not repair the damage. In fact, it adds to it. The way of forgiveness is the way of Jesus, the only path to real freedom. To forgive is to cancel a debt. As Jesus said, "Forgive us our debts as we also have forgiven our debtors." The friend who betrayed you owes you. But to forgive is to say, "You don't owe me. I'm moving on and closing the account." This does not necessarily mean the restoration of the friendship. But it does mean the restoration of your freedom.

*Today I will remember:*

- Forgiveness is the way of Jesus and the path to freedom.
- To forgive is to cancel a debt.

*Lord, You have forgiven me.*
*May Your power flow through me so that*
*I might forgive others. Your way is always best.*

# BEWARE OF JEALOUSY

*When the victorious Israelite army was returning home after David had killed the Philistine, women from all the towns of Israel came out to meet King Saul. They sang and danced for joy with tambourines and cymbals. This was their song: "Saul has killed his thousands, and David his ten thousands!" This made Saul very angry. "What's this?" he said. "They credit David with ten thousands and me with only thousands. Next they'll be making him their king!" So from that time on Saul kept a jealous eye on David.*

1 SAMUEL 18:6-9 (NLT)

One of the questions I must ask myself anytime I read this account in the Bible is whether I can celebrate the success of others. Do I really celebrate my friends' successes? Or do I just give lip service while I secretly stew in jealousy? Sinful jealousy is the mother of resentment, and she is an unrelenting witch who will kill gratitude and contentment in your life. Beware the witch of jealousy!

Saul is not known for his graciousness and celebration of what God was doing for the good of the kingdom. Rather, Saul's jealousy drove him mad. He would hunt David down and try to kill him. Concerned with keeping his crown, Saul didn't care what God was doing. At the end of the day, jealousy is not between us and the other person; it's between us and God. When we're jealous, we believe that God owes us what He has decided to give someone else. This is the thief of joy. The fastest way to kill the witch is to be grateful. What are you grateful for? Stew on that instead.

*Today I will remember:*

- Sinful jealousy is the mother of resentment, and she is an unrelenting witch who will kill your gratitude and contentment.
- I will focus on the things I am grateful for.

*God, forgive me for my jealousy at times.*
*Ultimately that's an issue between*
*You and me. You have been so good to me.*
*Help me to stew on what I am grateful for.*

# DAVID AND JONATHAN

*And Jonathan made a covenant with David because he loved him as himself. Jonathan took off the robe he was wearing and gave it to David, along with his tunic, and even his sword, his bow and his belt.*

1 SAMUEL 18:3-4

Have you ever just connected naturally with someone and became fast friends? Mark is like that. We both are the same age and from the South. We both like to hunt and fish and are avid readers. Our friendship came quickly and easily because of how much we have in common. But we've also had deep conversations. We've challenged each other from time to time, and I know Mark has my back. Some friendships come naturally. Some are forged in fire. David and Jonathan's friendship was both.

David was anointed by the prophet Samuel as the future king while Jonathan's father, Saul, still reigned. As a result, Saul felt great jealousy and animosity toward David. Like, bloodthirsty, murderous jealousy with a capital "J." Although Saul continually tested his son's loyalty to David, Jonathan stayed faithful to his friend. It was a covenant friendship, an unbreakable bond. The Bible says Jonathan "loved him as he loved himself." His love foreshadows Jesus' command for us to "love your neighbor as yourself" from Matthew 22:39. Real friendship means doing for others what you would want done for yourself. We want to have a few covenant friends. Men that we are committed to through thick and thin. Such was the friendship of David and Jonathan.

*Today I will remember:*

- Some friendships come naturally, and some are forged in fire.
- The best are both.

*Lord, please give me a friend or two like David and Jonathan. I need men to connect with and who choose to commit to me in a bond of friendship.*

# ELIJAH AND ELISHA

*Elijah said to Elisha, "Stay here; the LORD has sent me to Bethel." But Elisha said, "As surely as the LORD lives and as you live, I will not leave you." So they went down to Bethel.*

2 KINGS 2:2

I am a big fan of *The Lord of the Rings* trilogy. In fact, I just ordered a new set of the books from a fancy pants publisher. My wife and I own the movies and read the books. One of the many reasons is the friendship between Frodo and Samwise. Frodo carries the burden of a ring of power that must be destroyed, and Sam is his partner and friend in the task. Sam is fully devoted to Frodo. Through thick and thin, they stick together until (spoiler alert) the ring is ultimately destroyed. Middle Earth is saved! This is an epic tale of friendship and partnership in the battle of good versus evil. There is no victory without friends.

In our verse, Elisha is a loyal apprentice and friend to Elijah. He sticks by his side even in times of danger and doubt. Acquaintances will come and go, and some friendships will be fickle, but we all need one or two that are committed and, if possible, lifelong. Men, we are built for this. Far too many go it alone. This is not God's will. We all need a couple of great friends that stick with us and we with them through thick and thin.

*Today I will remember:*

- There is no real victory without friends.
- It is not God's will for me to go it alone.
- Friends stick together through thick and thin.

*God, I need good friends. I know that You do not want me to go it alone. Help me to pursue and find this real friendship—and be the kind of friend that You've called me to be.*

# FAST FRIENDS

*I am a friend to all who fear you,*
*to all who follow your precepts.*
PSALM 119:63

There's just something sexy about Africa. This is the continent of elephants, hyenas, zebras, giraffes, and lions. When driving in Africa, I've had to stop for a baboon crossing. It's just cool, man. I was speaking at a leadership conference just outside of Johannesburg and got to spend a few days in Pilanesberg National Park. Our tour guide and driver was funny and knew his stuff. There was also a kind sense of comradery between us that went below the surface. I knew he was a follower of Jesus before I asked him. It wasn't his piety or self-righteousness. It was his kind, joyful nature, which I knew to be the fruit of the Holy Spirit.

Here I was, on the other side of the world, talking to someone I'd never met and yet knew he was a brother. At the end of the ride, we spoke for a few minutes, shared our mutual faith, shook hands, and departed. It wasn't deep or profound, just real. When you gave your life to Jesus, you became part of a very large family. People from different cultures, different backgrounds, and different colors of skin are now part of your family all over the world. This is the beautiful connection of being part of the family of God.

*Today I will remember:*

- I am part of a very large, multicultural family.
- People from different backgrounds with different colors of skin from all over the world are now related to me in Jesus.

*Lord, thank You for my brothers*
*and sisters around the world. May we*
*experience unity in our diversity.*

# GOOD FELLOWS

*When Job's three friends, Eliphaz the Temanite,*
*Bildad the Shuhite and Zophar the Naamathite,*
*heard about all the troubles that had come upon him,*
*they set out from their homes and met together by*
*agreement to go and sympathize with him and comfort him.*

JOB 2:11

If you're in a hard season of life right now, one of the healthiest things you can do is have a plan. Just know what you're going to do each day. What time will you get up? What are you going to do after work? What are your plans for Saturday? Make some plans and stick to them. Don't go with your feelings each day. Go with the plan. Friends have taught me the value of this approach during rough seasons in my life. When I was hurting, several guys would come around me, one after the other, and divvy up the time to spend with me. I needed to be around people, so one guy took one night and another a different night. Over time, they just made plans for me and got me through the tough season.

These three dudes, these friends of Job, knew that he was going through hell, so they planned to go through it with him. Specifically, to "sympathize with him and comfort him." If you read the entire account, you'll see they didn't do everything right, but they did get the "being there" part right. That's what friends do; they're there for each other. If you have a friend going through a difficult time, get some other buddies and make a plan. Be there and walk through it with him. You don't have to know what to say. In fact, saying a lot might not be good. Just be there and be consistent.

*Today I will remember:*

- Walking with my friend through tough times is as simple as planning regularly to be together.
- There is value in being there and being consistent.

*God, help me to be a good friend,*
*especially in times of need.*
*Help me be there for my friends.*

# HEART AND SOUL

*Jonathan said to his young armor-bearer,*
*"Come, let's go over to the outpost of those uncircumcised men.*
*Perhaps the LORD will act in our behalf. Nothing can hinder*
*the LORD from saving, whether by many or by few."*
*"Do all that you have in mind," his armor-bearer said.*
*"Go ahead; I am with you heart and soul."*

1 SAMUEL 14:6-7

I was watching a movie the other night and there was a scene kind of like this one between Jonathan and his armor-bearer. A dude goes to his buddy's house and says he needs him; it's time to fight and there is no time for questions. The friend pauses, then looks at his buddy for a few seconds and says, "I'm in." Now I can't cheer on violence in general, but I do want to applaud the loyalty.

Jonathan is tired of waiting around. His father, Saul, has six hundred men but will not challenge the Philistines. He decides to take matters into his own hands. How does Jonathan's armor-bearer respond? "I am with you heart and soul." I dig that. The two go over and by themselves kill twenty enemy soldiers, striking terror into the heart of the Philistine army. Such is the power of two committed friends who are committed to God.

Loyalty is hard to come by these days. Commitment is low. A fickle apathy permeates the population, even in the church. Gentlemen, let's look out for each other and guard one another in a spirit of heart and soul commitment.

*Today I will remember:*

- Having committed friends who are committed to God is a powerful thing.
- Loyalty matters.

*Father, help me commit myself to a few friends in*
*both heart and soul. May we look out for each other,*
*guard each other, and fight for each other.*

# KIND ENOUGH TO BE BOTHERED

*"Anyone who withholds kindness from a friend forsakes the fear of the Almighty."*

JOB 6:14

At the end of your life, you won't look back at your time on this earth wishing you had watched more Netflix. You'll be thinking about your relationships with God, your family, and others. It is God's will for you to have a few good friends. If we're going to have that, we must work toward it. I meet guys all the time who gave up on one another when things got difficult. There was a disagreement or misunderstanding, and they just wouldn't make the effort to make things right. Be better than that.

Not all friendships will last, and some need to end. But many end because of a lack of grace, mercy, and plain, old kindness. It's easier to cut someone out than it is to work it out. Like all things in life worth having, friendships require work. Who do you need to have a difficult conversation with? Who do you need to forgive or ask forgiveness from? It's worth the effort when two men decide to fight for each other. Brothers disagree at times, and the tension of a good argument can deepen the relationship if we choose to work through it. Many times, this is the difference between having a good acquaintance or a good friend.

*Today I will remember:*

- It matters that I care enough to be bothered.
- It's easier to cut someone out than it is to work it out.
- Like all things in life worth having, friendships require work.

*Jesus, thank You for Your commitment to me, even when I disappoint You. Help me to be the friend You are. I choose to care enough to be bothered.*

# MIGHTY MEN

*These are the names of David's mighty warriors: Josheb-Basshebeth, a Tahkemonite, was chief of the Three; he raised his spear against eight hundred men, whom he killed in one encounter.*

2 SAMUEL 23:8

If you want to read about the exploits of some of the mightiest warriors in history, check out 2 Samuel 23. The warrior in our verse single handedly killed eight hundred men. This group of special forces that served David were known as his mighty men. They were like Navy SEALs, MMA champions, and John Wick all rolled into one. To say they were formidable is an understatement.

All of us need some mighty men. I don't mean guys who can kill hundreds but who are mighty in character. They faithfully love their wives, invest in their children, and strive to do what's right in the eyes of God for the good of others. We become like those we hang out with. If you wish to become mighty, then you must spend time with the mighty. A wise man chooses to emulate and learn from other good men. A foolish man is unintentional about such things.

How are you growing? Who are you becoming? What kind of man do you want to be in five, ten, fifteen years from now? Find a man who is already there and learn from him. I have lots of acquaintances. Men that I enjoy and laugh with, but I only have a few good friends. They aren't perfect, but they are committed to pursuing the right things, and they hold me accountable to do the same. We all need this. We all need some mighty men.

*Today I will remember:*

- I become like those I spend time with.
- The men I want to learn from are the ones who are where I want to be.

*Father, help me to choose my closest friends wisely, men I respect and admire and want to learn from. Help me to be that kind of man.*

# MOSES AND AARON

*"What about your brother, Aaron the Levite? I know he can speak well. He is already on his way to meet you, and he will be glad to see you. You shall speak to him and put words in his mouth; I will help both of you speak and will teach you what to do. He will speak to the people for you, and it will be as if he were your mouth and as if you were God to him."*

EXODUS 4:14-16

Moses and Aaron were brothers and partners in accomplishing God's purposes. Here are three things all great partnerships require:

1. *Humility*: God chose Moses to be His spokesman, but Aaron was the better communicator and so he was chosen to help. This required humility and mutual submission to each other's strengths. Partnerships require mutual submission.
2. *Trust*: Aaron trusted that Moses was hearing from God and that his testimony was true. Aaron put his life on the line as he submitted to Moses. All partnerships require great trust. If you lack trust, then don't partner.
3. *Competency*: The basis of any partnership is need. You need help and so does the other person. You realize you can do far more together than you could ever do alone. You lean into your partner's competencies. He leans into yours.

I have been privileged to work with friends for the last twenty years. Not all friendships are official partnerships, but a friend is a partner in life. Partnership with friends requires humility, trust, and understood competencies.

*Today I will remember:*

- Partnering with friends requires humility, trust, and understood competencies.
- The basis of the partnership is realizing that we can do far more together than we could ever do alone.

*Lord, I need partners in life beyond my spouse. Help me to be a good friend and to choose partners wisely.*

# IT'S NOT PRIVATE

*Therefore confess your sins to each other and pray for each other so that you may be healed. The prayer of a righteous person is powerful and effective.*

JAMES 5:16

There is a myth in the church world that says my walk with Christ is just between me and Him. That's not true. Our sin always affects others. We carry in our hearts the private sin that we think no one knows. It changes us and our relationships. This is true internally, emotionally, and spiritually. Sin splashes. It spills out onto our families and our relationships in ways that we cannot see or fathom.

To deal with this, every man needs a couple of other men. I'm not saying be a hundred percent authentic with everyone. When someone you don't know well asks you how you are doing, the response "I'm fine" is just fine. The truth is, he probably doesn't really want to know. However, you do need a couple of guys that you are a hundred percent real with. Look again at our verse for today. Overcoming sin and experiencing healing includes confession and prayer. Your faith walk is personal, but it was never meant to be private.

Have a couple of guys that you're regularly processing your thought life with. They will help you see what you can't see. This will protect you and help heal you in your time of need. Secret sin is like a vampire, strong in the dark and weak in the light. Confessing and praying with a couple of friends brings help and healing.

*Today I will remember:*

- My faith walk is personal, but not private.
- It is important to have a couple of guys to regularly process life with.

*Lord, give me the courage to talk about my sin with a couple of guys I trust. Help them to do the same with me.*

# ONLY A FEW

*He did not let anyone follow him except Peter,*
*James and John the brother of James.*
MARK 5:37

Who are your friends? I'm not talking about the kind on Facebook. I'm talking about the close kind. Men whom you spend regular time with, live life with, and men who know the real you. You can only have a few friends like that because real friendships take time, and there's only so much of that to go around. Jesus had His group of twelve, but He was closest to three: Peter, James, and John. Most scholars believe His closest friend was John. Who are your three?

We don't get to choose our family, but we do get to choose our friends. As you think about who you want to invest in to build a good friendship, think about three things: chemistry, character, and the guy's relationship with Christ.

Chemistry means you get along well. It's someone you like to hang out with. You have similar interests and goals; you probably laugh a lot together, and you care what he has to say. Second, he has character. He's someone you can trust. I want a friend who I can say whatever I want to, and it stays between us. There's a mutual respect in keeping private things private. He's a man of his word. He's trustworthy. Finally, I want someone who is as committed to following Jesus as I am. We have all kinds of acquaintances, Jesus had that, but your closest friends need to be on the same mission of following Jesus as you are.

*Today I will remember:*

- I don't get to choose my family, but I do get to choose my friends.
- My three closest friends must be on mission for God.

*Lord, guide me in building a circle of trust.*
*Please give me three friends I can live my life with*
*who will help me in my walk with You.*

# PAUL AND SILAS

*About midnight Paul and Silas were praying and singing hymns to God, and the other prisoners were listening to them.*

ACTS 16:25

I spoke to a man years ago who had survived Auschwitz. I toured the camp on a dreary, dark, cold, day. The stories were horrifying. As we stood there in the rain under our umbrellas, this man spoke of the horrible suffering he and some of his friends had endured, and how it was their bond that got them through. They spoke hope and encouragement to one another. They spoke reality to each other when they were on the verge of insanity. He said he owed those friends his life.

When Paul and Silas were in chains, they sang and gave testimony to God's faithfulness. They led church services in dungeons amid the stench, cold, rats, and rage. They demonstrated faithfulness and brotherhood. I'm not sure you can have one without the other. Faithfulness is more likely to endure when coupled with fellowship. Good friends help us endure the trials of life and even sing in the suffering.

*Today I will remember:*

- Good friends help me endure trials.
- Faithfulness is more likely to endure when coupled with fellowship.

*Lord, I need the fellowship of friends in the good times, and especially in the bad. Thank You that Paul and Silas had one another. Please give me a friend like that. Let me be a friend like that.*

# PAUL AND TIMOTHY

*To Timothy, my dear son: Grace, mercy and peace from God the Father and Christ Jesus our Lord. I thank God, whom I serve, as my ancestors did, with a clear conscience, as night and day I constantly remember you in my prayers. Recalling your tears, I long to see you, so that I may be filled with joy.*

2 TIMOTHY 1:2-4

Paul was a spiritual father and friend to Timothy. Paul's two letters to Timothy in the New Testament display the apostle's admiration and affection for him. At the same time, you see challenges, corrections, encouragements, affirmations, and a rebuke here and there too. It's the stuff of a real, mentoring friendship. Paul was discipling and coaching this young pastor. We all need this, and we all want to be that for others.

I have a spiritual father and friend named Larry. We met years ago at a leadership event. Larry was the mentor of a cohort I was placed in. I was immediately impressed by his ability to see patterns and speak wisdom and insight in pursuit of solutions. Larry also had the experience and moral authority of "been there, done that." I knew I needed his help, so I chased him until he caught me. If you're looking for a mentor, chase someone until he catches you. Take him to lunch and have your questions ready.

*Today I will remember:*

- I need the wisdom of older, more seasoned men.
- I must chase mentors until they catch me.

*Lord, please give me insight on finding mentors.*
*I need some men who are older and wiser.*
*Help me to chase them until they catch me.*

# SECRET SICKNESS

*Therefore confess your sins to each other*
*and pray for each other so that you may be healed.*
*The prayer of a righteous person is powerful and effective.*
JAMES 5:16

In places of recovery, there is a saying, "We are as sick as our secrets." Secret sickness permeates society, and it runs rampant in the church. Secret addictions of all kinds, from alcohol abuse to pornography, damage the souls of millions of men. The Bible says that we're to confess our sins to each other. Why? So that we may be healed. Confession is to be a normal practice in the Christian life. Not necessarily between a parishioner and a priest, but between brothers in Christ who guard and protect one another from the dangers that lurk in secret.

Is there anything in your life that you are pretending is not a problem? Secret sins are like vampires; they are strong in the dark and defeated in the light. Confess your sins to Christian brothers and have them pray for you. One friend says that confession is most powerful when you confess the sin that you're thinking about doing. He's right. The eye cannot see the I, so talk your thoughts through with trustworthy friends who are striving to follow Jesus. They can help protect you from doing something stupid. At some point, we made church the place you go to pretend, but this is not God's will. God desires that we have friends to whom we confess.

*Today I will remember:*
- Confessing to men I trust is part of God's will for me.
- Confession is most powerful when I confess the sin I'm thinking about doing.

*Lord, help me be courageous enough to confess my sin to a brother I trust. Let this become a normal practice in a couple of my friendships. Thank You for the healing power of prayer and confession.*

# THE STRONGEST OF MEN

*Two are better than one, because they have a good return for their labor: If either of them falls down, one can help the other up. But pity anyone who falls and has no one to help them up.*

ECCLESIASTES 4:9-10

Podcaster Joe Rogan asked a former Navy SEAL to name the most important characteristic of a SEAL. The answer surprised me. It wasn't physicality or mental toughness. While those things are extremely important, he said that as a commander he would look for the guys who were the best teammates. Strength is important, but it's the ability to work with others that sets a SEAL apart. The strongest of men are those who work well with other men. The combined strength of a team is always stronger than the strength of one.

In essence, he was talking about the power of our verses for today. Everyone eventually falls; we are all human, and strong men know they will need the strength of others. This is the power of real friendship. An isolated man is a vulnerable man. Perhaps the greatest lie of the enemy is the lie of isolation. The feeling that no one understands, and that vulnerability is weakness. It's the lie that we can make it on our own. Not true. Life is hard, and we all need a team. Brothers who watch our back and we watch theirs. Don't go it alone. That's the plan of the weak.

*Today I will remember:*

- An isolated man is a vulnerable man.
- The strongest men are those who work well with other men.
- The combined strength of a team is always stronger than the strength of one.

*Lord, I need other men in my life, and I am weakest on my own. Help me to commit to the strength of a few good friendships.*

# September

## COURAGE

"This is my command—be strong
and courageous! Do not be afraid or discouraged.
For the Lord your God is with you wherever you go."
*Joshua 1:9 (NLT)*

# SADDLE UP

*"Be strong and courageous, because you will lead these people to inherit the land, I swore to their ancestors to give them."*

JOSHUA 1:6

In the book that bears his name, Joshua is commanded repeatedly to be "strong and courageous." Most people think that strength and courage are feelings. That people who display courage are just naturally courageous. If that's the case, then why the command? The reason for the command is because to be strong and courageous is not about feelings, but decisions.

Any area of your life where God has called you to be a leader will require courage. Being a good husband, a good father, a good friend, a good boss, or a good employee requires courage. Life requires courage! Courage is not the absence of fear. I have a coffee mug with a picture of John Wayne and the quote: "Courage is being scared to death and saddling up anyway." Courage is not letting fear make the decision for you. Courage is being afraid and doing the right thing anyway. Courage and strength are decisions to not let fear be in charge.

Where in your life are you wimping out? Where are you letting fear make the decision? Is there a conversation or a person you've been avoiding in fear? Is there a calculated risk that you're too afraid to take? Don't let fear be in charge. Be afraid and then saddle up anyway.

*Today I will remember:*

- Courage is being afraid and doing the right thing anyway.
- It's a decision to not let fear be in charge.

*Father, grant me the wisdom to know the right thing to do and the courage to do it. Forgive me for being more faithful to fear than I am to You at times. Even when I feel afraid, help me do the right thing.*

# JESUS IS STRONG

*"Isn't this the carpenter? Isn't this Mary's son and the brother of James, Joseph, Judas and Simon? Aren't his sisters here with us?" And they took offense at him.*

MARK 6:3

A few years ago, at a church in Texas, I couldn't help but notice that on the back wall was a massive painting of Jesus. He had long, flowing, winged-back hair and seemed to be wearing eyeliner, mascara, maybe a little rouge, the whole nine yards. He looked frail, weak, and a little too dolled up. I thought to myself, *Jesus needs to man it up a bit*. When I was a kid, the pictures of Jesus I saw always seemed to look like that. He always looked wimpy. Is that really Jesus? Not according to the Bible.

Jesus was a carpenter before He began His three-year public ministry. A carpenter before there were power tools. Have you ever used a saw, like the traditional kind? No electricity. Just good, old fashioned, muscular manpower. Jesus worked like that all the time. He was muscular and strong. His hands were calloused. He spoke with a kind authority. When crowds wanted to kill Him, He would just walk right through the mob. That's stout. And that's just His physical presence. When it came time for Him to go to the cross, He laid down His life willingly in obedience to the Father and shed His holy blood to rescue sinners such as you and me. Make no mistake, Jesus is strong.

*Today I will remember:*

- Jesus is all-powerful.
- He is the Lamb of God through His sacrifice.
- He is the Lion of Judah by right.

*Jesus, thank You that in all Your power, You freely laid down Your life, so that I might know You. You are an example of great courage. Help me to see Your kindness and strength.*

# A GOOD DEATH

*Therefore, I urge you, brothers and sisters, in view of God's mercy, to offer your bodies as a living sacrifice, holy and pleasing to God—this is your true and proper worship.*

ROMANS 12:1

Two things are true of all of us. We're all born, and we're all going to die. This is the blessing and curse of humanity. Our verse is about death, but of a different kind. Look at it again. It says we're to be a "living sacrifice." How does that work? A sacrifice is about death. How do we live and die at the same time? To be a living sacrifice is to continually die to your will, so that you live out God's will. The Christian life is not to be self-led, but Spirit-led. Living, a godly man practices a type of death to self each day.

True worship is not about the songs we sing but the lives we live. This all begins with a proper view of His mercy. The more you understand His love and the sacrifice He made for you on the cross, the more you'll want to live for Him. Grace reveals two things: (1) we are great sinners, and (2) Jesus is a great Savior. When a man realizes the greatness both of his sin and of God's mercy, he will bow the knee. Not out of shame or guilt, but out of gratitude. This is God's will for you. That you understand His love, mercy, and grace over your life so fully that you are compelled to give Him your full devotion. Being a living sacrifice is motivated by being loved. It's a good death.

*Today I will remember:*

- Because of God's great love for me, I choose to live for Him.
- Worship is less about singing and more about how I'm living.

*Lord, help me to better understand Your mercy,*
*so that I might be more faithful in my obedience.*
*I choose today to submit my will to Yours.*
*May I live a life of true worship.*

# BOW THE KNEE

*"If we are thrown into the blazing furnace,*
*the God we serve is able to deliver us from it,*
*and he will deliver us from Your Majesty's hand.*
*But even if he does not, we want you to know,*
*Your Majesty, that we will not serve your gods or*
*worship the image of gold you have set up."*
DANIEL 3:17-18

Defying King Nebuchadnezzar's command to worship a golden statue, this is the battle cry of Shadrach, Meshach, and Abednego. Nebuchadnezzar had the best and brightest Jewish young adults brought to his Babylonian court to serve him. He likely made the men eunuchs (that part is not typically brought up in children's Sunday school classes), changed their names, gave them an education in the occult, and put them in places of service in his palace. Daniel is the most famous of this group, and these three men are his friends.

Notice their stance. They are aware that God can rescue them, but that He is not obligated to do so. Their loyalty is to God simply because He is God. Their allegiance is not to God's blessings or provision, but to God Himself. This is righteous courage. We *hope* He rescues us! But if we die, we're OK with that. In the story, Nebuchadnezzar has these three men thrown into an uber-hot fiery furnace. They walk around in the flames untouched. A fourth man, whose identity is a mystery, is also revealed in the flames. Shadrach, Meshach, and Abednego would not bow to King Nebuchadnezzar because they had already bowed their knee to another king. Their allegiance was to the Kings of kings, even to the point of their own lives.

*Today I will remember:*

- My allegiance is to the King of kings.
- I will serve God because He is God, regardless of the outcome.

*Father, I bow the knee to You today.*
*I am Your servant. Help me to*
*serve You above all things.*

# CHECK YOUR HEARING

*For the time will come when people will not put up with sound doctrine. Instead, to suit their own desires, they will gather around them a great number of teachers to say what their itching ears want to hear. They will turn their ears away from the truth and turn aside to myths.*

2 TIMOTHY 4:3-4

I'm hard of hearing. It's been that way since I was a kid. Once I became an adult, various people encouraged me to consider hearing aids, but my pride got in the way. I already wore glasses. To add hearing aids, I felt, was just too much. Finally, when I turned forty, I gave in, and you know what? It was life-changing! Every relationship I had improved. My wife says hearing aids are sexy. Apparently listening is extremely attractive. Imagine that.

We all need to check our hearing from time to time. Not just physically, but emotionally and spiritually. The Bible is God's primary way of speaking to us, and we are to submit ourselves under its authority. When we're taught the Bible, we need to confirm that what we're hearing is what the Bible is saying. It is good to question, to study, to not turn away from the truth but to seek it and mine God's Word for it. The apostle Paul tells Timothy in the verses above that truth can be hard for people to hear. Some will turn away. Instead of seeking the truth, they'll just find teachers who say what they want to hear. Let's not be like that. Let's turn toward, not away from, the hard things. Use the Scriptures as a hearing aid. God's will is found in God's Word. The Bible tunes us in to hear God's voice.

*Today I will remember:*

- God's will is found in God's Word.
- The Scriptures are a hearing aid that helps me know His voice.

*Father, Your will is found in Your Word. Help me grasp what the Bible teaches. Let me seek the truth and honor Your authority.*

# CHEERING YOU ON

*Therefore, since we are surrounded by such a great cloud of witnesses, let us throw off everything that hinders and the sin that so easily entangles. And let us run with perseverance the race marked out for us, fixing our eyes on Jesus, the pioneer and perfecter of faith. For the joy set before him he endured the cross, scorning its shame, and sat down at the right hand of the throne of God.*

HEBREWS 12:1-2

You have fans. Our verses say that we are surrounded by a cloud of witnesses watching us run our journey of faith. They ran and now they watch us run. I wonder who is in the crowd. Maybe King David is watching. Perhaps Abraham, Isaac, and Jacob are cheering you on today.

My family is really into fantasy football. You think in heaven those who have gone before us select their team and cheer us on? Probably not. But we're surrounded by witnesses, nonetheless. Sometimes the race of faith can be tiring. There will be moments when we want to give up. Some people on earth will cheer us on, and we'll get booed, too. Not everyone is a fan. The testimonies of those who have gone before us are there to help us persevere.

These few verses follow Hebrews 11, which many call the "Hall of Faith." The people who are mentioned aren't commended for living perfectly; they're commended for living faithfully. They persevered. I heard a pastor say that saints are just sinners who fall and choose to get up. Perhaps you've fallen. You've stopped running the race. Get back up. Keep going. You're not alone. The crowd is watching. Fix your eyes on Jesus, at the right hand of God. In Him, you've already won.

*Today I will remember:*
- I will keep running the race.
- I may not run perfectly, but I can run faithfully.
- Perseverance is a choice.

*Father, give me the wisdom and strength to complete the race You have for me. When I fall, give me the grace to get up and continue.*

# COURAGE NOT TO CONFORM

*Do not conform to the pattern of this world,*
*but be transformed by the renewing of your mind.*
*Then you will be able to test and approve what*
*God's will is—his good, pleasing and perfect will.*
ROMANS 12:2

Everyone is being trained and shaped by something. This is what the word *conform* means: to follow, to imitate, to be shaped. Who or what is shaping you? Our verse today tells us not to conform to the world.

Having the courage not to conform is about checking our patterns. The patterns we practice and the patterns of our ponderings. We must ask whether we are practicing the world's patterns. Two things immediately come to mind. First, how much television are we watching, and how much are we letting social media influence us? Neither is wrong in and of itself. But if we're not careful, we are letting the world shape us in unhealthy ways. What patterns of activity have you fallen into that are not healthy?

Second, we must watch the patterns of our ponderings, meaning how we think. The world follows a pattern of jealousy, envy, selfishness, lust, bitterness, and greed. What are the patterns of your thoughts? Do they include these things? If so, you must fight this and choose different patterns.

You've heard the adage, "garbage in, garbage out." What goes in our minds shapes our behaviors. If this is true, then "goodness in, goodness out" is also true. All of us are being shaped. Let us have the courage to fight conformity to the world, so that we might instead be shaped by our Savior.

*Today I will remember:*

- I must choose the right patterns in my practices and ponderings.
- I choose to focus on godly things, so that I might be formed in godliness.

*Father, renew my mind today. Forgive me for*
*being haphazard in my patterns. Help me to follow*
*Your patterns so that my character is shaped by You.*

# COURAGE TO ACT

*Moses answered the people, "Do not be afraid. Stand firm and you will see the deliverance the LORD will bring you today. The Egyptians you see today you will never see again. The LORD will fight for you; you need only to be still." Then the LORD said to Moses, "Why are you crying out to me? Tell the Israelites to move on."*

EXODUS 14:13-15

There have been many times when I thought I was waiting on God and later realized He was waiting on me. Many things that God asks us to do we will not understand until we obey. This is where the people of God are in the verses above. God is going to part the Red Sea and deliver them, but not until they move. Biblical faith is action oriented. At times it will require courage. It's more than just belief or mental assent. Biblical faith works like this: To believe is to trust, and to trust is to obey.

What have you been praying for? Is it possible that you think you're waiting on God, while He's waiting on you? Don't just pray for a job; go and look for one. We don't just pray for better marriages. We go to good counselors with our wives and get some coaching. Think about it this way: Pray as though it all depends on God, and work as though it all depends on you. God meets us in the middle. If Moses did not move forward with the people, there would be no account of the parting of the Red Sea. There are so many breakthroughs in life that are on the other side of the hard decision we're unwilling to make. Pray. Move forward. Obey God. That's courageous faith.

*Today I will remember:*

- Sometimes I think I'm waiting on God when He's waiting on me.
- Real faith includes action.

*Father, give me wisdom to move forward.*
*I choose to do my part and trust You with the rest.*
*Help me to practice real, action-oriented faith.*

# COURAGE TO BUILD

*I answered them by saying,*
*"The God of heaven will give us success.*
*We his servants will start rebuilding."*

NEHEMIAH 2:20

If God has called you to it, God will get you through it. Nehemiah was called to a seemingly impossible task—lead the Jewish people to rebuild the broken-down wall around Jerusalem. The wall represented legitimacy and stability for the city. A broken-down wall meant a broken people. Nehemiah was cupbearer to a king who was not Jewish and most likely would not allow him to do it. But not only did Nehemiah get permission, he got the king's financial backing. He was a spokesman to God's people who had given up hope. Nehemiah was the one guy with God's help when everyone said it couldn't be done. He moved forward in bold, winsome fashion and led the people to do it anyway. The powerful book of Nehemiah is a masterclass in leadership.

What about you? What's something you believe God has called you to but you won't even try because you're not sure it can happen? Have you ever heard the phrase "God will never give you more than you can handle"? Let me help you; that's not true. There are a lot of things that God calls us to do that we cannot accomplish in our own strength. This keeps us reliant upon Him; in the end, we know only He deserves the credit. God might be calling you to something difficult or seemingly impossible. Be afraid. Be scared. Then do it anyway. You're not responsible for results but for faithful obedience. Trust God and move forward.

*Today I will remember:*

- If God has called me to it, then God will get me through it.
- Some things that God calls me to I cannot accomplish in my own strength.
- I must rely on Him.

*Lord, I choose to trust You. I will be faithful*
*in obedience and leave the results to You.*
*Give me the grace to keep moving forward.*

# COURAGE TO FORGIVE

*But Joseph said to them, "Don't be afraid.*
*Am I in the place of God? You intended to harm me,*
*but God intended it for good to accomplish what*
*is now being done, the saving of many lives. So then,*
*don't be afraid. I will provide for you and your children."*
*And he reassured them and spoke kindly to them.*

GENESIS 50:19-21

Joseph was a gifted young man, loved by his father and hated by his brothers. They secretly sold Joseph into slavery and convinced their dad that he was dead. Joseph suffered a false accusation, spent years in prison, and then, by a miracle of God, was released to serve in the court of the Pharaoh, who was the most powerful man in the world.

There's a famine back in Joseph's homeland. The same brothers who literally sold him out years earlier now come to seek the help of Joseph, who happens to be the second most powerful man in the world. This is Joseph's moment to exact revenge, but he doesn't. Instead of hurting those who hurt him, he chooses to help. Forgiveness is not for weak people but for the strong.

Look at our verses again. Joseph acknowledges that God was working behind the scenes. He chooses to trust God. This is an amazing account of his understanding of the sovereignty of God and of the proper use of power. Men who are strong in their faith and secure in who they are can forgive the seemingly unforgivable.

*Today I will remember:*

- To forgive is to agree with heaven and align oneself with God.
- Strong men forgive.

*Father, may I trust You over my need to*
*exact revenge. Make me strong and secure so that*
*I might forgive others. I choose to be on Your side.*

# CROSSING THE LINE

*Simon Peter answered him, "Lord, to whom shall we go? You have the words of eternal life. We have come to believe and to know that you are the Holy One of God."*

JOHN 6:68-69

In every journey of faith, there's a metaphorical line that you cross and cannot go back. Why? You know it's real. You know it's true, and even though you may doubt, struggle, and wrestle, you can't abandon it. You've crossed the line.

This is one of those moments for Peter and the other disciples. Jesus has just said some hard things, and many choose to no longer follow Him. Jesus spins around and asks the twelve disciples if they are going to leave too. Peter doesn't always get it right, but he does here. There are things that Jesus asks of us that are hard, but to whom else will we go?

What is it for you? What is He asking of you that is shaking your faith? For me, it was forgiveness. I knew Jesus wanted me to forgive, and it was more than hard—it was seemingly impossible. I thought about throwing in the towel and giving up. I didn't want to be a follower if it meant forgiving the seemingly unforgivable! But Jesus had revealed Himself to me in real ways. I knew that He was with me, and I couldn't walk away. At some point in my journey, I had crossed the line. So I chose to trust Him. And you know what? His forgiveness flowed through me. His power showed up. Instead of abandoning the faith, I grew in it. How about you? Are you thinking about throwing in the towel? Cross the line. Follow Jesus. To whom else will you go? He is the Holy One of God.

*Today I will remember:*

- Jesus is real, and I can trust Him.
- I choose to cross the line of faith and keep moving forward.

*Jesus, increase my faith. I believe in You but struggle when following You is hard. You are the Holy One of God, and I trust You.*

# DEAL WITH IT

*Humble yourselves, therefore, under God's mighty hand, that he may lift you up in due time. Cast all your anxiety on him because he cares for you.*

1 PETER 5:6-7

Have you ever heard the adage that time heals all wounds? It's not true. If time healed all wounds, then anyone who is sick would just have to wait. Cancer? Wait it out. Broken leg? Just give it some time. Shot? No bandages needed; bleed out, and just let the bullet sit. Yet when it comes to cancerous, broken, blown-up matters of the soul, that's how we think. This is why fifty-year-old men are still walking around carrying wounds from their childhood. To heal from it you must deal with it. Time doesn't heal all wounds. Jesus does.

My wife is a nurse. I can't count how many stories she's told me of men who finally show up to the doctor's office once something is way out of hand. One dude had an issue with one of his personals. It was swelling and getting larger, and he didn't do anything about it for nine months. The day he walked into the doctor's office, it was the size of a large grapefruit! Gentlemen, that's ridiculous. The doctor dealt with it, and the next day the guy was back to normal.

What are you pretending is not a problem? Not just physically, but emotionally and spiritually. Courageous men do not ignore their problems. They deal with them. Want healing? Get the help you need.

*Today I will remember:*

- To heal from it we must deal with it.
- Courageous men do not ignore problems.
- Courageous men face them head on.

*God, give me the courage to face my problems.*
*Forgive me for ignoring important things.*
*I choose today to get the help I need.*

# DEFEATING GIANTS

*Goliath stood and shouted to the ranks of Israel, "Why do you come out and line up for battle? Am I not a Philistine, and are you not the servants of Saul? Choose a man and have him come down to me. If he is able to fight and kill me, we will become your subjects; but if I overcome him and kill him, you will become our subjects and serve us."*

1 SAMUEL 17:8-9

Almost everyone knows the story of how David, a shepherd boy, defeated the great warrior Goliath with a slingshot. Goliath took a rock to the forehead. The projectile was traveling approximately two hundred miles per hour thrown from David's sling. In essence, the giant brought a sword to a gunfight, he just didn't know it.

That's the climax of the story, the pinnacle when God's people win and David's trajectory to becoming king is set. Our verses tell us what was happening before that, the taunts of the giant Goliath. Before we get the hero David, we see hundreds of others quaking in their boots, paralyzed in fear.

There are wonderful breakthroughs on the other side of the giants we're unwilling to face. What are you afraid of? Is there a conversation you've been unwilling to have? A decision you know is right but have been unwilling to make? For many, the simple difference between success and failure is fear. Fear is a very good liar, and most people are good believers. Rarely is reality as bad as the falsely perceived eventuality. As sons of a God who loves us, we are not called to be men of fear but men of faith. Be wise. Be shrewd. Be bold. Face the giant!

*Today I will remember:*

- Fear is a liar.
- There is a breakthrough on the other side of the hard decisions I've been afraid to face.

*Lord, give me wisdom to see what You see.*
*Help me to be a faithful man, not a fearful one.*
*Fear will no longer make decisions for me.*

# DYING TO SELF

*Then Jesus said to his disciples,*
*"Whoever wants to be my disciple must deny*
*themselves and take up their cross and follow me."*
MATTHEW 16:24

All growth, maturity, and learning require death to self. There is no advancement without personal surrender. To learn a new skill, you're probably going to look a little foolish at first. So you must die to your pride. Anytime you follow a personal trainer or are being led by a coach, you must choose to die to your way and submit to his. You don't join a team and then tell the coach how things are going to go. You put on the uniform, shut your mouth, and receive instruction. You die in a way. You submit your wants and desires to the good of the team and the leadership of the coaches.

Dying to self is a daily decision to submit yourself to Jesus' way of life and leadership. I used to think this verse was all about suffering. It might include that at times, but it's mainly about submission. We die to ourselves and submit to His authority. To become a follower of Jesus is to invite Him to be the leader, coach, and trainer of your life. It's to submit your will to His because you trust that His ways are better. People make this type of decision each day, whether they believe in Jesus or not. Everybody is learning how to live from somebody. We all submit and trust that someone's way is better than ours. Jesus is the most brilliant person who's ever lived. He is God in the flesh. To submit to Him and follow His ways is the smartest thing you can do.

*Today I will remember:*

- Dying to self is less about suffering and more about submission.
- Everyone is practicing faith like this in various ways.
- Trusting Jesus is about submitting to His leadership.

*Jesus, Your way is best. I choose to trust*
*and follow You today. Not my will,*
*but Yours be done in and through me.*

# ENCOURAGING COURAGE

*Therefore encourage one another and build each other up, just as in fact you are doing.*
1 THESSALONIANS 5:11

To encourage someone is to speak courage into his or her life. We all need that, and we all need to do that. What happens to your soul when someone sincerely compliments you? It swells. I don't mean in an arrogant way, but in a healthy way. It fuels you forward. A complimented and encouraged soul is being built up. Why? Because encouragement fuels confidence and courage.

One of the best things we can do for our family and friends is speak courage into their lives. Especially our children. Dads, your words to your children carry massive weight. Compliment them, tell them they're doing a good job, cheer them on. God doesn't want us to be soul destroyers but soul builders. Soul builders encourage.

Who in your life needs some encouragement? Give it. You never know what God might do. So why not sincerely encourage three people today? They could be in your family, at work, or among your friends. Think of what you admire about each person and actually tell them how that quality inspires you to be a better person. See how they respond. Then make encouragement a habit. Carry around large doses of encouragement and serve them up regularly.

*Today I will remember:*
- To encourage is to speak courage into someone's life.
- I choose to build up rather than tear down.

*Father, I want to be a person who builds people up.*
*Make me an ambassador of encouragement.*
*May I speak courage into someone's life today.*

# FIGHT THE GOOD FIGHT

*For he has rescued us from the dominion of darkness and brought us into the kingdom of the Son he loves, in whom we have redemption, the forgiveness of sins.*

COLOSSIANS 1:13-14

Make no mistake. There's a war going on. It's a battle between the dominion of darkness and the kingdom of Jesus. These verses say that if you've given your life to Jesus, then He has rescued you. You were in the wrong place, with the enemy. You were a citizen of the place of darkness. But Jesus, through the power of His shed blood on the cross, has redeemed you from all sin for all time. Through His resurrection, He has defeated and destroyed death, hell, and the grave. You have been brought out of darkness and into the light! You're now a citizen in the kingdom of the Son through your faith in Him. So stay in the light. Don't visit the enemy's city.

The quickest way to lose a fight is to not realize you're in one. Don't get lazy. Stay alert. The challenge is that the darkness feels natural. Your very nature gravitates to it. So you must fight. Ultimately, we know the war is won. Jesus wins, but in this life, we're still in the battle. The enemy still has a foothold in this broken world, and we are to represent the kingdom of Jesus here. To follow Jesus is to fight for His kingdom. To love your enemy, bless those who persecute you, give to the poor, love your wife, train your children in the ways of God, stay sexually pure. All these things are part of fighting the dominion of darkness and representing the kingdom of the Son. Fight on!

*Today I will remember:*

- I represent the kingdom of Jesus.
- When I choose to do what's right, I'm winning the fight.

*Jesus, help me to stay alert. Forgive me for giving ground to the enemy at times. Today I will fight the good fight. I choose to follow You and take ground for Your kingdom.*

# GOD STRONG

*He gives strength to the weary*
*and increases the power of the weak.*
ISAIAH 40:29

The strength God wants for us does not come from us but from Him. God wants His strength in you. What are you tired of right now? Where do you feel weak? God's energy and strength are infinite, and He is not waiting for you to get your act together and show more willpower. The Christian life is learning to lean into His strength. We play a role, but it's more about trusting Him than trying harder.

If you're weary and tired right now, here are a few things you can do.

1. What is your part? What do you have control over? Make a list of those things and reduce it to small, doable, bite-size tasks.
2. Now make another list, this list covers the things that are out of your control. It's longer than you probably think. Write it out and pray through it. We usually get exhausted when we're trying to control things on that second list.
3. Give the "Out of My Control" list to God. Pray through it, ask God to search your desires, and then let it go and give it to Him. Let God be God. Let Him empower you and strengthen you as you trust in Him. It's exhausting when we try to be God. These items were not meant to be carried by you, but by Him.

*Today I will remember:*
- If it's out of my control, then God carries it.
- If it is in my control, I take care of it.
- I will give God what is His, and take responsibility for what is mine.

*Father, I get tired and stressed about so*
*many things that I can't control. I choose today*
*to let You carry those things. You are my strength.*

# GRACE GIVES GRIT

*It was about this time that King Herod arrested some who belonged to the church, intending to persecute them. He had James, the brother of John, put to death with the sword. When he saw that this met with approval among the Jews, he proceeded to seize Peter also.*

ACTS 12:1-3

There's a myth in westernized Christianity that if you do what God wants, then everything in your life gets better. I hate to burst another bubble, but that's not true. Faith in God doesn't fix everything. In fact, sometimes it can make things more difficult. This was true in the early church. Christians were martyred and arrested because of their faith in Jesus. It didn't make their lives easier, but it did make them eternally blessed.

A "health and wealth" version of Christianity, while popular, contradicts what the Bible teaches. It's driven by those who abuse the Scriptures, take things out of context, and sell lies to vulnerable people. Many of us know this, but somehow this approach rubs off on us anyway. The Christian life is not problem free, but it can be peace filled.

God's grace gives us grit. Those early disciples chose prison and even death because they knew the truth. Their souls were filled with a never-ending, eternal peace. Our God is bigger than our problems and pain. We have a forever hope in Jesus that cannot be snuffed out. Understanding His grace fills us with love and grit. We know that in this world we will have trouble, but we take heart because Jesus has overcome the world.

*Today I will remember:*

- Understanding God's amazing grace fills me with steadfast love and unwavering grit.
- There will always be problems, but in Jesus there is peace.

*Jesus, may Your grace give me the hope and grit I need in this broken world. Fill me with Your strength and peace even in my problems.*

# GROW THROUGH IT

*Not only so, but we also glory in our sufferings,*
*because we know that suffering produces perseverance;*
*perseverance, character; and character, hope.*

ROMANS 5:3-4

Most of us pray for comfort, blessings, and ease. I know I do, and doing this is OK. But reality is that we *grow* through times of difficulty. Think about any progress you've made. You got physically stronger because you pushed through the pain of exercise. You got emotionally stronger because you adjusted and adapted in response to emotional pain. The truth is, pain changes us. Ease leaves us as we are and weakens us. But for pain to change you for the good, you must choose to grow through it.

If you're in a difficult time right now, understand that growth will come if you make the right decisions. Even if you've made the wrong decisions, you can repent, change, and grow. The biggest lesson in times of pain is not to waste it. We waste pain when we medicate it rather than deal with it. Sometimes we drink too much alcohol. Some guys sleep around. Others buy stuff they don't need to impress people they don't know. There are all kinds of ways to numb the pain. But there's no growth in that. When we face and deal with the pain, we develop character, perseverance, and hope.

*Today I will remember:*

- I can choose to grow through what I'm going through.
- Pain is fertile ground for positive change if we choose it.
- Pain shouldn't be wasted!

*Holy Spirit, produce the necessary growth*
*in me in times of pain. I don't want to waste these*
*difficult times. I want to grow through them.*

# ONLY THE STRONG

*Be on your guard; stand firm in the faith; be courageous; be strong.*

1 CORINTHIANS 16:13

One guy told me he thought Christianity was for weaklings who need a crutch. I agreed with the crutch part but disagreed with the rest.

Christianity is for all who are willing to face the truth. Wimps are not willing to do that. The truth is, we're sinners. Most men are unwilling to acknowledge God because to do so would mean acknowledging ourselves, our failures, and our sin. I can't live up to my own standard, much less God's. The weak are unwilling to own up to a holy God or take a real look in the mirror. All of us are a mess in various ways. The strong deal with it; the weak ignore it. Don't look down on others when you're unwilling to take a good look at yourself.

Is it a crutch? Yes. But what's wrong with that? Crutches help you stand tall. They keep you moving even in your brokenness. The courageous grab the crutch and walk on while the weaklings whine and wander around fruitlessly as the world passes them by. Any pansy can drown his sorrows in alcohol, drift from woman to woman, or criticize others like an armchair quarterback. It takes a real man to sober up, commit to one woman for a lifetime, and care for others instead of criticizing them. A Christian man who is about the Lord's business stands firm, practices courage, and chooses to remain strong. Christianity is not for the faint of heart. Don't let the weak fools fool you.

*Today I will remember:*

- Christianity is for men who will face the truth.
- This requires strength, tenacity, and grit.

*Father, help me to walk in manhood today, face the truth, and fight to walk in it. Don't let me ignore my problems. Help me deal with them.*

# RIGHTEOUS REBELLION

*Now when Daniel learned that the decree had been published, he went home to his upstairs room where the windows opened toward Jerusalem. Three times a day he got down on his knees and prayed, giving thanks to his God, just as he had done before.*

DANIEL 6:10

Do you know why Daniel was thrown into a lion's den? Because he prayed at a time when prayer was outlawed. If you read the full account, you'll see that Daniel had jealous political enemies. Daniel was rising in both popularity and power, and these men were scheming to crush him. They tried to get some dirt on him, but there was none, so they devised a plan. These men knew that Daniel was committed to God and would not break His law, so they convinced the king to outlaw prayer. What does Daniel do? He does what he'd always done. He chooses to pray openly, to be righteously rebellious in his allegiance to God.

The king is heartbroken because he loves Daniel, but he's caught between a rock and a hard place. Daniel is sentenced to death by being thrown to hungry lions. While God miraculously rescues Daniel, you must remember that Daniel didn't know God was going to do that. Daniel's commitment to God and what was right was greater than his commitment to self-preservation.

*Today I will remember:*

- The righteous choice is always right.
- Trusting God is less about the outcome and more about my decision to be faithful.

*Lord, may I be courageously committed to You above all else. I am responsible for faithfulness, and You are responsible for the outcome. I trust You.*

# THE "WITH" WARRIOR

*When you go to war against your enemies and see horses and chariots and an army greater than yours, do not be afraid of them, because the LORD your God, who brought you up out of Egypt, will be with you.*

DEUTERONOMY 20:1

Sometimes I'm afraid. I'm afraid of taking the calculated risk God has led me to. What if it doesn't work out? What if I'm wrong? Sometimes I'm afraid of others' opinions. What will they think of me if I do this? Or if I don't do it? Sometimes I'm afraid of my wife. She's not all that scary, but I just don't want to let her down. Or have her be disappointed in me, or think less of me. What are you afraid of?

Our verse doesn't pull any punches. Yeah, the enemy is bigger and stronger, but do not be afraid! Why? The Lord your God will be with you. I'll tell you about a little secret for gaining courage. Here it is: The warrior is found in the "with."

I have a friend named Ted who was an umpire in Major League Baseball. Before that, he was a boxer and had sparred with Evander Holyfield, Mike Tyson, and George Foreman. He's about six foot four and weighs a lean two hundred sixty-five pounds. I will tell you this, when Ted is with me, I ain't afraid of nothin'! Ted's presence makes me brave. The same is true with God. Why won't I be afraid? He is with me.

*Today I will remember:*

- The warrior is found in the "with."
- God is with me, and He is for me.
- I will not fear.

*God, thank You for being with me. What shall I fear? You are greater and stronger than anything, and You love me. Today I will walk in courage with You.*

# WATCH YOUR THINKING

*"What I feared has come upon me;*
*what I dreaded has happened to me."*

JOB 3:25

I remember the first time I saw *Jaws*. I was young, too young. Not sure that as a five-year-old I needed to see it, but I did. For weeks, I was afraid to take a bath. I think that's when I switched to showers. Even now, when I water ski in a freshwater lake, while I'm waiting for the boat to get set, sharks will cross my mind. Big ones. Why? Because what we focus on is what we move toward. This is true physically, emotionally, and even spiritually.

Have you ever watched a scary movie and been terrified? Why are you afraid? You're not in danger. You're in a comfortable theater with your family or friends. You're drinking a soda and eating popcorn that you paid way too much for. All is well. Yet your heart beats fast, you're jumpy, uptight, and on edge. You are safe and yet afraid. That's the power of focus.

We all need to be thinking about what we're thinking about. How's your thinking been lately? Do you focus on good things or negative things? What is righteous and good, or what is wrong and sinful? Our minds take us places. Let's focus in the right direction.

*Today I will remember:*

- I will be conscious about the things I'm thinking about.
- Focus is powerful.
- It affects my emotions and decisions.

*Father, help me to think about Your love and*
*what is good and right. Be my focus today.*
*May Your peace reign in my heart.*

# ALL IN

*Going a little farther, he fell with his face to the ground and prayed, "My Father, if it is possible, may this cup be taken from me. Yet not as I will, but as you will."*

MATTHEW 26:39

This powerful verse reveals Jesus' devotion and love for the Father, and for you and me. He has always known this day would come. Yet when it's time for Him to go to the cross, He asks the Father if there is some other way. Then He concludes here with the beautiful words "Yet not as I will, but as you will."

Nothing reveals love like a freely surrendered will. You know you love someone when what that person wants is more important than what you want. Even if it comes with great cost. Jesus loves the Father even to the point of His own life. He surrenders what He wants to obey the Father and sacrifice His life as the Savior of the world. This is courageous love.

Are your will and the will of the Father on a collision course anywhere in your life? What has He asked of you that you really don't want to do? Maybe it's about money. Perhaps it's a secret sin. Is there something He has asked you to renounce that the thought of giving it up, or giving in, saddens or terrifies you? These things are the real test of trusting God. There is no resurrection without some sort of death. Life you've never known and freedom beyond your comprehension are on the other side of surrendering your will to His.

*Today I will remember:*

- Nothing reveals love like a freely surrendered will.
- You know you love others when what they want is more important than what you want.

*Father, I want what You want. Your way is better than my way. I surrender my will to Yours and choose to trust You.*

# HUMILIATING LOVE

*Then they spit in his face and struck him with their fists. Others slapped him and said, "Prophesy to us, Messiah. Who hit you?"*

MATTHEW 26:67-68

I'm always amazed at the audacity and immaturity of the religious leaders. It's shocking! They are sentencing an innocent man to death while mocking and slapping Him. Evil in the name of God is by far the worst kind.

I am especially amazed at the humility and courage of Jesus in allowing this abuse. Jesus is God. At any moment, He could obliterate these guys. Lions do not let themselves be slapped around by sheep. Yet Jesus, in great strength and great humility, allows the spitting, the mocking, and the slapping. His love for the Father and for you makes room for humiliation.

A couple of years ago, I felt that God wanted me to pray for a stranger. I was supposed to walk up, introduce myself, and ask if the person wanted me to pray. I didn't do it. I didn't want to look stupid. But then I read these verses and was convicted for being shallow, wimpy, and weak. Real love allows for looking foolish. God wants me to love Him and to love people enough that I am willing to forget my ego. The strong are not overly concerned with the opinions of the weak. To be strong in Him means I am willing to look foolish to others.

*Today I will remember:*

- Love is willing to look foolish in service to others.
- God wants me to love Him and to love people enough that I am willing to forget my ego.

*Jesus, help me be strong enough to look weak.*
*Help me love You and others more than my ego.*
*Thank You for Your humiliating sacrifice for me.*

# STEP INTO THE LIGHT

*This is the verdict: Light has come into the world, but people loved darkness instead of light because their deeds were evil. Everyone who does evil hates the light, and will not come into the light for fear that their deeds will be exposed.*

JOHN 3:19-20

I look great in the dark. Seriously, awesome. Not so much in the light, though. Light exposes. In the light, you can see my blemishes, my weight, and my aging body. Jesus is the light of the world, which is why many have a problem with Him. His light exposes our need. We like to keep our problems, our flaws, and our struggles hidden.

Sin is like a vampire. It grows in the dark and shrinks in the light of Jesus. Jesus is real, and He only operates in the context of reality. He cannot help or save who you are pretending to be; that person does not really exist. We must own up to our sin and struggles if we want Jesus involved. Any area of your life where you need God's help will require a courageous decision to step into His light. To heal from it, you must open yourself up and deal with it.

*Today I will remember:*

- To be healed by Jesus requires that I courageously step out of hiding.
- His light defeats the darkness of sin.
- Trusting Him in humility is where I find the power of His saving grace.

*Jesus, You are the light of this world. Help me to love and trust You more than my pride, so that I might get help in my time of need.*

# A COURAGEOUS ASK

*"Ask and it will be given to you; seek and you will find; knock and the door will be opened to you. For everyone who asks receives; the one who seeks finds; and to the one who knocks, the door will be opened."*

MATTHEW 7:7-8

I was on a plane and had a window seat. The guy next to me wore a knee brace. He winced in pain when he stood up to let me into my seat. It was obvious that moving was painful for him. But about midway through the flight, I had to go to the restroom. I looked over and the dude was sleeping. I waited and waited because I didn't want to bother him. There's no way I could climb over him. Finally, my eyeballs were floating, and I couldn't take it anymore. I asked and I received relief. He was gracious and kind. I made a much bigger deal out of asking than he did.

It takes courage to ask for something, and this is true with God. Sometimes we have not simply because we ask not. God is never tired, never bothered, and never put out by our requests. In fact, Jesus tells us here in the original Greek language to keep asking, keep knocking, and keep searching. You can't bug or bother God with your asking. A lot of times, we are wishing or hoping, but we haven't asked God for His help. So courageously talk to God about everything. Nothing is off limits as you express your heart to Him.

*Today I will remember:*

- I can't bother God.
- He wants me to seek Him and to ask Him for things.
- Sometimes I have not because I ask not.

*Father, many times I hope for something but do not ask for Your help. I'm wishing instead of coming to You and talking about what I want. Thank You that I can talk to You about anything and ask You for anything. Thank You that You are not bothered by my requests.*

# FEAR IS AFRAID

*For the Spirit God gave us does not make us timid, but gives us power, love and self-discipline.*

2 TIMOTHY 1:7

I memorized this verse as a kid. In fact, there were hand motions and everything. Only recently have I understood its meaning. Fear is not a fruit of the Spirit. The Holy Spirit does not make us afraid. He brings peace. So any fear we allow to control us is not from God but from another source. To let fear make our decisions is to worship something other than God.

Fear comes from two places: our own sin nature and from the evil one. Let's start with evil forces. Fear is a spirit. There are dark forces at work that want to intimidate us and keep us from doing what's right. What's right almost always requires courage. What do we do with a spirit of fear? We command it to depart in Jesus' name. Jesus is bigger and fear is afraid of Him. Then go do the courageous thing.

If the fear is coming from our own insecurities, we remind ourselves that our trust is in Jesus. We are not moving forward in our own power or worthiness, but in His. Jesus is the focus, and fear submits to His authority.

*Today I will remember:*

- Fear is a spirit, and it is afraid of Jesus.
- God's Spirit gives me power, love, and self-discipline.

*Jesus, grant me knowledge of the right thing to do and the courage to do it. Thank You that fear submits to the power of Your name. You are the Prince of Peace, and I trust in You.*

# TAKE COURAGE

*When the disciples saw him walking on the lake, they were terrified.*
*"It's a ghost," they said, and cried out in fear.*
*But Jesus immediately said to them:*
*"Take courage! It is I. Don't be afraid."*

MATTHEW 14:26-27

The sea was a place of mystery, myth, folklore, and danger. The disciples were floating in darkness in the middle of the night. Suddenly they see a mysterious figure and are terrified, as we would have been.

Do we take courage in the presence of Jesus, or do we find Him scary too? Maybe not scary, but perhaps annoying. If Jesus called and you saw His name on Caller ID and knew it really was Him, would you answer, or let the call go to voicemail? Many believe that real surrender to Jesus and His ways might mess up their lives. How about you?

Jesus is the Prince of Peace. His presence brings calm. To avoid Him is to avoid true serenity. He never ghosts us, but we tend to ghost Him. Because we're afraid. Where in your life are you avoiding Jesus? Take courage. All His ways are for your good. Don't avoid Him; include Him. The more you understand who He is, the more peace you will find. Take courage in the presence of Jesus.

*Today I will remember:*

- I can take courage in Jesus.
- Peace is found in welcoming Him into every area of my life.
- He will never ghost me, and His ways are best.

*Jesus, help me to know and understand You.*
*Forgive me for avoiding You and keeping You out*
*of certain areas of my life. In Your presence*
*there is peace, and I welcome You in.*

# ONLY GAIN

*I eagerly expect and hope that I will in no way be ashamed, but will have sufficient courage so that now as always Christ will be exalted in my body, whether by life or by death. For to me, to live is Christ and to die is gain.*

PHILIPPIANS 1:20-21

One of my friends was a Navy SEAL. He's one of the nicest, kindest, and most dangerous men I've ever met. He did several tours of duty in the Gulf War. He is the quintessential warrior and has proven himself in battle. If something went down, I am confident that this guy would not hesitate to act. In him, I have a certain hope, and I expect courage.

The apostle Paul had a certain hope and eagerly expected that he would be courageous when it came to his faith. Even death wasn't a threat to him; he considered it a bonus. He was all in because he knew he would glorify Jesus one way or another. He was battle-proven, a quintessential Christ follower. I want to be like that. To know in advance that, come what may, I will glorify Jesus. How about you?

My Navy SEAL friend would say that his training prepared him for the trials of war. I think the apostle Paul would agree. The more we read the Bible, spend time in prayer, share our lives with other brothers who hold us accountable, the more prepared we are when the trials come. Training in the Bible prepares us for the battles. A weak man is an untrained man. Keep training in Jesus. Keep going. Knowledge, wisdom, love, and courage are forged in the training.

*Today I will remember:*

- A weak man is an untrained man.
- Training in prayer, the Bible, and accountability to Christian brothers prepares me for future tests and trials.

*Jesus, I choose to train in You and work out my life with You. In all this, bring me knowledge, wisdom, and courage.*

# October

## STEWARDSHIP

Then God blessed them and said, "Be fruitful
and multiply. Fill the earth and govern it.
Reign over the fish in the sea, the birds in the sky,
and all the animals that scurry along the ground."
*Genesis 1:28 (NLT)*

# SALVATION AND STEWARDSHIP

*Then God blessed them and said, "Be fruitful and multiply. Fill the earth and govern it. Reign over the fish in the sea, the birds in the sky, and all the animals that scurry along the ground."*

GENESIS 1:28 (NLT)

The two big themes of the Bible are salvation and stewardship. Salvation is all about God's redemptive plan in Christ. You see it prophesied in the Old Testament and much of it fulfilled in the New Testament. The Bible ends in Revelation with the prophecy that God will eventually redeem all things.

The other theme is stewardship. God has given us the world to govern, beginning right here in His command to Adam and Eve. God has made you a steward. You have been entrusted with resources and responsibilities. You will either manage things God's way or your way. Obedience to the Master is always the goal of a good steward. Rebellion, on the other hand, always brings brokenness.

On every page of the Bible, you will see one of these two themes at work. Whether the passage is descriptive or prescriptive, it will highlight His salvation or how we are to manage things on His behalf. Pray that you will be the best of managers, prioritizing God's wishes and will.

*Today I will remember:*

- The two big themes of the Bible are salvation and stewardship.
- Obedience to the Master is always the goal of a good steward.

*Lord, thanks for Your salvation and for Your blessings. Make me a good manager of all that You have entrusted me to govern. Your ways are best.*

# ON LOAN

*So then, each of us will give an account of ourselves to God.*

ROMANS 14:12

I once heard another pastor say, "What we think we own is really just on loan." That is so true. We came into this world with nothing. No matter what you've acquired in your lifetime, you will leave this world with nothing. Even your very breath is borrowed. One day, God, the owner of all things, will take it back. We are stewards, simply managing what God has given us for a time.

This is not only true when it comes to our possessions. It's also true when it comes to our relationships. My wife does not belong to me. She belongs to God. One day, I will give an account for how I cared for, provided for, and loved her—or for how I did not. The same is true with my children. They belong to the Creator of all things. This reality is both heavy and helpful. Heavy because of the responsibility, but helpful because of the perspective. Our job is simply to manage what we have been given in the way the Owner wants.

Here are two questions to think about. Am I managing my relationships in a way that honors God? Am I obedient to God with the money and possessions that He has entrusted to me? Evaluate and make whatever changes you believe God wants.

*Today I will remember:*

- What I think I own is just on loan.
- I should manage my relationships in a way that honors God.
- I can obey God with the money and possessions that He has entrusted to me.

*Lord, thank You for trusting me with what I have. I'm grateful. Help me to know how I can better manage it all for You.*

# GOOD STEWARDSHIP

*He has shown you, O mortal, what is good.*
*And what does the LORD require of you?*
*To act justly and to love mercy*
*and to walk humbly with your God.*

MICAH 6:8

This is one of my favorite verses in the Bible because it's so clear. Being a good steward involves three things. You act justly, you love mercy, and you walk humbly with the Master.

To act justly means to live with integrity, fairness, and righteousness. We are ethical and honest, just in our relationships and decisions. It's not about laws and punishment, but about love. We serve the vulnerable and speak up for the voiceless. We defend the oppressed. We are good men who use our strength to serve others.

To love mercy means we are compassionate. This includes kindness, generosity, and a willingness to forgive. We don't walk around choosing to rub it in when people are wrong. Instead, we show mercy. Instead of giving people what they deserve, we give them what they need.

To walk humbly with God means to be a servant. Our lives are about serving His purposes in the world and being honest in our need for Him. We live authentically in the light of truth. There are no proud followers of Jesus—just those who know they need His grace and offer it to others.

*Today I will remember:*

- Good stewards act justly, love mercy, and walk humbly with God.
- Men of God are righteous, compassionate, and humble.

*Thank You, Lord, for who You are. Your ways are right and good.*
*Help me to walk in them. When I give an account before You,*
*help me to stand as a good and faithful servant.*

# A GREAT INHERITANCE

*For you know the grace of our Lord*
*Jesus Christ, that though he was rich,*
*yet for your sake he became poor, so that*
*you through his poverty might become rich.*

2 CORINTHIANS 8:9

The grace of God allows us to be part of God's family. We are adopted into royalty as sons of the King. Heaven is our forever home. We're just travelers in this life on a mission trip. Our family home is paved with streets of gold and is full of the glory of the full presence of God. To walk with Jesus is to walk in wealth.

Jesus gave all He had to serve the poor. That means men like you and me. We were dead broke in our sin and had nothing to offer God. But Jesus stepped into our broken, impoverished world and graciously gave us all He had. Jesus paid a debt He did not owe because of the debt that we could never pay. In His generosity, we are made rich!

Even though we are now free, many of us return to the poverty of our sin. Following Jesus is learning to walk wealthy in grace, in the wealth of His righteousness, in the power and prosperity of His Spirit, and in the presence of the Father, who is the King. Do you know who you are? In Jesus, you're an adopted son of the royal bloodline. Let's step into that dignity. Let's be gracious in humility and be about the family business.

*Today I will remember:*

- To walk with Jesus is to walk in the wealth of His grace.
- In Jesus, I am a son of the Kings of kings and Lord of lords.

*Father, thank You that I am Your son. Give me the insight*
*I need to walk through this life in the wealth of Your grace.*
*I am fully known and fully loved by You. Thank You!*

# A TEMPLE

*Do you not know that your bodies are temples of the Holy Spirit, who is in you, whom you have received from God? You are not your own; you were bought at a price. Therefore honor God with your bodies.*

1 CORINTHIANS 6:19-20

God has called us as stewards to care for our bodies. Most men do not take this calling seriously, but God does. When we gave our lives to Jesus, we acknowledged His ownership, including our physicality. We are temples of the Holy Spirit. We don't have to become health nuts, but we should strive to be healthy.

God gives us many blessings. Food is one. If you've ever thought that a meal tasted heavenly, then you were theologically correct. Good food is a gift from God. There will be food in heaven. However, if we practice gluttony and continually make poor or inappropriate eating decisions, we turn this blessing into a bummer.

Romance and sex are similar. They are blessings from God. Treat this area of your life right, then it is good; take it outside of God's design, and it can destroy you, your family, and your legacy. Much of stewardship is simply staying within the bounds of blessing. Honor God with your body today. Eat real food, exercise, and manage your body in purity.

*Today I will remember:*

- My body is not my own.
- It belongs to God.
- Much of stewardship is simply staying within the bounds of blessing.

*Lord, all of me belongs to You. My body is given to me for a time to manage. Help me treat it correctly in health and in purity.*

# BIG BLESSING

*Remember this: Whoever sows sparingly will also reap sparingly, and whoever sows generously will also reap generously. Each of you should give what you have decided in your heart to give, not reluctantly or under compulsion, for God loves a cheerful giver.*

2 CORINTHIANS 9:6-7

I often get asked whether Christians should give their tithe (10%) based on their gross or their net income. I always answer, "I don't know. Would you prefer a gross blessing, or a net one?"

Whether we admit it or not, our questions in this vein may be more about doing the minimum required to stay within God's good graces than about getting an accurate answer. The Bible, however, is not about rules as much as about relationship. Do we trust Him? Trusting God with our money is where the rubber meets the road. It's a litmus test for what we truly believe.

Our verses say that when we think about giving, we should think *investment*. It's not so much what we're letting go of when we give, it's what we stand to gain when we trust Him. God loves it when we cheerfully trust Him. Ultimately, everything comes from Him, so to tithe is to simply give back to God a small portion of what's already His. We're sowing back into the source. Sow generously. If ten percent is a stretch, what percentage can you start to trust God with? Do it regularly and increase it. God delights in a cheerful giver.

*Today I will remember:*
- Giving is a test of our trust in God.
- God loves it when we cheerfully trust Him.

*Lord, thank You for all that You have given me. Let my heart be aligned with Yours. Make me a cheerful giver.*

# CHARACTER AND COMPETENCY

*And the Lord replied, "A faithful, sensible servant is one to whom the master can give the responsibility of managing his other household servants and feeding them. If the master returns and finds that the servant has done a good job, there will be a reward. I tell you the truth, the master will put that servant in charge of all he owns."*

LUKE 12:42-44 (NLT)

John, one of my best friends, is also our financial adviser. Our relationship, both personal and professional, is built on trust, for two main reasons: character and competency. Character: We know he wants what's best for us. He doesn't move our money around based on his commissions. Competency: John has over thirty years of experience and has helped build wealth for hundreds of clients.

When John invests for us, it's not his money, but ours. He is simply a steward of what we entrust to him. However, he knows that the more faithful he is with his clients' money, the more he will be rewarded with other people's money. He's built a thriving business based on being competent and displaying an outstanding character.

This is the principle of good stewardship. When we manage well what God has given us, He will entrust us with even more. The owner rewards faithful stewardship.

*Today I will remember:*

- I must manage what God has given me with character and competency.
- Character is about my heart and motives.
- Competency is about my head.

*Lord, all that I have is Yours. Help me to manage it with a pure heart and clean hands. Make me a good steward, so that I can be trusted with more.*

# STEWARDING COMPASSION

*"Going over to him, the Samaritan soothed his wounds with olive oil and wine and bandaged them. Then he put the man on his own donkey and took him to an inn, where he took care of him. The next day he handed the innkeeper two silver coins, telling him, 'Take care of this man. If his bill runs higher than this, I'll pay you the next time I'm here.'"*

LUKE 10:34-35 (NLT)

Today's verses are from the Parable of the Good Samaritan. Jesus mentions religious leaders in this parable who have no compassion and then makes the Samaritan the hero because of his compassion; he uses what he must to serve someone in desperate need. Part of being a good steward for God is using what He has entrusted to us to care for others. Repeatedly the Bible teaches that God's heart is with the poor and hurting. When we give and serve those in need, we reflect the heart of our Master.

Generosity to the poor is one of the great indicators of real faith in Jesus. Where there is no generosity, there is no real understanding of who Jesus is. He gives to us, so we give to others. Every Easter, our church receives a special offering that we give to a charity we trust that serves the poor. Through the years, we've been privileged to give away millions of dollars. Good stewards reflect the heart of their Master. Look for competent, trustworthy Christian charities that serve and empower the poor, and give generously to them.

*Today I will remember:*

- Repeatedly the Bible teaches that the heart of God is with the poor and hurting.
- When I give and serve those in need, I show forth the heart of my Master.

*God, thank You that when I was spiritually bankrupt, You gave Your life for my salvation. May my heart and giving reflect Your generosity.*

# CONTENTMENT

*But godliness with contentment is great gain.*
1 TIMOTHY 6:6

The purpose of every billboard, every commercial, and every pop-up ad is to breed discontentment. Marketing exists to feed our greed. The world constantly wages war on our souls, telling us that we would be happy if only we had more.

The constant chasing of stuff to validate our lives is a treadmill that never stops. However, this verse teaches that great gain comes when you realize that less is more. The gain here is getting to a place where material things are necessary, but not defining. Where our net worth and self-worth are not the same thing. Where our valuables are not what make us valuable.

Contentment is great gain because it is peace. It's knowing that life is more than the clothes we wear, the car we drive, and the house we live in. Maybe the streets in heaven are paved with gold because gold doesn't have much value there. Heaven is heavenly because of right relationships with God and people. Heaven is a place of contentment. If you want a little heaven in this world, then look for life in the places where it actually resides. Godliness with contentment is great gain.

*Today I will remember:*

- Contentment is the most valuable thing I can own.
- My valuables are not what make me valuable.

*God, help me to see what You see. Life is not found in an abundance of possessions, but in right relationship with You and with others.*

# DILIGENCE

*The plans of the diligent lead to profit*
*as surely as haste leads to poverty.*
PROVERBS 21:5

A buddy and I hiked through the woods to our hunting spot to prepare for the deer hunt. As we were setting up camp, I realized I had packed the wrong sleeping bag. The one I packed is rated for warmer weather. That night it got down into the thirties, and we slept in the open air on backpack cots. Yeah, I froze my butt off.

You don't want to do something similar in your financial planning. Fools rush in. The wise think things through. A mistake in packing might make for an uncomfortable night, but a big mistake in our financial life could hijack things for years. Wise men are diligent. They think through the potential consequences of their decisions. They work hard at forming the plan and then work hard at executing it. Another friend of mine says we want to always be "minding our business," thinking through what we're doing with our money. The best way to predict the future is to create it, and we are all creating our futures one decision at a time. Will the decisions you made today make for a better tomorrow?

*Today I will remember:*
- Today's decisions affect my tomorrows, for better or worse.
- Fools rush in, while the wise think things through.

*Father, help me to see that I create*
*my future by the choices I make today.*
*Help me to be diligent in my decisions.*

# DIVERSIFY

*Invest in seven ventures, yes, in eight; you do not know what disaster may come upon the land.*

ECCLESIASTES 11:2

Have you ever heard the phrase "Don't put all your eggs in one basket"? It comes from this verse. Solomon, the wisest and wealthiest man who ever lived, is the author. His net worth in modern dollars would make him a trillionaire, so I'd say it's sound advice. Good stewards practice diversification.

Beware of get-rich-quick schemes and investing all your money in a "sure thing." There are no sure things except death, taxes, and the goodness of God. Your money is always up for grabs, and it will leave you in a second if you treat it foolishly. Wealth is usually built slowly. The more you invest wisely now, the more you will have later. Now occasionally someone does get rich quickly, but this is rare. What we don't hear are all the stories of the guys who lost their shirts.

You might not have enough money to invest in eight ventures. Then wisely invest in a few. The point is, don't put all your eggs in one basket. A good financial adviser will help you invest in several companies that do various things. Solomon was right thousands of years ago, and he's right today. Practice the principle of diversification.

*Today I will remember:*

- There are no sure things except death, taxes, and the goodness of God.
- I invest my money wisely when I use the principle of diversification.

*God, all I have is Yours. Help me to heed the counsel of Your Word and to invest wisely. Protect me from poor financial decisions.*

# FREEDOM NOT SLAVERY

*The rich rule over the poor, and the borrower is slave to the lender.*
PROVERBS 22:7

I spent my twenties doing stupid things with money. I thought money was primarily about buying stuff and that good financial planning was all about a good credit score. After all, the better the score, the more stuff you can buy! I remember being so excited to get envelopes in the mail that said "pre-approved" on the front. Of all the people that the credit card company could have chosen, it chose me! Little did I know how dumb that type of thinking is. I was just signing up for slavery.

Credit card debt is dumb debt. If you are paying off the balance every month, then it's fine. A credit card is convenient. However, if you are just making the minimum payment, then you are not experiencing convenience but incarceration. You are locking yourself in a prison of debt because you are being charged interest, and that interest is compounding. You are digging a deeper and deeper hole with every passing day. Your credit cards are the shovels.

The first step to getting out of the hole is to stop the spending. I spent my twenties getting chained to debt and my wife Katrina and I spent our thirties breaking free. Financial expert Dave Ramsey's books and courses helped us. Today I am in my early fifties, and we are debt free except for our house. It feels great! Don't chain yourself down with dumb debt. But if you have, take the steps to break free!

*Today I will remember:*
- Don't chain yourself down with dumb debt.
- Telling myself no is one of the keys to financial freedom.

*Lord, thank You for the book of Proverbs.*
*I choose to seek and practice Your financial wisdom.*
*Help me live in financial freedom.*

# GIVE FIRST

*Be sure to set aside a tenth of all*
*that your fields produce each year.*
DEUTERONOMY 14:22

If you take everything the Bible says about how we are to manage money, it breaks down to give first, save second, and live on the rest.

Giving first honors God. Any time you receive income, you should acknowledge first where it came from. We do this by practicing percentage giving. The most common percentage word in the Bible is the word *tithe*. It literally means "ten percent." I believe we are called to give God ten percent of everything we make to our local church. This is a principle established in the Old Testament and it continues in the New Testament.

Katrina and I have been doing this for the last twenty-four years. At the start of our marriage, we heard a sermon on tithing, and she suggested we start. I didn't think so. For me, it was simply a matter of math. She was still attending university. I was working for a nonprofit. We had more expenses than income. Taking out ten percent to give to God made absolutely no sense! Then she said something mean: "Why don't you pray about it?"

Well, reluctantly, I *did* pray about it, and soon after we started tithing. You know what happened? Ninety percent of our income went farther than the previous one hundred percent. Things worked out. I have never regretted trusting God with our finances. Back then I didn't think we could afford to tithe. Now I know we can't afford not to. Put God first in any area of your life that you want God to bless. This includes money. Maybe you should pray about it.

*Today I will remember:*

- Any time I receive income, I will first acknowledge where it ultimately came from.
- Giving first honors God.

*God, I want to trust You in all things.*
*I choose to put You first in my finances by giving*
*back to You a portion of what You've given me.*

# SAVE SECOND

*Go to the ant, you sluggard; consider its ways and be wise! It has no commander, no overseer or ruler, yet it stores its provisions in summer and gathers its food at harvest.*

PROVERBS 6:6-8

Yesterday, I wrote that if you take everything the Bible says about how to manage money, you can break it down to these three things: Give first. Save second. Live on the rest.

I believe we're to give God ten percent of everything we make, and I suggest that you save ten percent as well. Every time you receive income, give ten percent, save ten percent, and live on the eighty percent. Giving first honors God. Saving second, over time, will build wealth. Living on the rest teaches contentment. A lot of people spend more than they make by using credit cards and living on debt. If you're constantly spending more than you make, then you will never get ahead financially. The only way to build wealth is through saving and investing. You must plan for it to happen, and then make it happen.

Giving first, saving second, and living on the rest is a financial plan that has worked for thousands of years. If you want something, but don't have the money to buy it, don't! It's that simple. Learn these four magic words: I can't afford it. Instead of buying things you don't need, with money you don't have, to impress people you don't know, pay yourself! Paying yourself for all your hard work is called saving. The sooner you practice it, the sooner you'll build it.

*Today I will remember:*

- God wants me to give first, save second, and live on the rest.
- Saving and planning for the future are part of God's will for how I handle money.

*Father, thank You for providing for all my needs. Give me wisdom to save money well and to prepare for the future.*

# INVEST YOUR LIFE

*"Then the servant with the one bag of silver came and said, 'Master, I knew you were a harsh man, harvesting crops you didn't plant and gathering crops you didn't cultivate. I was afraid I would lose your money, so I hid it in the earth. Look, here is your money back.' But the master replied, 'You wicked and lazy servant! If you knew I harvested crops I didn't plant and gathered crops I didn't cultivate, why didn't you deposit my money in the bank? At least I could have gotten some interest on it.'"*

MATTHEW 25:24-27 (NLT)

Fearful and lazy stewards are rarely rewarded. Where there is an excess of excuses there is usually a lack of gain. In this famous parable, the master entrusts each of his three servants with money to invest. The first two multiply it, while the third buries it. Out of fear, he conceals what the master has given him. Is there anything that you have buried? A talent or gift that God has given that you are too afraid or lazy to use?

Jesus is not teaching about potential here. We will never know if we've reached our potential. In many ways, chasing this false god can keep you from God's purposes. What Jesus is teaching is stewardship. The Master entrusts us with talents and resources to use for His kingdom. Many do nothing with them. So invest your life. No one on his deathbed wishes he had watched more Netflix. Serve God by serving people. Don't waste your life. Invest it.

*Today I will remember:*

- Laziness and fear never accomplish anything.
- I can serve God by serving people.
- I won't waste my life; I'll invest it.

*Lord, forgive me for my fear and laziness. Help me not to sit and watch life go by, but to actually live and to invest my life in the things that matter most.*

# MANAGE THE GIFTS

*There are different kinds of spiritual gifts, but the same Spirit is the source of them all. There are different kinds of service, but we serve the same Lord. God works in different ways, but it is the same God who does the work in all of us.*

1 CORINTHIANS 12:4-6 (NLT)

Have you ever heard someone speak, sing, treat you with amazing hospitality, or care for the hurting in such a powerful way that you thought, *Man, that person is just gifted*? You would be correct. The Bible says that followers of Jesus are entrusted with gifts of the Holy Spirit. There are various things that each of us can do that are naturally supernatural. What are some of your gifts? If you're not sure, ask God. You can also ask your wife or people who know you well. They will probably see some things in you that you didn't.

One time I heard a pastor say something crass, but true: We must be careful not to "pimp out" the gifts of God. You'll remember that one. What he meant was these precious gifts are only to be used for *God's* purposes. When we leverage them for personal gain and forget God, we are cheaply selling out a prized gift. The gifts are for God, for the good of others, and to serve the church. They are from the Holy Spirit living in you. Manage them well. Treat them as precious and use them for God's glory.

*Today I will remember:*

- I am gifted by God for the good of others.
- This serves the church and His glory.
- The Holy Spirit resides in me.

*Holy Spirit, give me wisdom concerning the gifts You've given me. I want to naturally serve in supernatural ways as You work in and through me. Help me be a good steward of these gifts.*

# MEN AT WORK

*Lazy hands make for poverty,*
*but diligent hands bring wealth.*
PROVERBS 10:4

A young man recently told me about his big dreams for the future: driving expensive sports cars, owning several houses in beautiful places, and living the life of the rich and famous. But work is something he plans to avoid, in favor of get-rich-quick schemes. He is sure that his ship will come in! But God doesn't instruct us to wait for our ship to come in. He instructs us to swim out to the boat.

You were made to work. It's part of what it means to step into manhood. A lazy boy will always be restless and unfulfilled. God made us to plan and to work. This is how the wise create wealth. This is part of God's will for you. You might not be rich, but you must be responsible. Men are called to provide for themselves and their families. A boy becomes a man when he begins to produce more than he consumes. Until then, you're like a baby still nursing at someone's breast. You're sucking on the provision somebody else provided. That's fine for a child, but not for a man.

Now it could be that you're thinking of an exception right now. Someone who purchased a winning lottery ticket or bought bitcoin way back when. Fair enough. Proverbs is about how life *generally* works. However, even if you receive an unexpected windfall, God's will is not for you to waste it, but to work it!

*Today I will remember:*

- It's God's will for me to work.
- God doesn't instruct me to wait for my ship to come in but to swim out to the boat.

*Lord, thank You for Your gifts.*
*Guide me in the work You have for me.*
*Let me be diligent and work hard.*

# MIND YOUR BUSINESS

*Be sure you know the condition of your flocks,*
*give careful attention to your herds; for riches do not*
*endure forever, and a crown is not secure for all generations.*

PROVERBS 27:23-24

I was in Mexico with my wife last week at a pastor's gathering. One night they had Dave Ramsey speak to us. Dave is famous for helping people get out of debt and move to a place of financial freedom. At one point in the evening, we got to ask him questions. I didn't have any questions; I just wanted to express a sincere thank you to him.

In my twenties, I did a lot of dumb things with money. I would buy things I couldn't afford, with money I didn't have, to impress people I didn't know. I brought a lot of dumb debt into our marriage, and, as a result, we were upside down financially. We took a course that Dave taught called Financial Peace University that changed our lives. Today, the only debt we have is our house. I wish for you the freedom that comes with making wise financial decisions. I wish for you, financial peace.

Our verse for today is about minding your business, meaning you know your financial situation. You are running the business of you. There are three things you always want to have your eye on: what you make, what you own, and what you owe. As our verse for today teaches, the first step to getting where you want to be financially is knowing where you are right now. Are you minding your business?

*Today I will remember:*

- I can mind my business by knowing my financial reality.
- This includes what I make, what I own, and what I owe.

*Father, thank You for what You've given me.*
*Help me to manage it well. I cannot manage what I am*
*unaware of. Help me to mind the business of my life.*

# MONEY LOVIN'

*For the love of money is a root of all kinds of evil. Some people, eager for money, have wandered from the faith and pierced themselves with many griefs.*

1 TIMOTHY 6:10

Many think that this verse says that money is the root of all evil. That's incorrect. It's the *love* of money that is a problem. Think about it. How can money by itself be evil? It doesn't have a heart or soul. It's how all business is transacted, and everyone needs it to live. People who say they don't care about money are probably going to lie about other things too.

However, the *love and worship* of money is a huge problem. It's the source of great heartache. Our verse teaches that we're to *love* God and people and *use* money. But if we *love* money, we will try to *use* God and people to get more of it. This is the "prosperity gospel." It's not true and is shameful in many ways.

Money is simply a tool. We're not to worship or abuse it, but to use it. We use this tool to provide for our families, fund the work of God in the world, and build for the future. Love God and people and put money in its proper place.

*Today I will remember:*

- Love God and people and use money.
- Money is a tool to provide for our families, fund God's work, and build for the future.

*Father, give me a proper view of money.*
*Help me to love You and others*
*and manage money as You wish.*

# NO ONE'S BUSINESS

*Now it is required that those who have been given a trust must prove faithful. I care very little if I am judged by you or by any human court; indeed, I do not even judge myself. My conscience is clear, but that does not make me innocent. It is the Lord who judges me.*

1 CORINTHIANS 4:2-4

I recently met with a woman about buying a car. She and her husband had been faithful members of our church for a long time, but she was anxious about the purchase—but not because they wanted to buy something they couldn't afford. I realized that she was nervous about other people's opinions. We broke down their finances, she and her husband were faithful in their tithes, and I saw no problem with the purchase. It was something they had always wanted, could easily afford and that they would enjoy. She was suffering from a false sense of guilt.

Everybody has an opinion about how you spend your money. It's true in our extended families, and it can be true in the church. But at the end of day, it's nobody's business but yours and God's.

Being a good steward of what God has given is as simple as obedience. Obey God and enjoy your life. Everyone has an opinion about everything. I've learned that opinions are like armpits. Everybody has two and they all stink if not treated properly. Be faithful to God and enjoy the blessings He has given you. There is no need for false guilt.

*Today I will remember:*

- By obeying God, I can enjoy my life.
- It's no one else's business what I spend my money on.
- It's between me, my spouse, and the Lord.

*God, thank You for Your blessings.*
*They are given to me to enjoy.*
*Help me to be faithful and obedient,*
*and let no burden come with Your blessings.*

# YOU'RE NOT THE EXCEPTION

*Wisdom will save you from the ways of wicked men,*
*from men whose words are perverse, who have left*
*the straight paths to walk in dark ways, who delight*
*in doing wrong and rejoice in the perverseness of evil,*
*whose paths are crooked and who are devious in their ways.*

PROVERBS 2:12-15

I've come to realize that anyone is capable of doing anything. We are all just one bad decision from screwing up our lives and legacy. Have you ever been shocked at someone who blew up his life over an immoral decision? Like, you never thought in a million years that this guy you knew would decide to do that. Yeah, me too. Stories like this serve as a caution. You, too, are very capable of blowing up your life, and so am I. We are not the exception.

Wisdom is a daily decision, and daily decisions are leading us down a path. Decisions have destinations. The dark path is real, and walkers must beware. Even though it looks like someone made one bad decision that blew up his or her life, it was probably a bunch of little decisions that eventually led to the one big one. Brother, the journey into darkness is a path, not a light switch. It's a slow fade. Choose to be a good steward daily. If you're already on a bad path, repent and tell someone you trust. Get back on the right path! Decisions have destinations.

*Today I will remember:*

- Decisions have destinations.
- Being a wise steward and staying on the right paths are daily choices.
- I am not the exception.

*Lord, I choose today to stay off the dark paths. Give me*
*a pure mind and heart and the wisdom to see that*
*decisions have destinations. May I walk wisely each day.*

# PLAY YOUR PART

*How strange a body would be if it had only one part!*
*Yes, there are many parts, but only one body.*
*The eye can never say to the hand, "I don't need you."*
*The head can't say to the feet, "I don't need you."*
1 CORINTHIANS 12:19-21 (NLT)

I recently had a conversation with a Christian who doesn't go to church. He told me he connects with God in nature, and that nature is his church. He was clearly ignorant about what church is. I too connect with God in nature, but church is much more than that. To neglect church is to weaken both it and yourself.

The church is a body. Like a body, it consists of many parts. It is a gross misunderstanding to think that church is simply a meeting to be educated and entertained about God. You don't go to church; you are the church. You and I need people, and they need us. To say your church is separate from the body is like a foot saying it's fine by itself; no, it's gross. It's weird and rotting. Saying that you experience God best in nature is simply a lazy excuse. I'm glad you do. Now go back and play your part in the body of Christ.

*Today I will remember:*

- I don't go to church; I am the church.
- I need people, and they need me.
- I should play my part in serving the church.

*Lord, thank You that I am an important part of the body.*
*The church needs me, and I need the church.*
*Forgive me for thinking it's just about me.*

# PROSPEROUS PRIDE

*Command those who are rich in this present world*
*not to be arrogant nor to put their hope in wealth,*
*which is so uncertain, but to put their hope in God,*
*who richly provides us with everything for our enjoyment.*
1 TIMOTHY 6:17

When I was a kid, I really wanted a pair of Zips sneakers. Perhaps you remember their commercials. Zips were supposed to make you faster, quicker, and able to jump higher. In the commercial, when kids wore Zips, they won races and leaped over bushes. You even heard the same iconic sound featured on *The Six Million Dollar Man* whenever the bionic man did something super.

One day, after I begged my mom, she got me a pair. I put on those bad boys and instantly became cocky. Filled with ignorant arrogance because of these new shoes, I challenged a girl down the street to a race. She had beaten me many times. Guess what? I lost. I was still slow, and my vertical was still unimpressive. Those shoes gave me a false sense of pride, ability, and importance. Money and stuff always do.

Writing to a young pastor, Paul tells Timothy to warn people with money not to be arrogant. Why? Because wealth makes one cocky. Just because you have some material stuff doesn't mean you have all the smarts. Beware of prosperous pride; it can make you ignorantly arrogant. Choose a posture of gratitude, knowing that God put you in the right place, at the right time, with the right abilities to prosper. Be generous and humble. We all still have a lot to learn.

*Today I will remember:*

- Money can give a false sense of pride, ability, and importance.
- We must be humble and grateful for all that God has given.

*Father, thank You for the blessings.*
*I choose a posture of gratitude, knowing that*
*You put me in the right place, at the*
*right time, with the right abilities to prosper.*

# SOWING AND REAPING

*Do not be deceived: God cannot be mocked. A man reaps what he sows. Whoever sows to please their flesh, from the flesh will reap destruction; whoever sows to please the Spirit, from the Spirit will reap eternal life. Let us not become weary in doing good, for at the proper time we will reap a harvest if we do not give up. Therefore, as we have opportunity, let us do good to all people, especially to those who belong to the family of believers.*

GALATIANS 6:7-10

What I'm about to say is not that insightful. In fact, it has proven itself true for thousands of years and will continue to do so for thousands more. It's simple. It's common sense. Are you ready? Here it is: You reap what you sow. Life is clear, experience is clear, and the Bible is crystal clear that this is true. And yet sometimes we forget. Our decisions today will reap a harvest in the future, for better or for worse. Wise stewards make decisions today that will make for a better tomorrow.

The good news is, if you don't like where you are, you can change your trajectory. If you don't like the crop you are reaping, you can change the seeds you are sowing. The sobering news is that every decision has a consequence. While we cannot control all that happens to us, we are responsible for how we respond. Grown men get this and take responsibility for their decisions. Practice extreme ownership here. God owns it all but has given you the ownership of your choices. Choose to be a wise steward and repent when you are foolish.

*Today I will remember:*
- If I don't like the crop I am reaping, I can change the seeds I am sowing.
- I will take one hundred percent responsibility for my decisions.

*Father, thank You for Your grace. In Jesus, You have given me unmerited favor. At the same time, I choose to take responsibility for my actions. Help me make decisions today that create a better tomorrow.*

# THE STEWARDSHIP OF JOSEPH

*The LORD was with Joseph, so he succeeded in everything he did as he served in the home of his Egyptian master. Potiphar noticed this and realized that the LORD was with Joseph, giving him success in everything he did. This pleased Potiphar, so he soon made Joseph his personal attendant. He put him in charge of his entire household and everything he owned.*

GENESIS 39:2-4 (NLT)

You know what I've noticed? The men in my church who honor God, work hard, and treat people well get promoted. It's as uncanny as it is common. Being a good steward of what God gives us makes us a good steward of what people give us. They go hand in hand. Such is the account of Joseph. Everywhere he went, he succeeded.

Now in many ways the middle of Joseph's life is like a bad country song. His brothers reject him and sell him into slavery. Later, he is falsely accused of rape and thrown into prison. But in whatever situation he finds himself, Joseph seems to thrive. If he's a slave, he's the best slave he can be. If he's a prisoner, then he's the best prisoner he can be. Spoiler alert: Eventually God rescues Joseph, and he becomes Pharaoh's right-hand man. And you know what? He thrives in that role too.

God's ways are always best. In whatever situation we find ourselves, God's ways work. Being good stewards of God's gifts makes us good stewards of our families, our companies, or any situation in which we find ourselves.

*Today I will remember:*

- Being a good steward of what God gives us makes us a good steward of what people give us.
- In whatever situation we find ourselves, God's ways work.

*God, I always work for You first. Serving You well makes me a good father, husband, boss, or employee. Help me to serve You in all things.*

# THE STEWARDSHIP OF NEHEMIAH

*Then I said to them, "You see the trouble we are in: Jerusalem lies in ruins, and its gates have been burned with fire. Come, let us rebuild the wall of Jerusalem, and we will no longer be in disgrace." I also told them about the gracious hand of my God on me and what the king had said to me. They replied, "Let us start rebuilding." So they began this good work.*

NEHEMIAH 2:17-18

The book of Nehemiah is a classic study on great leadership. The walls of Jerusalem have fallen, and the city remains vulnerable. Not only is the city in shambles, but the people's morale is as well. A broken-down wall symbolizes a broken-down people. It is a disgrace. Nehemiah convinces the foreign king Artaxerxes to not only allow him to lead a movement to rebuild the wall but also to grant him the funding. Nehemiah is leading a comeback for the glory of God and the good of his people.

Christian leadership is always a service of stewardship. Leaders who serve the King of kings lead on His behalf. Our influence, the culture we build, and the goals we accomplish are a sacrificial gift to the glory of God and the good of others. Nehemiah led with integrity and wisdom. He took full responsibility to accomplish the seemingly impossible. He navigated low morale, financial struggles, and even violent opposition, and did it all in the name of the Lord.

*Today I will remember:*

- Christian leadership is always a service of stewardship.
- Leaders who serve the King of kings lead on His behalf.

*Father, give me the grace to lead well as I serve under Your leadership. I ask this first for my home and then in my church and career. May it all be in service to You.*

# THE STEWARDSHIP OF NOAH

*This is how you are to build it: The ark is to be three hundred cubits long, fifty cubits wide and thirty cubits high. Make a roof for it, leaving below the roof an opening one cubit high all around. Put a door in the side of the ark and make lower, middle and upper decks. I am going to bring floodwaters on the earth to destroy all life under the heavens, every creature that has the breath of life in it. Everything on earth will perish. But I will establish my covenant with you, and you will enter the ark—you and your sons and your wife and your sons' wives with you.*

GENESIS 6:15-18

One of the reasons I believe the Bible is true, and particularly the account of Noah and the ark, is the details. Look at the details in our verses for today. God gives Noah very specific instructions for the ark. The dimensions are exact as well as the design and in other verses there are specific instructions on how to keep the ark watertight. Legends lack detail; the Bible does not. Noah is a good steward of what God instructs him to do. And because he is, Noah's family, and ultimately the future human race, is spared.

Stewardship is a form of obedience. It is doing what God says in the way that He says it. When you and I prioritize obedience and faithfulness, we are good stewards. Examine your life. Anything that is outside of God's desire and design is poor stewardship. Adjust and serve Him faithfully.

*Today I will remember:*

- Stewardship is a form of obedience.
- When I prioritize obedience and faithfulness, I am being a good steward.

*Lord, Your ways are best, and the details of my life matter to You. Help me to joyfully live in obedience to Your commands. This is a blessing to me and my family.*

# THE STEWARDSHIP OF SOLOMON

*"Now, LORD my God, you have made your servant king in place of my father David. But I am only a little child and do not know how to carry out my duties. Your servant is here among the people you have chosen, a great people, too numerous to count or number. So give your servant a discerning heart to govern your people and to distinguish between right and wrong. For who is able to govern this great people of yours?"*

1 KINGS 3:7-9

This is the prayer of a man who desires to be a good steward. It is humble, grateful, selfless, and serving. After the passing of his father, David, Solomon ascends the throne. The Lord comes to the young man in a dream. God says that He'll grant Solomon whatever he asks for, and Solomon responds with this prayer. That's impressive and insightful to the wisdom he already possessed.

God grants his wish and gives Solomon more wisdom to manage the kingdom, and as a result, Israel thrives. Solomon's reign is still seen as the most prosperous time in Jewish history. Yet success would cause Solomon to drift. He begins to serve foreign gods and break his promises to the Lord God. The lesson? Let's stick with Solomon's first prayer. Let's stay humble, grateful, and selfless. God responds to such prayers.

*Today I will remember:*

- The humble, grateful, selfless, servant prayer is the prayer of a good steward.
- God responds to such prayers.

*God, give Your servant a discerning heart to govern all that You have entrusted to me. I am grateful and humbly ask for wisdom to serve Your purposes well.*

# THE ULTIMATE STEWARD

*In your relationships with one another, have the same mindset as Christ Jesus: Who, being in very nature God, did not consider equality with God something to be used to his own advantage; rather, he made himself nothing by taking the very nature of a servant, being made in human likeness.*

PHILIPPIANS 2:5-7

Erik has made a lot of money in real estate. If you met him on the street, you would never guess that he is a millionaire. He is humble, kind, and unassuming. He leads a local food bank. He also greets visitors and serves coffee at our church. Right now, he's working on a community project to serve adults with special needs. Erik understands stewardship. His life is not his own. He joyfully lays it down in service to God.

Jesus, the ultimate steward, gave all He had in service to the Father. He understood that His life and ultimately His death served a greater purpose. It was never about Him but always about the will of God through Him. The apostle Paul encourages us to have the same mindset.

If you're wondering if you are a good steward, ask yourself if you are good at serving others. We serve God by serving people. To have the mindset of Jesus is to take on the mind of a servant. Ironically, Jesus was always the most powerful person in the room, and He always chose to serve. You're never more like Jesus than when you give and serve. It is the very essence of what it means to follow Him.

*Today I will remember:*

- Jesus is the ultimate steward, giving all He had in service to the Father.
- I serve God by serving people.
- To have the mindset of Jesus is to take on the mind of a servant.

*Holy Spirit, give me the mindset of Jesus.*
*Help me serve Him by serving others.*
*This is the heart of good stewardship.*

# THE WIDOW'S OFFERING

*But a poor widow came and put in two very small copper coins, worth only a few cents. Calling his disciples to him, Jesus said, "Truly I tell you, this poor widow has put more into the treasury than all the others. They all gave out of their wealth; but she, out of her poverty, put in everything—all she had to live on."*

MARK 12:42-44

Several years ago, I purchased a small ancient coin that was advertised as a "mite." A mite was a small copper coin used in ancient Judea and was worth very little. This account in Scripture is usually referred to as the "Widow's Mite." Jesus celebrates her offering not for the amount given, but the percentage given. The wealthy gave larger amounts, but a smaller percentage of what they had. The widow gave one hundred percent, "all she had to live on."

Most of us never think of ourselves as greedy. I mean when was the last time you heard a sermon on greed? We think of ourselves as generous. We think back to Christmas time when we dropped two dollars into the Salvation Army bucket. Now we might make a hundred thousand dollars a year, but, you know, there were those two dollars last Christmas.

God's plan for giving is not about amount, but percentage. Studies show that the more someone makes, the less of a percentage he or she usually gives. Let's flip that. Give consistently the percentage that God has called you to give, regardless of amount. The widow was fully devoted to God, and her giving reflected that. Our giving reflects our devotion as well.

*Today I will remember:*
- Giving to God is not about amount, but percentage.
- My giving reflects my devotion.

*Jesus, thank You for Your generosity to me. You gave one hundred percent. May my heart be aligned with Yours. Help me to grow in generosity.*

# THEOLOGY OF STEWARDSHIP

*Each of you should use whatever gift you have received to serve others, as faithful stewards of God's grace in its various forms.*

1 PETER 4:10

There are three major theologies of money in the church. I believe one is right and the other two are wrong. You may disagree, but let's think about it.

Prosperity Theology: This says that God wants all Christians to be wealthy. I do not believe this for two main reasons. First, there are many people all over the world who live in poverty and love Jesus with all their hearts. Jesus affirms the widow who puts two cents in the offering at the temple. She is poor in money but rich in faith. Second, prosperity theology is not about loving God, but loving money. It's about using God to get more of what's really loved.

Poverty Theology: This claims that being poor is righteous and being rich is wicked. But there are righteous rich people in the Bible and wicked poor people in the Bible. Abraham was righteous and wealthy, and Proverbs highlights poor people who are poor because of laziness, gambling, or alcohol abuse. Money is neutral. It's our hearts and our actions that determine righteousness or wickedness.

Stewardship Theology: This says God owns it all, and we are simply temporary managers or stewards of what He has entrusted to us. We are to manage what we have God's way because it all belongs to Him anyway. This is what I believe the Scriptures teach.

*Today I will remember:*

- God is the owner, and I am the manager.
- Everything I have is entrusted to me for a time.

*God, help me to be a good steward of all that You have entrusted me. I am grateful and want to be a faithful manager in all that I have for the time You've given me.*

# November

## THE HOLY SPIRIT

*"But you will receive power when the Holy Spirit comes on you;
and you will be my witnesses in Jerusalem, and in all
Judea and Samaria, and to the ends of the earth."*
*Acts 1:8*

# NOT A GHOST

*"But the Advocate, the Holy Spirit,*
*whom the Father will send in my name,*
*will teach you all things and will remind*
*you of everything I have said to you."*
JOHN 14:26

From birth to about age 17, I was at church almost every weekend. I was also there most Wednesday nights for youth group as a teenager. I attended camps, went on mission trips, and did Bible studies during the week. I went to a Christian university and studied the Old and New Testaments. But despite all this, I rarely heard about the Holy Spirit and, if I did, He was referred to as the "Holy Ghost." That was always weird to me. The only ghost I knew anything about was the cartoon one named Casper. Otherwise, I thought of ghosts as dead people coming back to haunt the living. We stayed away from such things.

The Holy Spirit is not a ghost. He is a Person within the trinitarian fellowship of one God, who is Father, Son, and Holy Spirit, who are distinct and yet one. In the church I grew up in, we just talked about the Father, Son, and Holy Bible. The Spirit was left out. In this month of Thanksgiving, let's think about the Holy Spirit. He is comforter, counselor, and friend. He wants to guide you. The greatest gift of grace in this life is the presence of the Holy Spirit. He's not a ghost; He is God.

*Today I will remember:*

- The Holy Spirit is not a ghost; He is God.
- The Holy Spirit is a counselor, comforter, and friend.

*Holy Spirit, show me who You are and how*
*You want to guide me. You are God.*
*Teach me and direct me in all things.*

# A FAITHFUL SPIRIT

*Create in me a pure heart, O God, and renew a steadfast spirit within me. Do not cast me from your presence or take your Holy Spirit from me. Restore to me the joy of your salvation and grant me a willing spirit, to sustain me.*

PSALM 51:10-12

This is part of David's prayer of repentance after his affair with Bathsheba was discovered. He not only slept with her, but had her husband, Uriah, killed by ordering him to the front lines in battle. The prophet Nathan confronts David with his sin, and he responds with the prayer recorded in Psalm 51.

We live on the other side of the cross of Jesus and His resurrection. Jesus paid for all our sin for all time. Through our faith in Him, the Holy Spirit will never leave us nor forsake us. He is forever faithful. However, the prayer for a faithful new heart is very much applicable for today. When we sin, we do not lose our salvation, but we do walk away from its joy. To hold fast to what is right even when we feel like doing something different is to cling to the Spirit's work in our lives. To continually choose to sin makes us numb to His presence and dulls our heart's receptivity to His guidance.

To repent is to turn away. Turn away from your sin and turn toward the Holy Spirit's work in your life. Confess and leave the sin behind. Ask the Spirit to create in you a clean heart and renew your faithfulness.

*Today I will remember:*

- I cannot lose my salvation, but I can lose its joy.
- By turning away from sin, I can turn toward the Holy Spirit's work in my life.
- I will confess and leave the sin behind.

*Holy Spirit, I confess my sin. I repent and leave it behind. Create in me a steadfast and faithful new heart.*

# ANOINTED BY THE SPIRIT

*You know what has happened throughout the province of Judea, beginning in Galilee after the baptism that John preached—how God anointed Jesus of Nazareth with the Holy Spirit and power, and how he went around doing good and healing all who were under the power of the devil, because God was with him.*

ACTS 10:37-38

Jesus walked perfectly with the Holy Spirit. He never sinned. The fruit of the Spirit—love, joy, peace, patience, kindness, goodness, faithfulness, gentleness, and self-control—were hallmarks of His character and life. Jesus was not only filled with the Spirit, He was anointed by God with the power of the Holy Spirit. At His baptism, the Spirit came upon Him. This is different than filling, this is anointing, and it is stated here again in Acts. Jesus had the power to heal through the anointing power of the Holy Spirit.

This Spirit of Jesus is also the Spirit who indwells believers in Jesus. He moved in power then, and He moves in power now. We can ask the Spirit in the name of Jesus to do powerful things. Where in your life do you need the power of God? Ask the Spirit. Where in a loved one's life does he or she need the power of God? Pray and ask the Holy Spirit in Jesus' name to do a great work. God was with Jesus, and He is with you by His Spirit.

*Today I will remember:*

- Jesus had the power to heal through the anointing power of the Holy Spirit.
- This Spirit is also the Spirit who indwells believers in Jesus.

*Holy Spirit, move in power. Guide me in moments where You want to do a healing work and give me the courage to pray boldly. It is Your power and anointing. Make me a vessel to do whatever You wish.*

# BORN OF THE SPIRIT

*Jesus answered, "Very truly I tell you, no one can enter the kingdom of God unless they are born of water and the Spirit. Flesh gives birth to flesh, but the Spirit gives birth to spirit."*

JOHN 3:5-6

Those enjoying a relationship with God through faith in Jesus have been born twice. If you've ever wondered what the term "born again" means, the answer is found in these verses. The phrase "born of water" represents your physical birth. Being "born of the Spirit" represents your spiritual birth. God is spirit; there is no connection with Him apart from the Holy Spirit. When we receive Jesus, His Spirit enters us, and we are awakened to spiritual things. We are born again.

Question: What work did you do to be "born of water"? The answer is nothing. Your father may have participated nine months prior, but your mother did all the work. She carried you, your body fed off hers, and she went through great pain to bring you into the world. Being born is not the work of the birthed, but of the one giving birth. The same is true with the Spirit. You cannot earn or work for new birth. His will and work make you spiritually alive. Being born again is not the result of you earning, but of you receiving, new life in Jesus. God does the birthing of those who are born again.

*Today I will remember:*

- We can have a relationship with God only through faith in Jesus.
- To be born again is to be born twice, once of water and again of the Spirit.

*Father, thank You that I have been born into Your family by the Spirit through faith in Jesus. This was not my work, but Yours. Thank You for this new life.*

# FILLED WITH THE SPIRIT

*Do not get drunk on wine, which leads to debauchery. Instead, be filled with the Spirit, speaking to one another with psalms, hymns, and songs from the Spirit. Sing and make music from your heart to the Lord, always giving thanks to God the Father for everything, in the name of our Lord Jesus Christ.*

EPHESIANS 5:18-20

God desires that we be filled with the Holy Spirit. To be filled is to be full. We are to be so full of the Spirit that we are living under His influence, guidance, and empowerment. How do we do that? How are we filled with the Spirit?

Our verses today bluntly instruct us not to fill our bodies with alcoholic spirits, but to pour in the stuff of the Holy Spirit.

1. We ask Him to fill us. We simply pray that He would fill our inner being with His presence. We pray, "Holy Spirit, fill me."
2. We do what our verses instruct us to do. We speak the Word of God to one another, sing songs of God with each other, and give thanks in everything. Talk with your friends about what God is teaching you. Instead of conversations always revolving around the trivial, talk about things in the realm of truth. Choose to regularly attend church and participate in the worship of God through music. Focus on the words of the songs, and lift your hands in praise. The Lord inhabits the praises of His people.
3. Make gratitude your go-to response in everything. What are you grateful for today? Pray and thank God.

*Today I will remember:*

- We can be filled with the Holy Spirit.
- We should go to God for the filling.
- Talking and singing about godly things allows us to express thanks to God in everything.

*Holy Spirit, fill me. I want to be full of the things of You. Cause me to live under Your influence, guidance, and empowerment today.*

# GOODNESS, PEACE, AND JOY

*For the Kingdom of God is not a matter of what we eat or drink, but of living a life of goodness and peace and joy in the Holy Spirit. If you serve Christ with this attitude, you will please God, and others will approve of you, too.*

ROMANS 14:17-18 (NLT)

When I was young, I would evaluate whether someone was a good Christian or not based on what they *didn't* do. Good Christians obeyed certain cultural rules, and bad ones didn't. Good Christians didn't smoke, drink, or chew and they did not hang out with people that do. Can you relate? How is it that we were OK back then with people being total jerks as long as they didn't drink beer? This thinking is more cultural than biblical. We are the ones who picked arbitrary traits of holiness, not God.

Our verse today says you can spot a person in the kingdom not by what's on the table, but by what's in his heart. Goodness, peace, and joy are prime traits of those living out the fruit of the Spirit. He transforms our habits, yes, but He does this as He transforms our characters. Jesus' followers are likeable, with characters that are attractive to people both inside and outside the faith. There are no grumps for God. There are just grumps. The Holy Spirit brings goodness, peace, and joy.

*Today I will remember:*

- You can spot a person in the kingdom not by what's on the table, but by what's in the heart.
- Those living by the Spirit exude goodness, peace, and joy.

*Holy Spirit, forgive me for choosing arbitrary things to define holiness. Holiness is about character of heart. Thank You that Your fruit is holy, and it is in these traits of character that we know who belongs to You.*

# IN THE NAME OF THE SPIRIT

*"Therefore go and make disciples of all the nations, baptizing them in the name of the Father and of the Son and of the Holy Spirit."*
MATTHEW 28:19

Our church usually does five services of baptism a year. They are big celebrations of new life in Jesus. In our verse, the Greek word translated as "baptizing" suggests to "dunk under." It symbolizes the person dying to self, being washed in the grace of God, and rising to walk in a new way of life as a follower of Jesus. We are to baptize in the name of the Father, and the Son, and the Holy Spirit. Why? Because all three persons of the triune God are at work in salvation.

The plan of salvation was ordained by the Father, who established and commanded it. The work of salvation was accomplished in and through the Son, who died on the cross to pay for all sin for all time and then was raised on the third day. Salvation is sealed by the Holy Spirit, who connects a person to the Father and Son. Salvation is stepping into the fellowship of who and what God is, and He is triune. We can talk and listen to the Father through the Son by the Spirit. This is why we are baptized in the name of all three.

*Today I will remember:*

- All three persons of the triune God are at work in the work of salvation.
- Salvation is ordained by the Father, accomplished through the Son, and sealed by the Holy Spirit.

*God, salvation is a beautiful mystery. Thank You that I am invited into the fellowship of who You are. Help me to grasp the beauty and depth of my relationship with You.*

# MINDING THE SPIRIT

*Those who live according to the flesh have their minds set on what the flesh desires; but those who live in accordance with the Spirit have their minds set on what the Spirit desires.*

ROMANS 8:5

Some people think that things in the realm of the Holy Spirit are magical. It's hocus pocus! That's not true. Walking by the Spirit is not about magic, but about the mind. What we focus on is what we move toward. When we focus on things that please the Holy Spirit, then the things of the Spirit will be evident in our lives. It's not about hocus pocus, but focus.

What are some things that please the Holy Spirit? You know the answer. The Word of God. Songs that honor and help us worship Jesus. Things that encourage love, joy, peace, patience, kindness, goodness, faithfulness, gentleness, and self-control. All these things are pleasing to the Spirit. Fill your mind with the stuff of God, and the stuff of God will fill you. Think of the GIGO principle: garbage in, garbage out; this means goodness in, goodness out works too. Go the goodness route.

Set your mind on the Holy Spirit. Think about Him throughout the day. Ask Him regularly what He wants you to know and what He wants you to do. Following the Spirit is not a mystery, but a matter of the mind.

*Today I will remember:*

- Following the Spirit is not a mystery, but a matter of the mind.
- What I choose to think about is what will come out.

*Holy Spirit, fill me with Your thoughts.*
*Help me to think about what I choose to think*
*about and to focus on the things of You.*

# POURING OUT THE SPIRIT

*"In the last days, God says, I will pour out my Spirit on all people, Your sons and daughters will prophesy, your young men will see visions, your old men will dream dreams. Even on my servants, both men and women, I will pour out my Spirit in those days, and they will prophesy."*

ACTS 2:17-18

I was recently at a gathering of pastors. We get together every year to hang out, laugh, and learn from each other and from a common mentor. Eight of us are from different parts of the United States, and two are from Canada. The first night, we were asked to go around the circle and share what God was doing in our lives. Each of us talked about recent experiences we had with the Holy Spirit. Most of us have come from backgrounds of cessationism, a theological view that certain spiritual gifts, particularly those considered miraculous, ceased to exist. Yet despite these factors, all of us had reported those types of experiences.

God is pouring out His Spirit. I believe we will see more and more in the coming days of the miraculous work of God through the power of the Holy Spirit. In our verses, Peter is simply quoting a passage from the Old Testament book of Joel. He is preaching a sermon on the Day of Pentecost where three thousand people received Jesus through the power of the Spirit. These types of things are happening right now all over the world. The Spirit is being poured out.

*Today I will remember:*

- God is pouring out His Spirit.
- As time goes on, we will see an increase in the miraculous work of God through the power of the Holy Spirit.

*Lord, pour out Your Spirit.*
*Display more of Your power so that*
*many more would believe in Jesus.*

# TEMPLE OF THE SPIRIT

*Do you not know that your bodies are temples of the Holy Spirit, who is in you, whom you have received from God? You are not your own; you were bought at a price. Therefore honor God with your bodies.*

1 CORINTHIANS 6:19-20

A few years ago, I was in Jerusalem and got to hear a lecture from a Jewish Professor about the Temple Mount and its importance to the Jewish people. I also got to participate in a moving prayer ceremony at the Wailing Wall in Jerusalem. This, the holiest site in Judaism, is the only portion of the temple that remains after AD 70. Jewish people go there to pray and to mourn. It was a powerful experience.

In the Old Testament, the temple was where God's presence dwelt. In the New Testament, God dwells in followers of Jesus by the Holy Spirit. If you are a Christian, you are a temple. Everywhere you go, you bear in your body the presence of God. Therefore, we should honor God with our bodies. You would never want to defile the temple, so do not defile yourself. Commit yourself to purity and good stewardship of the temple of God. Treat your body as holy to the Lord.

*Today I will remember:*

- Holy ground is not about a place, but a Person.
- The Person of the Spirit lives in me.
- My body is the temple of the Holy Spirit.

*Holy Spirit, thank You for residing in me. Holy ground is wherever I give You my attention and surrender to Your presence. Help me take better care of my body, which is Your temple.*

# THE ADVOCATE

*"If you love me, obey my commandments. And I will ask the Father, and he will give you another Advocate, who will never leave you. He is the Holy Spirit, who leads into all truth. The world cannot receive him, because it isn't looking for him and doesn't recognize him. But you know him, because he lives with you now and later will be in you."*

JOHN 14:15-17 (NLT)

When Jesus ascended into heaven, He did not leave the disciples alone. Ten days after the ascension and fifty days after the resurrection, on the Day of Pentecost He sent the Advocate, the Holy Spirit. In Greek, the word translated as "Advocate" is the word *paraclete*. It means "comforter," "helper," and "counselor." One of the primary ministries of the Spirit for a follower of Jesus is to help, to counsel, and to comfort.

1. The Holy Spirit helps in that we do not follow Jesus in our strength. The work of the Spirit in our souls is what transforms us. Christianity is less about trying harder and more about trusting in the Spirit. The more we allow Him to fill us, the more He transforms us.
2. The Holy Spirit counsels us into all truth. When you're not sure what to do, ask Him to guide you and press upon your mind the steps you should take. Everything He says will agree with the Bible.
3. The Holy Spirit comforts us with the peace of His presence. He helps us to know and experience God. Be still, close your eyes, and ask Him to fill you with His peace and love.

*Today I will remember:*

- Jesus never leaves His disciples alone.
- The Holy Spirit helps, counsels, and comforts.

*Holy Spirit, fill me with Your peace and love.*
*Empower me to follow Jesus and guide*
*my steps in the way You want me to go.*

# THE ETERNAL SPIRIT

*How much more, then, will the blood of Christ,*
*who through the eternal Spirit offered himself*
*unblemished to God, cleanse our consciences from acts*
*that lead to death, so that we may serve the living God!*

HEBREWS 9:14

Thinking about eternity in heaven as a kid always boggled my mind. How can something never end? Add to that the cartoons that pictured the heavenly experience as people floating around on clouds, wearing diapers, and playing harps, and it just sounded like a never-ending bummer. But we need to understand that when the Bible talks about eternity, it is not addressing a measurement of time, but a state of being.

The Holy Spirit is eternal because He is God and outside of time. In fact, God transcends space, matter, and time. He created these things and lives outside of them. Someone may ask, "When did God begin?" The question is irrelevant. For something to begin, it would have to already be in the construct of time, which God is outside of. The Spirit has always been and He always will be because He is eternal.

When people give their lives to Jesus, they receive God's eternal Spirit. The Holy Spirit covers us with the life of Christ and His holiness. We remain unblemished before God forevermore. We join the Father, Son, and Spirit in fellowship with the triune God in the state of eternity. This is what makes heaven heavenly, and it will be better than we can possibly imagine.

*Today I will remember:*

- When someone gives his life to Jesus, he receives God's eternal Spirit.
- The Holy Spirit covers us with the life of Christ and His holiness.
- We remain unblemished before God forevermore.

*Thank You, Holy Spirit, that You are with me for*
*all eternity. This is what my soul is ultimately*
*longing for. It is what makes heaven heavenly.*

# THE FRUIT OF THE SPIRIT

*But the fruit of the Spirit is love, joy, peace,*
*forbearance, kindness, goodness, faithfulness, gentleness*
*and self-control. Against such things there is no law.*
GALATIANS 5:22-23

Trees do not try to produce a certain type of fruit; they just produce what they are. Fruit is the natural product of the roots from which it springs. Apple trees produce apples. Orange trees produce oranges. These trees are not trying for the fruit; they are just producing from their roots.

The apostle Paul is not telling us in this passage to try and be more kind, good, and loving. He's not saying that we should put a plan together so that we might be considerably more loving this time next year. The passage has nothing to do with trying, just as trees don't try. Instead, he is teaching us that the right roots will produce the right fruit.

Everything begins with a seed. Including the fruit in our lives. There is the fruit of sin and there is the fruit of righteousness, and both begin in the seeds of our thoughts. If you don't like some of the fruit in your life, then change the roots. Change your thinking and change your life. The fruit of the Spirit is the product of your mind's focus. Give the Holy Spirit your focus today, and you will produce good fruit.

*Today I will remember:*

- Good thoughts produce good fruit.
- The fruit of the Spirit is the product of what I focus on.

*Holy Spirit, let all of my thoughts be rooted in*
*You today. Produce in me whatever You wish.*
*I give You my heart, my mind, and my focus.*

# THE GOOD GIFT

*"If you then, though you are evil, know how to give good gifts to your children, how much more will your Father in heaven give the Holy Spirit to those who ask him!"*

LUKE 11:13

I remember talking with a friend in college about the Holy Spirit. He grew up in a denomination in which the gifts of the Spirit were taught on and practiced, and I did not. I thought him strange in some ways, and yet I was jealous. He seemed to have a special connection with God that I didn't. Especially in times of prayer. He didn't just speak to God; he felt His presence. It's been over thirty years, and I can tell you today that I now understand and experience what my friend did.

If you want to understand and experience more of the Holy Spirit, then pray and ask God. Your Heavenly Father wants you to experience the good gift of His presence. Ask God, study the Scriptures, and give the Spirit some room in your prayer life. Talk less and listen more. Ask the Spirit to fill you and speak to you—and then wait. He will always guide you in the truth. Whatever He says will agree with the Bible. It may help to turn your palms up in a posture of receiving.

*Today I will remember:*

- God wants me to experience the good gift of His presence.
- I can pray and ask God for this.
- The Holy Spirit can fill me and bless me.

*Father, give me a better understanding of Your Holy Spirit. Teach me how to experience His presence.*

# THE SEAL OF THE SPIRIT

*Now it is God who makes both us and you stand firm in Christ. He anointed us, set his seal of ownership on us, and put his Spirit in our hearts as a deposit, guaranteeing what is to come.*

2 CORINTHIANS 1:21-22

In ancient times, the king would wear an insignia ring bearing his own symbol or coat of arms. Wax would be heated. As it melted, it would drip onto a royal document or letter. The king would then press his insignia ring in the wax. When it dried, it would bear the mark of the king, signifying its authenticity.

The Holy Spirit is the mark of the King of kings and Lord of lords upon our lives. The Spirit is proof that we belong to God and represent His kingdom. It is the seal that sets us apart and guarantees our place in the age to come. As knights bore the insignia of the king on their shields, so men of God bear His insignia on their souls.

Anything found now with the insignia of an ancient king is considered extremely valuable. Brother, you are marked with the seal of God. His Spirit is impressed upon your soul, and you are valued beyond measure.

*Today I will remember:*

- The Holy Spirit is the mark of the King of kings and Lord of lords upon our lives.
- As knights bore the insignia of the king on their shields, so men of God bear His insignia on their souls.

*Thank You, Lord, for the marked seal of Your Spirit upon my life. Help me reflect Your character and represent Your kingdom well.*

# THE SPIRIT AT CREATION

*In the beginning God created the heavens and the earth. Now the earth was formless and empty, darkness was over the surface of the deep, and the Spirit of God was hovering over the waters.*

GENESIS 1:1-2

The Holy Spirit was there at creation. In the original Hebrew, our verses could have the sense that the Spirit "fluttered over the waters." That reminds me of the Holy Spirit fluttering over and descending upon Jesus like a dove at His baptism. There's a connection between the baptismal waters and the deep waters mentioned here in Genesis. The Holy Spirit is at the creation of the world and also at the start of the new creation that Jesus' ministry would usher in.

The triune God remains a mystery. Many have tried to explain the unexplainable reality of God as trinity. Some say He's like an egg with a shell, yoke, and the white. Yeah, that doesn't really cut it. The better illustration is water, $H_2O$, which can be liquid, solid (ice), and vapor (steam). That still doesn't quite work because the Father, Son, and Spirit are individual persons. We can't really explain it, but the Bible reveals it. God is one and yet three, three and yet one. "God created the heavens and the earth," which includes the creative work of the Holy Spirit.

*Today I will remember:*

- The Holy Spirit is God.
- He took part in creating the heavens and the earth.
- God is one and yet three; He is three and yet one.

*Holy Spirit, You are God, and I praise and thank You for creation. Help me understand who You are and how You want to work in my life.*

# THE SPIRIT INVITES

*The Spirit and the bride say, "Come!" And let the one who hears say, "Come!" Let the one who is thirsty come; and let the one who wishes take the free gift of the water of life.*

REVELATION 22:17

I was going to try to make it through this devotional without mentioning that I am a Cowboys fan, but I guess I've failed. I grew up in Dallas, and my wife learned American football by watching the Cowboys. So, yes, we are big fans of "America's team." The tight ends coach was attending our church and invited us to a game. It was amazing! We saw the team practice and walked through the locker room. We sat in seats reserved for friends and family. Then we went to a dinner with the players and former players. It was legit! One of the best invitations ever!

The Holy Spirit offers an even better invitation. Our verse today teaches that He does this in partnership with the bride, also known as the church. The invitation is for anyone and everyone to come and receive the water of life found in Jesus. This invitation is at the heart of the ministry of the Spirit, and of any church on mission with Jesus. An invitation to a backstage tour with the Cowboys is good. Receiving this invitation from the Spirit is far better.

*Today I will remember:*

- The Spirit partners with the church to invite people to Jesus.
- I am invited to receive the invitation and to invite others.

*Holy Spirit, thank You for Your invitation to me. I want to join You in inviting others to Jesus.*

# THE SPIRIT IS QUENCHED

*Do not quench the Spirit. Do not treat prophecies with contempt but test them all; hold on to what is good, reject every kind of evil.*

1 THESSALONIANS 5:19-22

People will regularly come to me, a pastor, and say they have a prophetic word from God for me. Sometimes that indeed is true, but many times the word is not truly from God. It is from them or someone else. How do we ensure that we do not treat prophecies with contempt and quench the work of the Spirit? Here are three thoughts:

1. Be open to God's guidance. Some believers have the gift of prophecy, and God might choose to speak through them. Be humble and intentional.
2. Use discernment. Recognize that not all prophecies are from God (1 John 4:1). Whatever is from God will align with Scripture. What does the Bible say?
3. Avoid cynicism. God still speaks to us through other believers by His Spirit. Avoid dismissing prophetic words in a knee-jerk fashion. This causes spiritual dullness. Beware of becoming callous and rejecting His leading.

If you know a word is evil, reject it. If you know it is good, apply it. If you're not sure, test it. Be open to the work of the Spirit through the people of God. Be open to the work and be wise as well. Let's not quench the movement of the Spirit.

*Today I will remember:*
- If I know a thought is evil, I should reject it.
- If I know a thought is good, I should apply it.
- If I am not sure, I should test it.

*Holy Spirit, make me sensitive to Your leading. I never want to stifle or quench what You want to do. Make me discerning and wise.*

# THE SPIRIT OF ADOPTION

*The Spirit you received does not make you slaves,*
*so that you live in fear again; rather, the Spirit*
*you received brought about your adoption*
*to sonship. And by him we cry, "Abba, Father."*

ROMANS 8:15

One of the greatest mysteries of salvation is that we have become adopted sons of God. We are welcomed into the trinitarian fellowship of Father, Son, and Spirit. Just like Jesus, we can call God "Abba, Father." The Holy Spirit brought about your sonship. You no longer have to be afraid of the Almighty but are welcomed into His throne room as His child.

Son of God, the Father loves His boys, and He loves the real you. You need not be fearful of His mighty and loving hand. You have never surprised or shocked Him. Because He is outside of time, He has seen everything you ever did or will do. His mercy and grace were already there waiting.

Knowing these truths does not give us a license to sin. Instead, it compels us to lovingly obey. Responding to such a great salvation involves a choice: You either reject it in ignorance or fully embrace it in joy. Adopted sons do not desire rebellion. In gratitude, they strive for righteousness. Thank God today for your adoption. Think about His love and grace, and in gratitude lovingly live for Him.

*Today I will remember:*

- One of the greatest mysteries of salvation is that we become adopted sons of God.
- We are welcomed into the trinitarian fellowship of Father, Son, and Spirit.
- We can, just like Jesus, call God "Abba, Father."

*Holy Spirit, thank You for bringing about my adoption*
*into the family of God. I am so grateful for this*
*amazing grace. Help me to live for You.*

# THE SPIRIT OF CHRIST

*Concerning this salvation, the prophets, who spoke of the grace that was to come to you, searched intently and with the greatest care, trying to find out the time and circumstances to which the Spirit of Christ in them was pointing when he predicted the sufferings of the Messiah and the glories that would follow.*

1 PETER 1:10-11

The Holy Spirit was working on behalf of Jesus Christ long before He came on the scene. The Spirit worked in the hearts of the prophets of old who foretold of the coming Messiah and the salvation of men. The words *Messiah* and *Christ* are interchangeable titles. Messiah is a Hebrew word, and Christ is the Greek counterpart. Both mean "anointed one." The Spirit of Christ is the Spirit of the Messiah, and He has proclaimed and is proclaiming the salvation of the Lord.

The Holy Spirit has always been in the salvation business. The Spirit of Christ was proclaiming the salvation of Christ before the arrival of the Christ. Hundreds of years before the coming Messiah, the Old Testament recorded many prophecies about His life and the grace that would be found in Him: where He would be born, how He would die and rise again to usher in a new kingdom, and many more. The ministry of the Spirit of Christ is not new, and He continues to work on the behalf of Jesus in saving souls.

*Today I will remember:*

- The Holy Spirit has always been in the salvation business.
- The Spirit of Christ was proclaiming the salvation of Christ before the arrival of the Christ.

*Thank You, Holy Spirit, that You have always been in the salvation business. May You continue to draw people to Jesus in salvation.*

# THE SPIRIT OF GOD

*For who knows a person's thoughts except their own spirit within them? In the same way no one knows the thoughts of God except the Spirit of God.*
1 CORINTHIANS 2:11

Years ago, I purchased a bookmark with a quote from Albert Einstein that said, "I want to know God's thoughts. Everything else is just detail." To have the Holy Spirit is to have access to God's thinking. Just as your spirit knows your thoughts, so the Holy Spirit knows the mind of God. If you want to know what God is thinking, ask His Spirit. Here are some questions you might want to ask Him:

What does God think of me?
How does God feel about me?
What does God want me to know right now?
What does God want me to do right now?
What does God think about this situation?
Where am I doing well right now?
What are some things I need to work on?

Write down what the Holy Spirit brings to your mind. You can make this a regular practice in prayer. Talk to God and then ask, wait, and write. If you want to know what God is thinking, ask His Spirit.

*Today I will remember:*

- To have the Holy Spirit is to have access to God's thinking.
- Just as my spirit knows my thoughts, so the Holy Spirit knows the mind of God.
- Talk to God and then ask, wait, and write.

*Holy Spirit, help me understand the will of God. I am grateful for the Bible, as a general guide for life. Please also help me to walk with God in the specific details. May my thoughts be in line with His.*

# THE SPIRIT OF LIFE

*Therefore, there is now no condemnation for those who are in Christ Jesus, because through Christ Jesus the law of the Spirit who gives life has set you free from the law of sin and death.*

ROMANS 8:1-2

Religion is about trying. Biblical Christianity, by contrast, is about trusting. The difference maker is the life we receive through the Holy Spirit. Religion is not what the New Testament teaches. In fact, most of the New Testament is dedicated to the reality that religion doesn't work. The heart of religion is a list of things you must do or not do to work your way to God. The theme of religion is try harder and do better. That's not what Jesus came to give us. In fact, we already had a religious list in the law of God. Jesus changes everything.

We couldn't keep the rules, so Jesus kept them for us. When we trust in Jesus, He takes on our penalty for breaking God's laws and gives us His life. His life is His Spirit, the Holy Spirit. The Spirit sets us free from the rules and allows us to walk with Him in relationship. Biblical Christianity is a relationship with Jesus by the Spirit, not a list of rules that we must follow.

*Today I will remember:*

- Religion is about trying, while biblical Christianity is about trusting.
- The rules bring death because we cannot keep them.
- Jesus brings life in the Spirit as we trust in Him.

*Jesus, thank You that there is no condemnation in You. Show me the way of the Spirit. May His life be in me and flow through me as I learn to trust in You.*

# THE SPIRIT OF THE LORD

*"The Spirit of the LORD is on me, because he has anointed me to proclaim good news to the poor. He has sent me to proclaim freedom for the prisoners and recovery of sight for the blind, to set the oppressed free, to proclaim the year of the LORD's favor." Then he rolled up the scroll, gave it back to the attendant and sat down. The eyes of everyone in the synagogue were fastened on him. He began by saying to them, "Today this scripture is fulfilled in your hearing."*

LUKE 4:18-21

The ministry of Jesus is the ministry of the Holy Spirit. The Father, Son, and Spirit work together to fulfill the will of the triune God. It's simple to understand that they work together and it's also a profound mystery in how they are three distinct persons and yet one God. Notice what the anointing of the Spirit is for and what the Spirit cares about. He cares for the poor, the prisoner, the blind, and the oppressed. These things are both literal and symbolic. Some people face these conditions physically. All of us face them spiritually.

The Spirit of the Lord cares about people. His ministry is for their good. Where there is no love or concern for people, there is no anointing of the Spirit. Jesus is the fulfillment of this prophetic word from Isaiah spoken hundreds of years earlier. God came to save people. This is the ministry of the Spirit of the Lord.

*Today I will remember:*

- The Spirit of the Lord cares about people.
- Where there is no love or concern for people, there is no anointing of the Spirit.

*Holy Spirit, make my heart like Yours.*
*Help me care about what You care about.*
*Help me to love and serve people the way You do.*

# THE SPIRIT OF THE RESURRECTION

*The Spirit of God, who raised Jesus from the dead, lives in you. And just as God raised Christ Jesus from the dead, he will give life to your mortal bodies by this same Spirit living within you.*

ROMANS 8:11 (NLT)

The Holy Spirit's power raised Jesus from the dead. He is the source of life and was part of creation way back in Genesis 1:2. This same power lives in you. Our hope for eternal life is the hope of the resurrection power of the Spirit. Just as He raised Jesus to life, so He will raise us.

If you are a follower of Jesus, you are carrying around this tremendous power. The Holy Spirit lives in your being. The miracles of Jesus, the healing of the blind, the deaf, and the lame, the walking on water, the raising of Lazarus from the dead, and eventually the resurrection of Jesus were all accomplished through the power of the Holy Spirit. It's not your power; it's His. But you have access to the same power in Jesus' name by His Spirit.

Walk humbly in the strength of the Lord. Fear not. Pray boldly. You are a blood-bought, adopted son of God indwelled by the Holy Spirit. This does not make a man cocky, but it does make him humbly unafraid. Ask the Holy Spirit to give you wisdom about how He wants to work in and through you. The power of the Spirit is the resurrection power of Jesus.

*Today I will remember:*

- The Holy Spirit's power raised Jesus from the dead.
- Through faith in Jesus, the Holy Spirit now lives in us.
- Christians are to walk humbly in the strength of the Lord.

*Holy Spirit, teach me how You want to work in me and through me. Help me to humbly walk in Your strength.*

# THE SPIRIT OF TRUTH

*"But when he, the Spirit of truth, comes, he will guide you into all the truth. He will not speak on his own; he will speak only what he hears, and he will tell you what is yet to come."*

JOHN 16:13

Have you ever wished you could just talk with Jesus? I'm not talking about in prayer, but in person. Like have a cup of coffee with Him, face to face, and ask whatever you want. Most of us would probably have a few weird trivial questions about things we have pondered. But probably all of us would ask for guidance and wise counsel.

Jesus calls the Holy Spirit the Spirit of truth. He is there to guide us through life. While in His humanity Jesus cannot not be everywhere at once, He can be all-present by His Spirit. You always have access to His counsel. When you pray, ask the Holy Spirit to guide you. Then just be quiet. Ask Him what He wants you to know and do. Maybe He will bring a verse of Scripture to mind, or a word, or even a picture. Everything the Spirit guides you to do will fall in line with the teachings of the Bible. The Spirit will not contradict the Word. Jesus wants to talk to you and guide you, and He does so by the Spirit.

*Today I will remember:*

- Jesus wants to talk to me and guide me by the Spirit.
- I always have access to God's counsel.

*Holy Spirit, please guide me in truth. Many of the decisions I must make are not specifically addressed in the Bible. What would You like me to know and do?*

# THE SPIRIT PRAYS

*And the Holy Spirit helps us in our weakness. For example, we don't know what God wants us to pray for. But the Holy Spirit prays for us with groanings that cannot be expressed in words. And the Father who knows all hearts knows what the Spirit is saying, for the Spirit pleads for us believers in harmony with God's own will.*

ROMANS 8:26-27 (NLT)

I've been in situations so dire, with the pain so great, that I was speechless. My grief was so heavy that I couldn't even pray. I've also faced times of desperation and shock and had nothing to say. In other moments, of course, I experienced such amazing joy that no words could possibly do it justice. In all these times of pain, confusion, and joy, the Spirit has prayed for me, and He prays for you. Even more amazing, He does so in connection with our spirits. He represents us in harmony with God's will and pleads on our behalf.

Therefore, it's OK when you don't know what to pray. Be at peace when you feel as if you should have said something different. In all of it, the Holy Spirit prays in your stead. We say something to God, the Spirit corrects it, and that correction is what actually gets said to God. Thank God!

*Today I will remember:*

- It's OK when I don't know what to pray.
- The Holy Spirit connects with my spirit and prays on my behalf.

*Holy Spirit, thank You for praying for me. Many times I don't know what to say, or don't have anything to say. I'm grateful that You plead on my behalf in harmony with God's will.*

# THE SPIRIT REVEALS

*But whenever someone turns to the Lord, the veil is taken away. For the Lord is the Spirit, and wherever the Spirit of the Lord is, there is freedom. So all of us who have had that veil removed can see and reflect the glory of the Lord. And the Lord—who is the Spirit—makes us more and more like him as we are changed into his glorious image.*

2 CORINTHIANS 3:16-18 (NLT)

The Holy Spirit reveals the glory of God in our lives. In Old Testament times, Moses encountered God, and the people would have him cover his glowing face with a veil because the glory reflected there was too much for them. God's glory wasn't freeing; it was scary, and they would hide from it. Now in Jesus, the Spirit not only reveals the glory to us, but causes it to flow through us. The glory of God is revealed by the Spirit of God as we place our faith in the Son of God. This changes us from the inside out and transforms our hearts to reflect His.

Ask the Holy Spirit to reveal the glory of God to you. Pray to understand God's character. For the more you understand Him, the more you will love Him, and the more you love Him, the more you will obey and reflect Him. There is freedom in knowing God. The glory of God is not a burden, but a blessing. It sets us free from fear and grounds us in His grace.

*Today I will remember:*

- The glory of God is revealed by the Spirit of God as we place our faith in the Son of God.
- His glory is not a burden, but a blessing.
- It sets us free from fear and grounds us in God's grace.

*Holy Spirit, reveal to me the glory*
*of the grace of God in Christ Jesus.*
*Help me see Him for who He really is.*

# THE SPIRIT SPEAKS

*I came to you in weakness with great fear and trembling. My message and my preaching were not with wise and persuasive words, but with a demonstration of the Spirit's power, so that your faith might not rest on human wisdom, but on God's power.*

1 CORINTHIANS 2:3-5

As a preacher I am very grateful for our verses for today. Even the best of communicators can struggle with speaking thirty-five to forty new messages each year. Add to that the reality that the most highly attended church services usually contain the same biblical material. The Christmas story is the same every year. Sometimes I feel like saying, "Well, I got no new material for you. Remember when we read the Christmas account last year? Yeah, it hasn't changed." I wonder if the people who only attend Christmas or Easter think I preach only two sermons. I'm grateful that people's lives are not changed through how good or bad I communicate, but through the power of the Holy Spirit.

The same is true with you. You may not stand on a stage speaking to a crowd each week, but you are called to share your faith. Your faith in Jesus is personal, but it was never meant to be private. Men way overthink this. When you share your faith, just ask the Holy Spirit to speak through you. Love the person well and talk about how Jesus has changed your life. The apostle Paul admits he was afraid and that he trembled. It's not about your words but the Spirit's power. You don't have to be slick; you just have to be real. Ask the Spirit to speak through you.

*Today I will remember:*

- My faith in Jesus is personal, but it was never meant to be private.
- I don't have to be slick; I just have to be real.
- I must daily ask the Spirit to speak through me.

*Holy Spirit, any time I have opportunity to speak to someone about my faith in Jesus, please take over. Let it be my vocal cords and Your voice.*

# THE SWORD OF THE SPIRIT

*Take the helmet of salvation and the sword of the Spirit, which is the word of God.*

EPHESIANS 6:17

Every warrior needs a weapon. For the Christian man, the weapon is the sword of the Spirit. But you will find that most of the armor of God in Ephesians 6 is protective and defensive. It guards our minds and our hearts. But when we attack the enemy, we strike with the offensive power of both the Word and Spirit. The Holy Spirit coupled with the Word of God cuts through the lies of the enemy. A weaponless man is a weak man. We must learn to wield the sword.

The Word of God gives us knowledge. The Spirit of God gives us understanding. You can be a good student of the Bible and still not have the Spirit. It is the Spirit who moves you past religious studies to a relational encounter with the living Jesus. The truth of the Word is enlightened by the Spirit's revelation. When you read the Bible, ask the Holy Spirit for understanding. Invite Him to join you in the study. Apply what He says, and you will be wielding the sword.

The Devil is a liar, and let's give the Devil his due; he's good at it. To fight the good fight of the faith, we must be training regularly so that when the lie comes, we cut the lie down with the Word of God in the power of the Spirit. Brothers, wield the sword!

*Today I will remember:*

- Every warrior needs a weapon.
- The weapon for Christian men is the sword of the Spirit.
- The Holy Spirit coupled with the Word of God cuts through the lies of the enemy.

*Lord, give me wisdom about Your Word. As I study it, may the Holy Spirit give me understanding. Teach me to wield the sword of the Spirit.*

# THE WAR OF THE SPIRIT

*So I say, let the Holy Spirit guide your lives.*
*Then you won't be doing what your sinful nature craves.*
*The sinful nature wants to do evil, which is just the opposite*
*of what the Spirit wants. And the Spirit gives us desires*
*that are the opposite of what the sinful nature desires.*
*These two forces are constantly fighting each other,*
*so you are not free to carry out your good intentions.*

GALATIANS 5:16-17 (NLT)

There are two forces at work in you. There is your old nature, the sin nature; and then there is the Holy Spirit. These two are at war with each other. Each day, you decide which one will win. Have you felt this? There is a struggle between the old and the new that reside in you.

First, the struggle is a good sign. It means you have the Holy Spirit. Where there is no struggle, there is no new life. When I first met Jesus and got serious about following Him, I became very aware of my sinfulness. Things that never bothered me before started to bother me. The war had begun.

Second, we must decide which direction we will go. Do we go the way of the Spirit and let Him guide us, or do we go the way of our sinful nature? The one that gets your focus wins the fight. Focus on the things of the sinful nature, and that nature will guide you. Focus on the things of the Spirit, and He will guide you. The fight is about focus.

*Today I will remember:*

- There is a war going on between my sin nature and the Spirit.
- The one that gets my focus wins the fight.

*Holy Spirit, let me focus on You today.*
*Help me to turn away from sinful*
*thoughts and toward the things of You.*

# December

## FOLLOWING JESUS

"The thief comes only to steal and kill and destroy;
I have come that they may have life, and have it to the full."
*John 10:10*

# ROCK SOLID PRACTICE

*"Therefore everyone who hears these words of mine and puts them into practice is like a wise man who built his house on the rock. The rain came down, the streams rose, and the winds blew and beat against that house; yet it did not fall, because it had its foundation on the rock."*

MATTHEW 7:24-25

At the end of the Sermon on the Mount, Jesus talks about two kinds of people. One is rock solid, and his house is built on a firm foundation, unshakable in the storms of life. The other is wobbly and built on the sand. When the big bad wolves of life huff and puff and the storms blow, the house on the sand goes down. The only difference between the rock solid and the wobbly is the willingness to put Jesus' words into practice. Application is everything.

Many in the modern church think the Christian life is all about education, about learning what the Bible says. It starts there, but Jesus did not say, "Come listen to me." He said, "Come follow me." The goal is not education but transformation. We hear the words and put them into practice. Many treat church like a gym. They know a lot about exercise, but they never actually exercise. There is no transformation without application.

This month, we're looking at practicing the words of Jesus. The right information plus the right application leads to transformation. If you want to be rock solid, the power is the practice.

*Today I will remember:*

- The right information plus the right application leads to transformation.
- The only difference between the rock solid and the wobbly is the willingness to put Jesus' words into practice.

*Jesus, help me not just to know but to do what You say. I don't want to just be Your listener. I want to be Your follower.*

# A NEW DAY

*Jesus said to the servants, "Fill the jars with water"; so they filled them to the brim. Then he told them, "Now draw some out and take it to the master of the banquet." They did so, and the master of the banquet tasted the water that had been turned into wine.*

JOHN 2:7-9

Have you ever wondered why Jesus turned water into wine for His first miracle? Pretty cool because with this miracle He reveals that He is the master of molecules. Turning $H_2O$ into merlot is slick, but why the wine thing? Think back to your Sunday school days for a moment. Moses' first miracle in Egypt was turning water into blood. Yeah, there's a connection. Moses would usher in the religious law; Jesus ushers in God's grace. It's two different covenants and two different ways of relating to God. Under Moses, it was religion—keep the rules and good luck. With Jesus, it is relationship—I am with you by my Spirit, so come follow me. Water to blood is a curse. Water to wine is a blessing. Jesus changes everything.

To follow Jesus is to walk in His grace. Wine symbolizes joy. Jesus would make things right between us and God through His death, burial, and resurrection. On the cross, He paid for all sin for all time. We do not have to work our way to God through obeying religious rules that are impossible to keep. Instead, God has worked His way to us in Jesus; we trust Him and follow Him. It's a new day!

*Today I will remember:*

- We do not have to work our way to God.
- Religious rules are impossible to keep and can't save us.
- God has worked His way to us in Jesus, whom we trust and follow.

*Jesus, thank You for ushering in hope, joy, and peace with God. Thank You that You did for me what I could never do.*

# IT'S JESUS

*"Then the righteous will answer him, 'Lord, when did we see you hungry and feed you, or thirsty and give you something to drink? When did we see you a stranger and invite you in, or needing clothes and clothe you? When did we see you sick or in prison and go to visit you?' The King will reply, 'Truly I tell you, whatever you did for one of the least of these brothers and sisters of mine, you did for me.'"*

MATTHEW 25:37-40

I wonder how many times I've missed Jesus. In my busyness going from here to there, have I missed Him? Passing by the homeless man who is passed out on the street still drunk from the night before, did I miss Jesus? As I hurriedly paid for my groceries as the special needs young man bagged them and tried to make conversation, did I miss Jesus? When I ignore the request of the beggar holding the sign at the stoplight, am I ignoring Jesus? Maybe. Quite possibly. When we serve the "least of these brothers and sisters," we serve Jesus.

As time goes on, I am learning to pray more often for the ministry of noticing. It sounds strange, but people are in awe when you notice them. In the modern world, many go unseen. Recently in Great Britain, the government addressed the epidemic of the unnoticed by establishing the office of the "Minister of Loneliness."

To care for someone in need is to care for Jesus. To see and speak to the least of these is to converse with Him. Sometimes we pray to hear a word from Him, when the truth is He is all around us. Do we recognize Him? It's Jesus.

*Today I will remember:*

- I miss Jesus when I ignore the needy.
- When I serve the "least of these brothers and sisters," I serve Jesus.

*Jesus, help me not to miss You in the people who go unnoticed. May I enter the ministry of seeing people. To serve them is to serve You.*

# A GRATEFUL ONE

*One of them, when he saw he was healed, came back, praising God in a loud voice. He threw himself at Jesus' feet and thanked him—and he was a Samaritan. Jesus asked, "Were not all ten cleansed? Where are the other nine? Has no one returned to give praise to God except this foreigner?" Then he said to him, "Rise and go; your faith has made you well."*

LUKE 17:15-19

It always bothers me when a man is ungrateful. When he cannot offer a simple "thank you" or a returned smile, it smacks of entitlement and self-centeredness. That's how I feel about the nine lepers in this passage. Jesus heals them from a debilitating disease, and they just take it for granted? Unbelievable.

It's easy to get self-righteous and stand in judgment of the nine; that is, until I think about my own life. There are hundreds of blessings that I take for granted every day. Most of my prayers are not expressions of gratitude but requests for more. Rarely overwhelmed by the obvious goodness of God, I am usually focused on what else I could get. If we're honest, we're a whole lot more like the nine than we care to admit. May we learn the gratitude of the one. Jesus owes us nothing. We owe Him everything. Let us live today in gratitude of His grace.

*Today I will remember:*

- Jesus owes us nothing.
- We owe Him everything.
- Today we can live in gratitude for His grace.

*Jesus, You have been so good to me. Thank You for Your blessings. I choose throughout this day to name them and to thank You. Make me a man of gratitude.*

# HAVE MERCY

*"Blessed are the merciful, for they will be shown mercy."*
MATTHEW 5:7

In its simplest form, mercy is choosing not to give someone what he deserves. God does not give us what we deserve. He gives us what we need. It is His mercy that compels me to want to live for Him. The more I understand His mercy, the more I love God and trust what He says.

Mercy is not about enabling, but empowering. It lives in the tension of a swift kick in the pants and giving an opportunity for a new start. For example, God never winks at sin. He will let us feel its consequences without letting it destroy us. He gives us a myriad of second chances. Mercy lives in the tension of tough and tender love. He doesn't rub it in when we do wrong. He lets us feel the pain and then polishes it out.

Who needs mercy from you right now? What would it mean to deal with reality and then empower this person to start fresh? Mercy requires security, strength, and wisdom. Thank God that He has an infinite supply. People who receive His mercy are good at giving it to others.

*Today I will remember:*

- God does not give us what we deserve.
- He gives us what we need.
- Receiving His mercy empowers us to be merciful.

*Father, thank You for Your mercy. I would be dead without it.*
*Give me wisdom in showing mercy. To not give people*
*what they deserve, but what they need.*

# KEEP PRAYING

*"Keep on asking, and you will receive what you ask for. Keep on seeking, and you will find. Keep on knocking, and the door will be opened to you. For everyone who asks, receives. Everyone who seeks, finds. And to everyone who knocks, the door will be opened."*

MATTHEW 7:7-8 (NLT)

While I don't understand everything about prayer, I know that perseverance is important. I'm not sure why. I think it's because it reveals our hearts. We continue to pray for what we are truly passionate about. I must admit that many times I think I prayed, but I didn't. I just hoped or wished. Praying is different. It is seeking God for requests and counsel. Do we really seek and knock, or do we just hope and wish?

My sons used to do this with me all the time. They were young and fickle, and I didn't take them seriously unless they began to continually bring up something. Maybe that's what Jesus is teaching here. Most of our prayers are halfhearted. But if we are really after something from God, then we will show it in passionate prayer. Authentic prayer, passionately seeking Him, reveals the heart. What is it that you seek, man of God? Keep on seeking. What do you want from Him? Keep on asking. Passionate prayer perseveres.

*Today I will remember:*

- We continue to pray for what we are truly passionate about.
- There is a difference between hoping, wishing, and really praying.
- Passionate prayers involve perseverance.

*God, sometimes I think I have prayed when I've really just hoped or wished. Authentic prayer reveals what I am truly passionate about. May I seek Your face about such things.*

# MERCY IS BETTER

*"But go and learn what this means:*
*'I desire mercy, not sacrifice.' For I have*
*not come to call the righteous, but sinners."*
MATTHEW 9:13

I was talking with a new friend the other night about his daughter's ex-husband. We were sitting out by a firepit at his house, and he was telling me the story of his daughter's ex-husband, who is an addict and a deadbeat dad. He owes thousands in child support, continually breaks promises to his children, and has been dishonorable and disrespectful to my friend's daughter. I asked my friend, "Don't you want to go hurt this guy?" He responded, "No. I feel sorry for him." My friend is helping his daughter and is righteously protective of his grandkids. At the same time, he doesn't want the guy hurt; he wants him to get help. That's strength; that's mercy, and it's one of the quintessential traits of a follower of Jesus.

When Jesus says, "I desire mercy, not sacrifice," it means that your character is a better sign of your relationship with God than your religious practices. Many a man reads his Bible, goes to church, takes part in a men's Bible study, but remains a jerk. There are no jerks for Jesus. There are just jerks. Our religious practices are meant to change and transform us so that our hearts begin to look like the heart of Jesus, and Jesus is full of mercy.

*Today I will remember:*
- My character reveals my relationship with God better than my religious practices.
- Jesus is full of mercy.
- So are His followers.

*Lord, thank You for Your mercy to me and for the way*
*You change and transform me. My religious disciplines help*
*me to know You better, so that I might reflect You more.*

# NOT THE JUDGE

*"Do not judge others, and you will not be judged. For you will be treated as you treat others. The standard you use in judging is the standard by which you will be judged."*

MATTHEW 7:1-2 (NLT)

After seeing me on a YouTube show, a state Supreme Court Justice began attending my church. We soon became friends, and I've grown to respect him for being kind, but fair. His desire is to serve God and care well for the people of Arizona. Through his example I've seen what healthy Christian judgment should look like, even in the most difficult cases.

People misunderstand what the Bible says about followers of Jesus and judging. Ask any person outside the faith, and he will quickly remind you, "Jesus said not to judge!" That's not entirely accurate. There are several places in the Bible that tell us to judge. We must regularly make judgment calls about people and whether they can be trusted with a particular job, responsibility, or relationship. That's just common sense. Judging is a normal part of life.

What Jesus is talking about is passing self-righteous judgment on people. It's in the "you reap what you sow" category. If you are a judgmental jerk, people will respond in kind. How you dish out will be how it's dished back to you. Go ahead and make judgment calls, but be a person of mercy and compassion. Know right and wrong, and love people well. You can love people you disagree with. Jesus did it all the time.

*Today I will remember:*

- I can make judgment calls without being judgmental.
- I can love people I disagree with.
- Jesus did this all the time.

*Jesus, help me to make judgment calls without being judgmental. Give me the grace to love those I disagree with. May I know right from wrong and treat people well.*

# ONE PERCENT FAITH

*The apostles said to the Lord, "Increase our faith!"*
*He replied, "If you have faith as small as a*
*mustard seed, you can say to this mulberry tree,*
*'Be uprooted and planted in the sea,' and it will obey you."*

LUKE 17:5-6

I was on my way to perform a memorial service for a young man who had died from a drug overdose. His family had attended our church for years, but I had only briefly met the young man. As I drove, I asked the Lord for some words of wisdom and comfort. The family was not sure of the young man's relationship with Jesus. In the past several years, it had become obvious that he was not following Him.

When people used to ask me how much faith is enough, I would respond, "Fifty-one percent." You just had to believe a little more than you doubted. But as I drove to the funeral that day, the Lord corrected me. It's not fifty-one percent—it's just one percent. The smallest mustard seed of faith is big enough to unleash the everlasting flow of God's grace. I believe the Holy Spirit whispered to me in my truck that day that this kid had one percent faith, and that was enough. The grace of God is so big, it can be unleashed with something that small. You see, the secret of faith is not the amount, but the object. Just a little faith in God is powerful. Even just one percent.

*Today I will remember:*

- The power of faith is not in the amount, but in the object.
- The smallest mustard seed of faith is big enough to unleash the everlasting flow of God's grace.

*Lord, thank You that my smallest*
*belief in You unleashes Your infinite grace.*
*Teach me to trust You and increase my faith.*

# PEACEMAKER

*"Blessed are the peacemakers,*
*for they will be called children of God."*
MATTHEW 5:9

I've never met a blessed troublemaker. How about you? This dude I knew in college seemed to cause trouble wherever he went. He'd be in the gym getting into arguments; eating in the cafeteria, he would manage to start a fight; he even caused a ruckus in the library. Once, he started to raise his voice once again to one of our buddies. My friends and I finally had had enough, so we all surrounded him. I thought for a moment that he was going to take us all on, but he chose a more civil option. Probably because one of my friends was six four and pushing three hundred pounds. As he calmed, we challenged him on what his constant problem was, and we found out his dad was the same. For some of us, violence and volume are the natural responses to conflict, but this isn't the way of God.

Followers of Jesus are called to make peace. It seems in our day, especially online, Christians feel the need to fight. Avoid this temptation. It is not honoring to God, it rarely changes anyone's mind, and it's not the way of Jesus. It's almost as if some think this verse is talking about peace *taking* instead of peace *making*. Friend, you do not have to defend truth; it can take care of itself. Just lovingly share it. Peacemaking is part of what it means to be a son of God.

*Today I will remember:*

- There are no blessed troublemakers.
- Men of God are called to be peacemakers.

*Father, help me bring peace to those I disagree with.*
*Help me to walk in Your ways and to represent You well.*

# POOR NO MORE

*"Blessed are the poor in spirit,*
*for theirs is the kingdom of heaven."*
MATTHEW 5:3

This is the opening line of the greatest sermon ever preached, the Sermon on the Mount. I've been on the hillside where scholars believe Jesus gave this famous address and when I was there, I sat down and read the sermon in Matthew 5–7. I encourage you to read the whole thing. Try to forget the chapters, verses and headings, which were all added later and can sometimes hinder our understanding. We need to remember that it's all one sermon, and today's verse is the opening line.

To be "poor in spirit" is to be humble. Why are we blessed if we're humble? Because humility is the first step in receiving Jesus' salvation and mentorship toward a better way of life. Jesus is brilliant. He knows everything about everything. He knows the ways of heaven. If we choose to humbly learn from Him, we too will know those ways as we get to know *the* way, Jesus Himself. Only the poor in spirit can accept Jesus' way. When we receive Jesus, we become rich in His Holy Spirit, trusting His guidance as we learn the ways of His kingdom. The rest of the sermon describes how His kingdom operates. Read it, study it, and apply it.

*Today I will remember:*
- Experiencing Jesus and the way of His kingdom begins with humility.
- Jesus is brilliant and knows everything about everything.

*Jesus, I want to know You and learn from You.*
*Teach me the ways of the kingdom of heaven.*
*May I humbly receive and apply Your teaching.*

# POWER IN THE NAME

*When they came to Jesus, they saw the man who had been possessed by the legion of demons, sitting there, dressed and in his right mind; and they were afraid.*

MARK 5:15

Some people who say they do not believe in God still believe in evil. Atheists may not believe in a literal Devil, but most believe in literal evil. Just ask them about the Holocaust, Hitler, and a host of other things. We're quick to identify evil and dismiss good.

I encourage you to read all of Mark 5. The demons are afraid of Jesus, and it is obvious that they are no match for Him. His power, position, and authority are recognized immediately, and he defeats a legion of them with a simple command. The name Jesus means "the Lord saves." Any time you proclaim it, you proclaim that truth. When I am afraid, or sense that I am in the presence of evil, I trust in the power and authority of Jesus. He makes the darkness tremble. There is power in His name.

*Today I will remember:*

- The name Jesus means "the Lord saves."
- Demons are afraid of Jesus, and they are no match for Him.
- Jesus makes the darkness tremble.

*Jesus, Your name is above every name. All power, authority, and dominion are Yours. I never need to fear evil because You are with me. You make the darkness tremble, and there is power in Your name.*

# RICH DIFFICULTIES

*Then Jesus said to his disciples, "Truly I tell you, it is hard for someone who is rich to enter the kingdom of heaven. Again I tell you, it is easier for a camel to go through the eye of a needle than for someone who is rich to enter the kingdom of God."*

MATTHEW 19:23-24

Celebrate Recovery (CR) is one of my favorite ministries because of the change that takes place in people's lives as they work the twelve steps. CR was founded by Rick Warren from Saddleback Church and is based on the beatitudes in the Sermon on the Mount. While it's likened to Alcoholics Anonymous, in CR, Jesus is always the higher power.

There are not a lot of rich people going to CR. It's not because the rich do not struggle with alcohol, drugs, sex, gambling, or porn. Money does not keep you immune from such things. It's just that the rich have the luxury of pretending. They haven't lost their jobs yet; things haven't hit rock bottom. Money gives them an out from having to deal with reality.

It's harder for the rich to experience real redemption because they're not convinced that they need it. A broke and broken man is ready for salvation, while the wealthy man remains unsure. Jesus loves the rich and people with Bentleys and Rolexes. But no one cares much about those things in the kingdom. After all, the Owner uses gold for pavement. All are welcome, but humility is the only key that allows you in.

*Today I will remember:*

- Sometimes money is a hindrance to dealing with reality.
- Humility is the key that allows us to experience the kingdom.

*Lord, thank You that You see the real me and love me as I am. Help me to not ignore my brokenness, but bring it to You. I always need Your grace.*

# STORM NAPPING

*A furious squall came up, and the waves broke over the boat,*
*so that it was nearly swamped. Jesus was in the stern,*
*sleeping on a cushion. The disciples woke him and said to him,*
*"Teacher, don't you care if we drown?" He got up, rebuked the*
*wind and said to the waves, "Quiet! Be still!" Then the*
*wind died down and it was completely calm.*

MARK 4:37-39

I am most stressed when I need to make a decision but am not sure what to do. That scenario usually keeps me up at night. I toss and turn in a self-made storm thinking of various negative outcomes. I fret at the possible ripple effect of my decision or the opinions of others. How about you? I wish I were more like Jesus, who can be in a boat in a storm and still go take a nap.

Worry is meditation in the wrong direction. It's focusing on potential negative outcomes that we have little to no control over. In the Sermon on the Mount, Jesus essentially asks why we waste our time on worry. Why indeed? It does us no good.

The antidote to worry is to adjust your sails. Move your mind in a different direction. Focus elsewhere. When you boil it down, worrying about things you can't control is really the fear that God might get it wrong. That the all-powerful, all knowing, and ever-present King of kings might not know what He is doing. Pretty silly. When you're worried, choose to adjust your trust. Do your best, give the rest to God, and go take a nap.

*Today I will remember:*

- Worry is meditation in the wrong direction.
- When I am worried, I can choose to adjust my trust.
- I will do my best, give the rest to God, and then go take a nap.

*Lord, You are great, and You are good.*
*Help me to make the best decisions*
*I can and trust You with everything.*

# THIEF OF FAITH

*But the other criminal protested, "Don't you fear God even when you have been sentenced to die? We deserve to die for our crimes, but this man hasn't done anything wrong." Then he said, "Jesus, remember me when you come into your Kingdom." And Jesus replied, "I assure you, today you will be with me in paradise."*

LUKE 23:40-43 (NLT)

The thief on the cross never did anything to make amends. He didn't return whatever He had stolen. He made no restitution. He wasn't baptized. To our knowledge, He never even prayed. Meanwhile, Jesus never sinned. He caused the blind to see, the lame to walk, and the deaf to hear. He preached history's greatest sermon, prayed all the time, and taught all of us how to pray.

How did the thief, who had no good works, and Jesus, who had only good works, wind up in the same place after they died? How did the thief make it to Paradise too? Amazing grace. He owned his guilt and simply asked Jesus to remember Him.

There are two things I know for sure. We are all great sinners, and Jesus is a great Savior. There is more grace in Jesus than there is sin in us. We must simply acknowledge this and trust in Him. I am so grateful that Paradise is not for the perfect, but for the person who trusts in Jesus and has the faith of the thief.

*Today I will remember:*

- It's amazing grace.
- There is more grace in Jesus than sin in me.

*Jesus, there is none like You. You are a great Savior. I trust and receive You and thank You for receiving me.*

# LIVING WATER

*Jesus answered, "Everyone who drinks this water will be thirsty again, but whoever drinks the water I give them will never thirst. Indeed, the water I give them will become in them a spring of water welling up to eternal life."*

JOHN 4:13-14

I was speaking with someone in the hospital recently who has a terminal illness. What struck me was how upbeat and at peace this person was. Lying there dying with a smile. The body was wasting away but the soul was thriving, nourished, and fueled with living water.

Our verses are part of a longer conversation between Jesus and a Samaritan woman. Socially, He breaks all the rules. He crosses a racial line, as Jews and Samaritans did not speak to one another. Jesus, a rabbi, also crosses a gender line, as rabbis would never approach a lone woman. He cares more about the woman's soul than He does society's rules.

All souls long for living water. Most seek it, tragically, in the mirages offered by the world. They equate net worth with self-worth, thinking money will slake the thirst of the soul. Or perhaps they think the thirst can be quenched through romance, so they go looking for love in all the wrong places. That's the plight of the Samaritan woman. What the soul really longs for, however, is God. Everything else is a mirage that perhaps gives a brief reprieve, but the deep thirst remains. Water cannot be found on the outside, but it can well up on the inside by God's Spirit. The soul longs for God, and the invitation of Jesus is to come and drink.

*Today I will remember:*

- The soul longs for God, and the invitation of Jesus is to come and drink.
- Living water is found in Him.

*Holy Spirit, fill me. Water my soul today with Your presence. Let me experience Your love. I want to drink from this fount that never runs dry.*

# THE BLIND MAN

*As he went along, he saw a man blind from birth.*
*His disciples asked him, "Rabbi, who sinned,*
*this man or his parents, that he was born blind?"*
*"Neither this man nor his parents sinned,"*
*said Jesus, "but this happened so that the*
*works of God might be displayed in him."*

JOHN 9:1-3

You ever feel like you're being punished? You get an illness or lose your job. Life seems to be broken all around you. You wonder what you did wrong. Or perhaps you know you did something wrong and assume this is the punishment. Yes, the Bible teaches that we reap what we sow, but not as a form of punishment. Reaping and sowing is just how life works. Punishment, the disciples assumed, is about God piling it on because He knows you're guilty. That's how many of us think.

The truth is, life is hard because we live in a broken world. It is that simple and that difficult. This account of the blind man is something special. Jesus says here that the man was born blind "so that the works of God might be displayed in him." He was born for a miracle that would be discussed for all time. It was part of God's purpose for him. That might sound cruel to some, but I doubt the blind man thinks so. His gratitude and astonishment over the touch of Jesus would be his for all eternity. Life is about purpose, and this was part of his. There is nothing more beautiful and fulfilling.

*Today I will remember:*

- Life is about living out God's purposes for me.
- There is nothing more beautiful and fulfilling.

*Lord, help me through the highs and lows*
*of life to live out Your purposes for me.*
*May Your works be displayed in me.*

# WATER WALKING

*"Lord, if it's you," Peter replied, "tell me to come to you on the water." "Come," he said. Then Peter got down out of the boat, walked on the water and came toward Jesus. But when he saw the wind, he was afraid and, beginning to sink, cried out, "Lord, save me!"*

MATTHEW 14:28-30

Many read this passage and think about how Peter should have had more faith. I would like to make the argument that out of all the disciples present, Peter had the *most* faith! After all, there are only two men in history who have walked on water. One was Jesus. The other was Peter.

I wonder if later in his life Peter sat around the campfire and reminisced. "Hey guys, remember that time I walked on water? Yeah, that was awesome." We are quick to pass judgment on those who try new things. Let's change our criticism to admiration. After all, if you want to walk on water, you have to get out of the boat.

Critics are often most critical of the truly courageous. Water walkers will always be criticized by the comfortable boat bums. What have you been thinking about trying, but have been too afraid to start? Brother, life is not in the boat, but out on the water. Never let fear make your decisions. If you want to walk on water, you must get out of the boat.

*Today I will remember:*

- We should never let fear make decisions for us.
- If we want to walk on water, we must first get out of the boat.

*Father, lots of guys just talk smack in the boat.*
*Very few have the courage to get in the water.*
*Don't allow me to live the life of a critic.*
*Let me be one of the courageous.*

# MAT CARRIERS

*Some men came, bringing to him a paralyzed man, carried by four of them. Since they could not get him to Jesus because of the crowd, they made an opening in the roof above Jesus by digging through it and then lowered the mat the man was lying on.*

MARK 2:3-4

Can you picture it? As Jesus is teaching, dust begins to fall from the ceiling. He looks up with the crowd, and they all see that the house suddenly has a sunroof. A man is being lowered right in front of everyone. Jesus is interrupted by the dramatic entrance. All eyes are on Him. Does He chastise them for the interruption? No, He commends their faith. Jesus sees an opportunity to teach another lesson, and the paralyzed man is healed. The formerly paralyzed man walks home carrying the very mat he was lowered on.

May we have the audacity and tenacity of these four friends. May we be less concerned about the pomp and circumstance of religion and more with the power of God to change lives. The man was healed because the power of Jesus combined with the love and faith of his friends. Both were at work, and this is how God works. Let's be mat carriers for the broken and do whatever we can to get people to Jesus.

*Today I will remember:*

- May we be less concerned about the pomp and circumstance of religion and more with the power of God to change lives.
- Let's be mat carriers and get people to Jesus.

*Jesus, thank You for healing power. You forgive sin and heal the brokenhearted. May I be a mat carrier who brings as many as I can to You.*

# THE WORK IS FINISHED

*When he had received the drink,*
*Jesus said, "It is finished." With that,*
*he bowed his head and gave up his spirit.*
JOHN 19:30

The biggest difference between biblical Christianity and all other religions is the finished work of Jesus. Christians don't work their way to God through religious activities. Christians trust in the finished work of Jesus and receive Him in a relationship.

"It is finished" in the original Greek language is the word *tetelestai*, an accounting term. It also means "paid in full." The word was written on receipts to indicate that a debt had been paid off. On the cross, Jesus paid the full debt of our sin. Peace with God is not *something* you can achieve through your good works. Peace with God is *someone* you can believe and receive in the person of Jesus.

Christianity is not about earning anything, but there is effort in the Christian life. All relationships require effort. Our religious activities are not about earning, but learning. We put forth effort to know Him better, so that we might trust Him more. We are motivated by loving gratitude for what He accomplished on the cross. Because He loved me and gave His life for me, I choose to live for Him. Thank God that in Jesus the work is finished.

*Today I will remember:*

- Christianity and following Jesus are not about earning anything.
- Jesus paid it all.
- There's no earning; we work to know Him and follow Him.

*Jesus, thank You for paying it all. I gratefully*
*choose to live for You because of Your death for me.*
*I praise You today that the work has been finished.*

# MIC DROP

*Every day he was teaching at the temple. But the chief priests, the teachers of the law and the leaders among the people were trying to kill him. Yet they could not find any way to do it, because all the people hung on his words.*

LUKE 19:47-48

I often wonder what it was like to sit at the feet of Jesus. To hear the author of life discuss the meaning of life. Of course, much of His teaching is recorded in the New Testament, and we can read and study it. But it would have been amazing to actually hear the greatest communicator of all time talk about the meaning of all time. Luke says, "all the people hung on his words." Everything He said was a mic drop.

Even so, the leaders, teachers of the law, and chief priests wanted to kill Him. Why? Well, one reason was because "all the people hung on his words." They were jealous with a capital "J." The madness of their jealousy kept them from receiving the brilliance of the Master. It's embarrassing and sad. They were so focused on protecting their power that they missed the truth of the power of God in their midst.

I wonder if you and I ever do that. Do we sometimes get so focused on ourselves that we miss the power of God when it is at work around us? I pray that we wouldn't miss it, but would surrender to it. Jesus still speaks through His Word, the Bible, and through the Holy Spirit. Everything He says is still a mic drop. Don't miss it.

*Today I will remember:*

- Everything Jesus says is a mic drop.
- I should be careful not to miss the power of God at work.

*Holy Spirit, help me to listen to You. Help me not be so focused on myself that I miss what You're doing. Give me eyes to see and ears to hear.*

# IN THE FLESH

*The Word became flesh and made his dwelling among us.*
*We have seen his glory, the glory of the one and only Son,*
*who came from the Father, full of grace and truth.*
JOHN 1:14

"What if God was one of us? Just a slob like one of us? Just a stranger on the bus ...?" These are lyrics from the song "One of Us" by Joan Osborne. Now Jesus was never on a bus, and there are other lyrics in the song that do not fit at all, but, in the person of Jesus, God was, and is, one of us.

God transcends our understanding. He is the Creator while we are the created. He is large and infinite in every way; we are small and finite. Yet we are created in His image and, like God, have intellect, personality, feelings, and will. If you want to know what He is like, then look at Jesus. He is God made flesh.

Watch how Jesus interacts with sinners, the religious leaders, the poor, the wealthy, the wise, and the foolish. As you read about Him in Matthew, Mark, Luke, and John, you are reading about God. When Jesus speaks, God is speaking. When Jesus chooses to remain quiet, God is choosing silence. To know Jesus is to know God.

*Today I will remember:*
- God has intellect, personality, feelings, and will.
- These are all revealed in the person of Jesus.
- Jesus is God made flesh.

*Thank You, God, for making Yourself known in Jesus.*
*Any time I want to know Your thoughts and*
*feelings about something, I can look to Him.*
*Thank You, Jesus, for revealing the heart of God.*

# THE WONDROUS "WITH"

*All this took place to fulfill what the Lord had said through the prophet: "The virgin will conceive and give birth to a son, and they will call him Immanuel" (which means "God with us").*

MATTHEW 1:22-23

A man I was talking to about Christmas asked me some profound theological questions: "Hey, why did Mary have to be a virgin? Is that a big deal? Why is that so important?" The answer has to do with our sinful nature. God created Adam with a choice to sin, but without the propensity to sin. Since then, all of Adam's sons and daughters have been born with a sin nature. For example, you don't have to teach a child how to tell a lie. Instead, you must teach him *not* to lie. It's in his nature.

In 1 Corinthians 15, the apostle Paul calls Jesus the "second Adam." Through the first Adam, we are born with a sin nature. Through the second, by faith in Jesus, we are born of a life-giving Spirit. The virgin birth is necessary for Jesus to be the sinless sacrifice on the cross.

Through faith in Jesus, God is with us by His Spirit. The wonder of it all is found in the "with." You are never alone, and He will never leave you or forsake you. He is the sinless sacrifice that paid for all sin for all time so that you might be with God.

*Today I will remember:*

- Through faith in Jesus, God is with us by His Spirit.
- God is with me, and I am never alone.

*Lord, thank You that You are with me.*
*This is the wonder of Christmas.*
*I praise You that I am never alone.*

# THE FIRST MOVE

*God showed how much he loved us by sending his one and only Son into the world so that we might have eternal life through him. This is real love—not that we loved God, but that he loved us and sent his Son as a sacrifice to take away our sins.*

1 JOHN 4:9-10 (NLT)

The Christmas account is God saying that He loves you. When you and I were hopeless and helpless in our sin, God made the first move by making a way for us in Jesus. The secret to loving God is found in remembering that He loves you. Our biggest problem is not that we don't love God enough, but that we do not realize how much He loves us.

This Christmas, let's continually focus on the gift of God's love. In the hustle and bustle, slow down and fix your eyes on Jesus. In all of this world's brokenness and craziness, there is a hope and a light that burns. God loves you and Jesus saves. The more you think about the love of God, the more you will trust Him and do what He says—and the more loving you will be. It's not that you loved Him, and He responded. It's that He loves you, and now you respond. He made the first move.

*Today I will remember:*

- The Christmas account is God telling us that He loves us.
- The secret to loving God is found in remembering that He loves us.

*Lord, help me to know Your love so that I might trust You. Thank You for loving me first. May my life be a response to Your love.*

# THE REASON FOR THE SEASON

*While they were there, the time came for the baby
to be born, and she gave birth to her firstborn, a son.
She wrapped him in cloths and placed him in a manger,
because there was no guest room available for them.*

LUKE 2:6-7

Merry Christmas! Usually at Christmastime Christians are quick to say, "Jesus is the reason for the season." That's true, as far as it goes. But Jesus is really the reason for everything. Colossians 1 says that "all things have been created through him and for him." Christmas, however, is specifically about Jesus coming to do the will of the Father to rescue people. Seen in this light, we can say with sincerity that *people* are the reason for the season.

When God wraps Himself up in flesh to be born of the virgin Mary, He is not flexing. His arrival is not a power move, but a relational one. He is quietly entering the world without any pomp and circumstance. That silent night is the new dawn of His redeeming grace. If it were solely about Jesus, it would have gone differently. It's not about His glory in that arrival, but about His obedient sacrifice so that you might be gloriously saved. God gave His Son to the world so that whoever believes in Him would not perish but have everlasting life. People are the reason for the season.

*Today I will remember:*

- Jesus enters the world without glory, so that we might be gloriously saved.
- People are the reason for the season.

*Thank You, Jesus, for Your sacrifice. Thank You that You took
on my sin and covered me with Your righteousness. I will spend
all eternity glorifying You! Thank You for the gift of Christmas.*

# HE KNOWS LIFE

*"Roll the stone aside," Jesus told them. But Martha, the dead man's sister, protested, "Lord, he has been dead for four days. The smell will be terrible." Jesus responded, "Didn't I tell you that you would see God's glory if you believe?"*

JOHN 11:39-40 (NLT)

The Bible is not so much an ancient book as a timeless one. It contains wisdom for the ages. Its stories will forever grip the minds of men. In the narrative above, notice the details. Martha is worried about the smell. Her dead brother, Lazarus, has been in the tomb for four days. The author of life and the Savior of the world has told her that He is "the resurrection and the life," and what is she focused on? The odor.

I remember watching a play that depicted this account artistically. In the play, Jesus says that Lazarus is just asleep. A woman looks at Jesus and says, "Do you think we do not know death when we see it?" Jesus responds, "You know death, but I know life!" Then He goes in and raises Lazarus from the dead. It was awesome!

Jesus knows life. He will one day come again, wiping out all evil for all time. All who believed in Him will rise again. The bummer for Lazarus is that he died twice. Jesus raised him from the dead, and then he surely died again. But at the final resurrection, death will forever be destroyed. Do you believe this?

*Today I will remember:*

- Jesus knows life.
- He will one day come again, wiping out all evil for all time.
- All who believe in Him will rise again.

*Jesus, You are the resurrection and the life. Death had no hold on You, and it will be defeated forevermore. I trust You as both Savior and King.*

# HOUSE OF PRAYER

*Jesus entered the temple courts and drove out all who were buying and selling there. He overturned the tables of the money changers and the benches of those selling doves. "It is written," he said to them, "'My house will be called a house of prayer,' but you are making it 'a den of robbers.'"*

MATTHEW 21:12-13

Most people see Jesus as weak, frail, and mild mannered—maybe because of the paintings through the years of Him holding lambs and petting sheep. But Jesus is not a ninety-pound weakling, emaciated and lifeless. Jesus was a man's man. Any time He chose humility and sacrifice, it was not because He was a wimp, but because it was the will of the Father.

Jesus drives out the money changers and those who were selling because they were ripping people off. In that day, you bought your animals for sacrifice at the temple. It was a holy moment, but some unscrupulous people saw it as an opportunity to take advantage of vulnerable worshipers. This is why Jesus called the exploiters "robbers." They were preying on the weak in the house of prayer.

I'm grateful for Jesus' response. He gets angry when they use God to the detriment of others for personal gain. The worst evil of all is the religious kind. Men of God honor Him, protect the vulnerable, and do it in the name of Jesus.

*Today I will remember:*

- The worst evil is the religious kind.
- Men of God honor Him and protect the vulnerable in the name of Jesus.

*Lord, may I honor You and protect the weak.
The worst type of evil is evil done in Your name.
It is unacceptable, and it's right to speak out against it.*

# BIG LIFE

*"The thief comes only to steal and kill and destroy; I have come that they may have life, and have it to the full."*

JOHN 10:10

Jesus wants for us what we all ultimately want for ourselves. Pick any desire that any man has ever had. Beneath it is a desire to "have life and have it to the full." In our verse, Jesus is teaching that who you follow will determine where you'll go and what you will experience. Follow the thief and there will be destruction, or follow Jesus and experience fullness of life.

The problem with the thief is that he is not obvious. He is sneaky. Jesus calls him the "father of lies" in John 8:44. He doesn't come to us dressed in a red suit with horns and holding a pitchfork. He comes as a slick salesman offering something that's seemingly missing from our life. He tells the age-old lie that God can't be trusted. The Devil's ways feel natural while the way of Jesus feels strange. The Devil would never tell you to "love your enemy." That's the stuff of Jesus and it is counterintuitive to us. You and I decide each day which way we will go. The big lies of the thief are enticing, but the big life is found in the way of Jesus. Your move.

*Today I will remember:*

- Everyone wants fullness of life.
- The question is who we will look to in finding it.

*Jesus, help me to trust You even when I don't understand. Please guard me against the lies of the enemy. I choose to follow You.*

# TREASURE IT

*"The kingdom of heaven is like treasure hidden in a field. When a man found it, he hid it again, and then in his joy went and sold all he had and bought that field."*

MATTHEW 13:44

My good friend Mark has lived two lives. There was his life before meeting Jesus and now there is his life after meeting Jesus. Mark is a radically different man than he used to be. He was a drug addict, alcoholic, and philanderer. Now he is a pastor, is faithfully married to his wife, and has helped thousands of people break free from addiction.

When Mark first met Jesus, he was one hundred percent, no holds barred, prime time in love with Jesus. He did a cannonball into the Christian pool and has not looked back since. Why? God's grace got ahold of him. He knew what he had discovered. The purely distilled, high-octane love of God quenched his soul better than any whiskey ever could. He left it all to follow Jesus.

I have followed Jesus longer, but I think Mark is ahead of me in the pursuit. He gets grace in a way that I don't. I'm grateful and jealous, all at the same time. Grateful that I haven't experienced some of his pain and jealous of what Mark has learned in facing that pain. We've both bought the farm with Jesus, I just think Mark better understands the deal.

*Today I will remember:*

- God's grace is the most valuable thing in the universe.
- To truly discover it is to go all in.

*Thank You for Your grace, Jesus. Help me truly grasp its value. Let me be an all-in investor, and one who shares it too. Teach me the wisdom of the man who bought the field.*

# TRUE TREASURES

*"Do not store up for yourselves treasures on earth, where moths and vermin destroy, and where thieves break in and steal. But store up for yourselves treasures in heaven, where moths and vermin do not destroy, and where thieves do not break in and steal. For where your treasure is, there your heart will be also."*

MATTHEW 6:19-21

I love to read, and I love books. Physical books. I've tried to read from an iPad and a Kindle, but it's not the same. I love how books look, smell, and feel in my hands as I read them. A few years ago, I was thinking about starting a book collection. I started shopping on eBay for rare first editions and signed copies. I began with Larry McMurtry, the author of *Lonesome Dove* and one of my favorite story tellers. But as I was about to make the purchase, our verses for today came to mind. Is there anything wrong with collecting rare books? No. But for me, as I thought and prayed over it, I realized I was treasuring the wrong thing. Books will pass away, even the good ones. But what we do for God will not.

Choose to treasure what is really valuable. A child is more important than a work of art. Empowering a poor woman living overseas is more valuable than a 1965 Mustang. In the end, all that will matter is what we do for God and for people. Let's not get sidetracked with the trivial. Stuff will pass away; souls will not. Let's invest in true treasures.

*Today I will remember:*

- My heart follows my treasures.
- Choose to treasure what promotes the glory of God and the good of people.

*Lord, help me to see what You see and to value what You value. Life is short. Help me not to get sidetracked with the trivial, but to invest my life in what matters most.*

# COMING SOON

*He who testifies to these things says,*
*"Yes, I am coming soon." Amen. Come, Lord Jesus.*
*The grace of the Lord Jesus be with God's people. Amen.*
REVELATION 22:20-21

These are the last two verses in the Bible. They constitute a final affirmation of the return of Jesus, a prayer for His coming, and a blessing of grace upon all believers. Jesus is coming back, and His second coming will look vastly different from His first. In the first coming, He arrived as a baby nursing at the breast of His mother, Mary. In His second, He will arrive as a warrior to wipe out all evil for all time.

When Jesus comes again, He will ride a white horse and bear the name "Faithful and True." He is described in Revelation 15 as having an inscription on His thigh that says, "King of kings and Lord of lords" and a sword protruding from His mouth. He comes to wipe out all death, crying, mourning, and pain. Evil will be defeated, and He will prevail!

Man of God, the Bible ends in victory for all who have trusted in Jesus. The overall message of the book of Revelation is "we win." This is a certain hope, and we need not fret over what tomorrow will bring. Be a man of kind courage. Love and lead your family well. Give generously to those in need. Leave a legacy of faithfulness. Fight the good fight of faith and finish your race! His grace prevails.

*Today I will remember:*

- Jesus will come again as a warrior to wipe out all evil for all time.
- This is a certain hope.
- There is no need to fret about what tomorrow will bring.

*Come quickly, Lord Jesus! I long for the*
*day when evil and its consequences are no more.*
*In the meantime, may I be a man of faith who represents*
*You well and finishes the race You have marked out for me.*

# ABOUT THE AUTHOR

*Chad Moore*

Chad Moore is Lead Pastor at Sun Valley Community Church in Gilbert, Arizona, one of the largest and fastest growing churches in America. With over twenty-five years of pastoral experience, Chad is passionate about serving the church. Chad and his wife, Katrina, a native of Scotland, have been married for over twenty-three years. They are the proud parents of a young adult son and a teenage son. Chad enjoys fly-fishing, hiking, long dinners with his wife, and motorcycle riding. He also serves churches and business leaders as a leadership coach and consultant. You can follow Chad at @pastorchadmoore on Instagram and listen to teaching at sunvalleycc.com or at the *Loving God. Loving People* podcast.